A POWERFUL OBSESSION

MARY WRIGHT

PROLOGUE

Frances Wilkins met Harold Jones at the Crystal Palace movie theatre in Christchurch's Cathedral Square when she was sixteen. From then on, they were inseparable. They both had good jobs: Frances was a bookkeeping machinist and Harold worked in a woodworking shop. They both enjoyed rock 'n' roll music and dancing. They went to dances every Saturday night. They married when Frances was seventeen and Harold was nineteen. Nine months later, their daughter Cindy was born, and they were ecstatic. Sixteen months after that, their son Peter was born, and their family was complete.

They lived in a loving relationship until August 1964, when Harold had a stroke three and a half years after they were married. Frances was twenty and Harold was twenty- two and became partially paralyzed in the lower back and top of his legs, an injury from which he never fully recovered. It was a tragedy, but Frances supported Harold completely during his recovery. On the surface, they were doing well, but deep down, Harold's paralysis forever changed him. He became determined to undermine Frances' confidence and self-esteem.

In 1976, Harold coerced her into moving away from Christchurch to live in Auckland. He said the weather in

Auckland would be beneficial for his health. She was completely unaware that this was his way of separating her from her family and friends. He wanted her all to himself.

After moving to Auckland, Frances ascended through the workforce from being a bookkeeping machinist, to a data entry clerk, to a computer operator, and finally becoming a systems administrator. She became the breadwinner, as Harold contributed little to their finances. She had no idea that Harold was jealous of her income.

The years flew by, and Frances thought they were generally happy, although she found it difficult to make new friends. Harold pointed out that she was aloof and didn't make friends easily. Frances felt there was something wrong with her, as people were always making covert remarks to her, they used put-downs and gave her a feeling of self-doubt. Her self-esteem diminished with the passing of time.

Thirty-four years later, Frances read the book *Emotional Blackmail,* by Doctor Susan Forward, and she came to the realization that there wasn't anything wrong with her. Harold had conditioned her to feel that way. He was playing mind games with her using emotional blackmail. He was an expert manipulator, deploying smoke screens and fog to hide the insidious abuse and calling in his own set of troops for reinforcement. All the hurts and humiliations in her past were by Harold's design. Frances wondered how she could have been so blind.

This book follows the last two years of their marriage and the following four years, revealing the extreme lengths Harold went to in a bid to control Frances. The incidents detailed are based on real events.

All names, cities, and town references have been changed to protect identities.

CHAPTER
ONE

As Frances readied herself for flight AA2 to Los Angeles on Friday night, fifteenth August 1997, she tried vainly to brush aside the humiliation and psychological abuse she had been subjected to by the company she had worked for recently.

The Daphne-patterned drapes nestled next to the opened ranch slider door of the dining room. A wooden wrap-around deck outside the door looked serenely over vacant land. On the other side of the dining room was the lounge with a light green corner lounge suite and two rimu China cabinets set in one corner. A television sat on a cream two-door cabinet that held dozens of videotapes, most of them Harold's; he was an avid movie buff.

Seated at the dining table, Frances was a small, slim woman in her late fifties. She flicked through her documents quickly, checking and rechecking. Her green eyes glanced at the TV. She sighed. She was only allowed to watch when the TV was free. It was too uncomfortable to watch the small TV in the bedroom. Nervously she chewed her fingernails and smoked one last cigarette.

"I intend to enjoy this trip," she whispered, completely

unaware that her nightmare was about to begin, one far beyond the realms of reality that would last six whole years.

"Frances!" Harold yelled from the garage. "It's time to leave."

"Won't be long," she replied as she stubbed the butt into the ashtray and rushed down the hall which led from the dining room to the bedroom for her luggage. She dragged it to the garage and rushed back to the dining room.

He never helps me.

Harold was five foot ten, stood with a slight bend at his waist, and walked with a limp. Three and a half years after they married Harold had a stroke and was left partially paralyzed.

His bushy grey hair half covered his ears and his sharp eyes pierced right through you. He had a long-hooked nose and above these cruel thin lips, he had a bushy moustache.

In the privacy of his home, he was impatient, distant, aloof, and self-destructive. Frances sometimes thought he had two personalities -; lots like his father, a Jekyll and Hyde. He never wanted to socialize with France and at times was a loner. Harold's appearance was all too deceiving.

He was popular, self-confident, and a plausible person. He delighted in humiliating Frances in public whenever he could. He was unfeeling to her sensitive nature despite her persistent complaints. She had learned to cope with his hurtful, sharp cutting barbs and sarcastic remarks. She loved him so much.

Harold entered the dining room from the hallway and closed the ranch slider. He picked up the flowers Frances' colleagues had given her yesterday, her last day at work.

"I will put these on the bookshop counter," he said as he limped off.

They drove in almost silence to Auckland Airport in Harold's 1996 Toyota Hi Ace van, and she mused to herself that at least she would have a well-earned break.

Away from grumpy. He never wants to do anything or go anywhere.

Harold drew into the curb outside the terminal. The wide glass doors opened immediately as she stepped on the rubber pads and struggled inside with her luggage. Queues of impatient people waited at airline booths which lined the back wall.

Harold went and parked the van while Frances joined the queue to book in. Then Harold returned to the terminal to meet Frances.

Do not help me. Frances thought.

Harold leaned against a pillar as she joined him, her boarding pass gripped tightly in her hand. With a meager peck on her right cheek, he left.

"Rather unusual, but at least I get a break from your sarcasm," she whispered.

With time to fill, she entered the departure lounge and browsed the duty-free shops where merchandise was displayed on neat and tidy shelves. Liquor, perfumes, toiletries, films, and cameras.

"Ma'am, can I help?" enquired the young male assistant who approached her.

"I'll have a bottle of JB Gold, Black Heart Rum, and a bottle of Drambuie. Thank you." Frances said.

"Also, a carton of mild cigarettes." She added.

"These I'll collect on arrival, take a carton with me."

"Arrival date, please." The assistant asked her.

"Tuesday, second September"

The young man completed the documents and handed her a receipt.

"I've put thirty-first August, ma'am. The date does not matter. You never know what can happen," he said.

Strange remark, she thought as she cringed inside while she tucked the receipt into her wallet and headed towards the departure gate. She quickly brushed aside the remark and climbed the steep stairs of the aircraft up to the cabin with its pink and green interior and settled herself in the economy seat she had been allocated.

"All passengers, fasten your seat belts. We will depart soon for Los Angeles for a twelve-hour flight" the captain said over the intercom as she relaxed in her seat.

Frances sat idly gazing out the window as the plane ascended into the dark cloudy sky.

Frances was meeting her friend Rita in a few days' time in Los Angeles. Rita had flown from Auckland to Memphis for the twentieth anniversary of Elvis Presley's death, now Rita was flying back to Los Angeles to meet Francis.

Frances hoped to visit Catalina Island a one-hour boat trip from Los Angeles and walk Hollywood Boulevard, and visit the Yosemite Valley nestled in the Sierra Nevada near Yosemite National Park. From there they were traveling to San Francisco and then Las Vegas to see the shows.

Houses and buildings below grew smaller. Their lights twinkled in the dark beneath her as the 747 glided into the clouds for the twelve-hour flight.

When she woke with a start, she stretched and yawned. Her cares and worries of the last few months were no longer on her mind. The breakfast trolley rattled past. The crew, dressed in smart, fresh uniforms that matched the interior of the plane, stopped, and served passengers as they moved along the aisle.

Frances became concerned when the hostess bypassed her but consoled herself, she would be served soon.

"Pancakes or eggs and bacon, ma'am?" the hostess inquired.

"Pancakes, thank you," Frances replied as she lowered the tray table from the seat in front of her.

"Enjoy," the hostess said as she placed the tray down in front of Frances.

Frances was astonished when she lifted the aluminium warming cover off and peered at her breakfast. Pancakes inedible hard brown burnt offerings and a dirty orange juice container sat on her tray. Not one to complain, she bypassed her breakfast and rested until arrival at LAX,

Visibility was poor due to fog and the descent slow, but at last they landed. The customs arrival hall was a big barn that had to cope daily with large volumes of passengers. She found her wait in the alien queue long and arduous.

Hot and muggy weather greeted Frances as she stepped outside the terminal pushing her trolley. The courtesy van for her hotel, Halswell Inn LAX, was parked at the curb and she climbed aboard.

Twenty minutes later, the door of the Inn swung open automatically and she was propelled into a smart tidy reception area, the lobby desk on the far side in front of her. Nervously she handed her voucher over and waited while a woman with a pin that said her name was Jean tapped on the keyboard to confirm her reservation.

It didn't take long to find her room. She swiped her card in the slot in the door and pushed it open. A double bed, bedside cabinet, small table, and chair greeted her as she walked into the pleasant room. A kettle, sachets of coffee, tea, milk and sugar sat on the table beside the cups.

She heaved her luggage onto the rack set into the wall near the open wardrobe and unzipped one. She pulled out a few clothes and hung them on hangers. Then she slipped off her shoes, reached for some brochures on the table, and lay down on the soft bed.

Deep blue water with the sun shining on the ripples as the ferry cruised over huge waves formed in her mind as she read about Catalina Island. Frances was agitated so she jumped off the bed, slipped on her shoes, and left her room, quickly turning back to make sure her door was locked before rushing towards the lift.

The doors swung open she stepped inside the lift and pushed the button to take her to the lobby.

"How do you get to Catalina?" Frances asked the lobby clerk.

"You can use our courtesy van to LAX," the clerk said, pointing towards the entrance. "The coach to the ferry is from Long Beach."

Back in her room she lay down exhausted and fell into a deep sleep.

When she woke suddenly and glanced at her watch she reached for the compendium and perused the meal service menu and decided on a light meal in the Blue Room Bar. Wandering into the bathroom, she eyed herself in the mirror, applied fresh lipstick, and quickly combed her hair. Then she grabbed her handbag and closed the door behind her. The handle rattled as she checked the door, then she walked along the hallway to the lift. She entered the lift after a couple stepped out, then pressed the button for the Blue Room Bar.

The doorway to the Blue Room Bar was straight ahead when she stepped out of the lift. She strolled into the room. Bright blue walls dazzled her as she seated herself in a booth. It was a pleasant room. Booths with seating for six lined the walls. After studying the menu, she decided on a steak sandwich on rye, with chocolate fudge cake for dessert.

A pleasant blonde waitress dressed smartly in cream and blue approached with her notebook ready.

"Are you ready to order?" she asked in a soft, twangy voice.

"Yes, thank you," Frances replied and placed her order. "I'd like a glass of dry white wine, too," she added.

"Your wine, ma'am," the waitress said as she set the glass on the table a few minutes later. Ten minutes after that, her meal arrived.

———

After she had finished, she sat and watched other guests as she sipped the last of her wine. Then she signalled to the waitress for the bill.

She felt relaxed and calm and couldn't wait to get to her bed and relax on the soft mattress. Before she went to bed, she rang the cafeteria and ordered her breakfast for room service the next morning.

**CHAPTER
TWO**

A loud knock on the hotel room door woke Frances suddenly.

"Room service, ma'am," a deep voice boomed from the other side of the door. What time was it? She could tell by the light slipping around the heavy curtains that she had slept through the night. It seemed to be morning. She slipped on a robe and opened the door. A tall, dark-skinned man strode in, and she watched as he set her breakfast on the table.

"Too much for me," she murmured to herself, surveying the tray of two fried eggs, sausages, a hash brown, two slices of bacon, some baked beans, two slices of toast and jam, a pot of coffee, milk and sugar, and a banana. She picked up the banana and placed it on the table.

After breakfast, Frances showered. The water flowed piercingly, tiny needle pricks soothing her weary body. Choosing a pair of cream slacks and a light blouse, she dressed quickly and left the room, shaking the handle before walking to the lift. She took the courtesy van to LAX.

"Where to, ma'am?" the olive-skinned driver enquired with broken English.

"Aotea Airlines, sir." Frances knew she would get her

bearings there. She settled in the van as he drove away from the Inn. The big dome of the Theme Building high in the sky appeared on the horizon, then she dozed off. She woke with a start as the van lurched to a stop, surprised to see that she was the last passenger.

"Where to?" the driver mumbled as he approached her down the aisle of the van.

"I said Aotea Airlines," she replied, annoyed with his illiteracy as he turned and walked back to the front of the van.

He drove round again and stopped at an unfamiliar terminal. Confused and disturbed, she climbed out afraid that she would miss her connection for Catalina.

Disorientated, she stumbled into the building. She noticed a bathroom and stepped inside. Why had he dropped her off here? She decided to go outside again and get her bearings. Once outside again in the daylight she noticed the van still parked at the curb.

She saw the sign Aotea Airlines in the distance and walked towards it but not before she saw the driver watching her. When he saw her noticing him, he drove off? She located the coach terminal near the Aotea Airlines terminal and found the bus she was to catch the ferry with.

Seated in the uncomfortable coach as it rattled towards Queensway and the ferry, dolphins and whales appeared in her mind. The sun peeped out through the fog, and with temperatures in the seventies the weather looked good.

Frances stretched her legs into the aisle as the coached pulled into the curb. She stepped off the coach and walked towards the terminal. The boat was a sleek two-decker cruiser painted blue and white. She settled in on the lower deck, and the waves gently rolled in the sea, as the sun touched the white tops. She smelled the salt air drifting in the breeze as she sipped a glass of wine in the small bar during the two-hour trip to Avalon, one of the two cities on Catalina Island.

She disembarked and was confused as to which way to walk. She turned right and walked towards the trendy shops.

The trendy shops excited her as she explored Avalon, and the crystal-clear water of the beaches beckoned her when she stopped for a cappuccino and light lunch. As the day wore on, in her confusion she no longer felt at ease and became agitated. Then she wondered if she was followed or even hunted. She felt other people's eyes on her and couldn't relax.

On the ferry ride back, the swirling waves increased in size, the wind rushed up around the deck, and the salt air stung her eyes.

Back in her room an hour later, she stared puzzled at the table. The banana had vanished. 'Why would the maid take her banana,' she intended to eat it when she arrived home from Catalina. I am safer here she thought with relief.

After a restless night, full of dreams that haunted her, she ate breakfast at McDonald's. She paused and gazed out the window as she remembered the hurts of the past few months, and all the abuse she had endured during her last months at work. She couldn't comprehend why they were treating her this way.

Peter would come in and say things that he did which was exactly what Harold had done. She felt that was a coincidence. He said his wife had the radio station phone number on recall and she hit the redial button and answered the question they asked. She always got it right. That was what Harold had done at his book shop. Audrey made it hard for Frances to do her work. She would smoke outside and speak to every work person who crossed her path. She spent a long- time smoking and talking, which that meant that Frances was behind with her work at the end of the month as Audrey had to finish her work before Frances could process month-end. The staff would abuse Frances every time they could.

––––––

The haze of Los Angeles loomed back at her with increasing density. She decided to have a restful day.

She was meeting her friend Rita later that night at the Roosevelt Lodge, one block from Hollywood Boulevard. From there they were travelling to the Yosemite Valley by plane and coach, in the Sierra Nevada not far from Yosemite National Park. Frances flew out two days later to Los Angeles.

They were staying in a cabin in the valley, surrounded by a rocky range.

"Are one-dollar bills, okay?" the desk clerk asked as she settled her account for check out.

"Fine," Frances replied worriedly. His attitude alarmed her as he handed her ten one-dollar notes. He kept looking at the notes and made remarks about them maybe they were counterfeit as they didn't have the working strip on them. She remembered Richards remarks about one-dollar bills not having the working strip on them, without the this they were counterfeit. Richard was one of Harold's friends, he was a builder and had short grey hair and stood at 5 foot ten.

Why did he make me feel this way? she thought as she walked away.

Fear crept into her as she sat waiting in the lobby for her taxi and gazed aimlessly at the guests. Suddenly she became aware of the staff quietly watching her. Her uneasiness increased, and she made a decision as she glanced around. She saw the phone on a table.

Frances wasn't sure what was going on around her so she decided to fly home due to her uneasiness.

Frances strolled quietly to the table and used the white pages. Then she picked up the receiver and dialled.

Confused and unable to comprehend what was happening to her, Frances had trouble concentrating and was fearful with severe anxiety that made her want to fly home.

"Aotea Airlines," the soft voice answered.

"I'd like to change my flight," Frances said.

"Yes, ma'am. What flight are you booked on?"

"Flight AA1, second September. I'd like a flight tonight instead."

The sound of tapping keys came through the receiver as the assistant located her booking.

"Yes, ma'am. We can rebook." More tapping. "Report to the flight desk at seven p.m. The fee will be fifty-five dollars."

Frances thanked the assistant and felt relieved as she hung up. She would be glad to be home with her beloved Harold. She had been glad that she was having a holiday away from Harold and his sarcasm but now she was pleased to be going home.

On arrival at Roosevelt Inn Hollywood, she found the lobby desk across from the staircase after she wended her way through the small, dark hallway. She eyed her surroundings as she approached the desk.

"Ma'am, do you have a booking?" enquired the pleasant black woman.

"Yes, Frances Jones, two singles. My friend arrives tonight."

The woman left the counter and went out the back. Instantly a man appeared, he lounged against the door and stared at her. He unsettled her. She assumed he was the manager.

After the bellhop delivered her bags to her room, Frances took the lift to the lobby.

"I won't be staying," Frances said nervously to the same woman.

"But, ma'am, you've just arrived," she replied, surprised.

"I don't feel well. I'm going home tonight. Give these slips to my friend," she asked as she handed over the documents. They were receipts for some of their trips they were taking and also receipts for their accommodation and flights. Frances had no way of contacting Rita to let her know her change of plans. Rita was on a plane from Memphis to Los Angeles. She was going home because she was agitated and confused about what was happening to her.

With time on her hands, Frances set off towards Hollywood Boulevard. Wearing a t-shirt, shorts, and comfortable walking shoes, she strolled aimlessly.

Fear crept in as she became aware of the stares of people, and she felt she was being followed. A man dressed in police uniform held a walkie talkie. He spoke into it as she passed.

Further along the boulevard there was a woman dressed similarly. She too held a walkie talkie. Instantly she became alert. These people were using the walkie talkies to follow her.

As she passed McDonald's, she passed a young man preaching from a soapbox. Frances barely listened to what he was saying, but he suddenly jumped from the box and approached her, shoving a pamphlet into her hand.

Fire and brimstone and threats of hell for those who sin leapt up at her as she glanced down at the paper. She spun around and glared at him as she crossed the road. She tossed the crumpled paper into a bin as her mind wandered back to a remark made months ago by Harold's friend Richard.

She was unsettled about having the one -dollar bills in her purse and wanted to get rid of them

"New strip with wording on all US notes," he'd said. "Without that strip, they are counterfeits."

"Get rid of those one-dollar notes," she whispered as she fled to her room. She lay on her bed and drifted into a restless sleep. Fear crept in; her dreams were of frightful images that came back to haunt her.

She was anguished about the way she had been treated at work. They had forced her to resign and she would need to find another job to support her and Harold as Harold only earned a pittance and could not support them. She recalled the man at the duty- free shop and his remark about going home early and also the burnt breakfast. She could see the work staff at Auckland Maintenance abusing her. They would go out to lunch and would not invite her but they freely talked about it when they got back from lunch. *Why did they do that? She couldn't comprehend that?* She was sent to Coventry and that hurt her and isolated her from the other staff members.

Frances woke at 2 p.m. distressed and pondered her predicament. She removed the notes from her wallet and fingered them. She was obsessed with destroying the one-dollar notes. She felt she had to get rid of them because they had been planted on her at the hotel.

Back on the boulevard at 3 p.m., her feet pounded the pavement as she held the notes tightly in her pocket. Should she bin them? She dismissed the thought, all too aware of eyes watching her every move.

Someone somewhere was stalking her. She crossed the road at the lights and went back the other way, her feet pounding the pavement as she returned to the sanctuary of her room at 4 p.m. lay down and had a restless sleep

At 5 p.m., she checked out after booking a shuttle to LAX. Using her foot to hold the door open, she dragged her luggage behind her and settled herself on the low concrete wall that ran beside the hotel.

Aware of silently being watched, she noticed a young man walk into her vision. He held a walkie talkie to his ear as he talked into it. He stared at her as he chatted then suddenly walked off as a large black limousine swept into the driveway and parked in the courtyard in front of her.

She whirled around, aware of movement at the hotel entrance. There were several middle-aged women talking. One woman who was laden with cameras stood and stared at her.

The woman then moved behind the limo and raised her arms, her camera aimed at the wall behind Frances. She became alarmed but consoled herself that she would soon be whisked away to the airport.

She didn't like leaving Rita but she had no choice.

Finally, the shuttle approached, and Frances boarded with several other passengers. The driver made several other stops to pick up more.

Back at the airport, Frances presented her ticket to the clerk at the desk on the far wall of the terminal. She had short, dark hair and wore fashionable glasses.

"I've changed my flight, rebooked for tonight," Frances explained.

After the woman tapped at the keyboard, a printer spat out a boarding pass and receipt.

"That will be fifty-five dollars," the clerk said, handing the document to Frances.

Blast, I am right at the back, Frances thought as she glanced at her seat number—33D—as she struggled away with her luggage.

She felt relieved after checking her bags through the x-ray and sent on for loading onto the plane.

She located a café and was sipping a cappuccino when a young boy approached her and thrust a tin in her face.

"Any change for the poor?" he asked innocently.

"I can find something," she said as she delved into her bag. She pulled out the one-dollar bills and stuffed them into the slit on the lid and felt relieved.

"Flight AA1 now boarding at gate 23A," the husky male voice boomed out over the intercom.

There was a long queue in the aisle of the plane as passengers settled themselves, stowing parcels, and briefcases into the overhead lockers. Frances reached her seat exhausted, and as the plane departed, she fell quickly into a deep sleep.

When she awoke in her seat early the next morning, she began to fret. She wondered what Harold would say when she arrived home so early. She would tell him the truth.

As she sat resting in her seat on the plane, strange images spun around in her mind, those notes, that enduring power of attorney for the investment unit on the market that Harold had forced her to sign.

Before she left the plane, she quickly made a note for the customs officer to jog her hazy memory, as she was unsure of what was happening nor why she felt this way. "My husband made me sign an enduring power of attorney before I left Auckland so he could sell the unit."

She got ready to depart the plane when it had landed and sat resting while the other passengers departed then she left the plane and looked for a customs officer.

On arrival at Auckland Airport, she handed the note to the customs woman.

"Could you please search my bags because I feel unsafe" Frances told the woman.

Before she left for her trip Harold had made her sign an enduring power of attorney so if a buyer was interested in buying their investment unit, he could use the power of attorney to sell it.

When Frances had been made redundant a few years before they had invested her redundancy money in a rental unit. The rent paid for the mortgage, insurance, and Inland Revenue tax.

"I'm not going to sell everything; I'm only going to sell the investment unit we brought with your redundancy money" he had grunted.

"I think you should seek legal advice," the woman said as she handed back the note.

Frances left her luggage in the depot to pick up later. She didn't want to be burdened with her luggage as she decided to surprise Harold. She walked out into the cold mist of the early morning and boarded a taxi.

"No luggage," the grumpy taxi driver mumbled.

"No," she replied.

"Where you been?"

"Los Angeles"

As they drove towards the west, she dozed off as the driver continued his barrage of questions. Inquisitive bastard, she thought to herself.

After paying her fare, she climbed out of the back of the taxi and crept quietly up the driveway and on to the deck. When she turned the handle, it was locked. So, she tapped on the door. It seemed ages before Harold appeared. He was surprised and gave her a big hug.

"Why are you home so early?" he asked. "Were you afraid I might kill myself?"

She simply said yes.

She paused. It was much easier to agree than to give the

real reason.

"Gee, I am shivering," Harold said cuddling her as he jumped up and down.

The house was not cold. Harold only used that as an expression of his attitude.

Frances sat at the table and recounted her experiences to Harold as she swallowed a Calm-U tablet.

"I came home because I was confused, and people were doing horrible things to me. They made me feel uncomfortable. I was uneasy and it upset me, and I just had to come home.

"I've let Rita down," she cried as she put down the glass of water. "I'll have to go back," she moaned. "What'll she think?"

"I have left a letter for Rita in the hotel telling her why I came home. I told her about the things that people were doing to me."

Frances grabbed the phone and dialled the airline to rebook for that night and for a return ticket on the second of September.

"Collect your tickets at the airport," the assistant informed her.

She booked the tickets on her Diners Club Visa and said to Harold, "I will have to cash in my bonus bonds to pay for this when I arrive home. We will still make our connections."

"Yes, you don't want to disappoint Rita," he replied.

Frances rang the Rooselvelt Hotel and left a message for

Rita to tell her to meet her at the Aotea Airlines terminal so they could catch their flight to Fresno.

"I am tired, I will have a nap," she said as she left the dining room.

***

That night at the airport, the reservation officer greeted them.

"Ma'am, you will have to wait," he said. "Your ticket is coming by courier."

"They might think you are a drug runner," Harold said slyly as they stood waiting. She quickly brushed that remark aside as she ran her finger through her fine, limp hair. "Bye," Harold said as he flung a newspaper at her.

"Fraud," the headlines blared at her as she sat in the smokers' lounge. Astounded with the headlines of the newspaper, she flung the paper aside.

As Harold limped off, he was pleased with himself.

***

Your mind will be muddled with all that cocaine you have been fed, let you think you have committed fraud, Harold thought as he limped away.

Frances felt she received special attention from the crew during the flight after being seated near first class.

She woke early to find two enormous brown eyes peering at her from the woman beside her. Frances felt uncomfortable and gazed out the window as she cringed inside.

As Frances stood in the queue at LAX, she idly observed the golden Labradors with their handlers. Suddenly one of them rushed to her bags and sniffed keenly as the man pulled sharply on the lead. She stiffened slightly and suppressed her terror as the dog sniffed her body and handbag. In her confused mind the reality of the incident frightened her.

Harold's words about looking like a drug runner flew through her mind, and she sensed imminent disaster. "I have to feel safe," she whispered to herself.

"Ma'am, can I have your documents?" asked the gruff black woman at the check-in counter.

"I don't feel well. I would like my baggage searched because I am paranoid, I am suffering severe anxiety and need to feel safe. I feel hazy in the head and am worried that someone has planted something illegal in my suitcase" Frances said as she pushed them towards the woman.

"This way," replied the woman, leading her to a small room.

Rough black hands ran over her body inside her legs and up to her groin. The woman was searching for illegal substances.

"How much money have you, ma'am?" the woman inquired.

Frances pulled out her travellers' cheques and gave them to her. As the woman flicked through them, Frances caught a glimpse of her pink palms.

"Would you sign this declaration?" the woman requested as she wrote down the amount.

When Frances finally walked through the exit doors from the airport, Rita was patiently waiting outside. She gave Frances a big hug and smiled at her.

Rita's modest lifestyle concealed the family's wealth. She had big green eyes and wore her long dark brown hair tied back with a ribbon. She was quite attractive. Like Frances she was shy. They were both Elvis fans, and Rita a fervent devotee, cluttered her house with Elvis memorabilia.

"What happened?" Rita asked.

"Tell ya later," she replied. "I just had my own adventure." She laughed nervously.

"We will just make it," Rita said as they dashed down the corridor to the gate for their flight to Fresno.

After checking their bags, they boarded a small sixteen-seater plane. As they stepped into the cabin, a hostess in a crumpled brown uniform welcomed them and seated them next to the emergency door. The woman looked sad and scruffy; her dark blond hair needed a comb.

Frances rested against the headrest, trying hard to suppress her agitation as the plane flew slowly into the sky. There was a lush green wilderness below. A river meandered through and blended into the valley below.

After disembarking at Fresno, they collected their luggage and stopped at the information desk.

"Is there a coach for the Yosemite Valley in the Sierra Nevada?" Frances enquired.

"No more today," said the short, dumpy woman behind the counter.

"Stay in a motel, get a coach tomorrow," she told them. "Or take a taxi. The stand is outside."

They almost wilted as they stepped outside the terminal into the hot August sun. Frances walked to the row of taxis as Rita sat on the lush grass and leaned against the side of the brick building, their luggage dumped beside her.

"Too far today," said the first driver when Frances told him they wanted to go to the Yosemite Valley in the Sierra Nevada. "Try the next taxi."

"That's a long way," the next driver said. "Sure can. Cost one hundred dollars."

"I'll see my friend," Frances replied. She reported to Rita how much the ride would cost.

"We'll go tonight," Rita replied, annoyed.

On the highway, the driver headed out of the sprawling city of Fresno and headed towards the Yosemite Valley. He drove past shady rest areas dotted with picnic tables and walking trails leading through the forest.

As they drove through the entrance of the Valley, there were Sequoia trees everywhere. They followed the road through the forest as they relaxed in the back of the taxi. They reached the cluster of cabins by 7 p.m.

Dusk was falling and the surrounding forest was eerily lit as Frances made her way to the lobby. It was a large rustic building which housed the check-in facilities.

"Won't be long, ma'am," the clerk said as he left the counter.

Your keys, ma'am," he grinned as he handed her two keys.They struggled with their luggage past the entertainment area set on a grassy knoll and made their way to their rustic cabin set against a backdrop of trees on the hillside behind them.

There were twenty rustic cabins which were quaint rustic buildings. They were built in blocks of four. There were two single beds and a large bench for putting their suitcases on and a small table. Frances lay down and found it was nice and comfortable. There was a shared kitchen and bathroom not far away. There was a food court with several different types of food, hamburgers, fish and chips, pizzas and a chicken outlet.

There were crowds of people lined up at the café as darkness fell. People bustled around everywhere in the village. They made their way to the food court and ate pizzas and chips at their table as the trees swayed gently in the breeze.

A large black woman approached their table.

"Could I share with you?" she enquired. "Where you from?" she asked as she seated herself.

"New Zealand," Frances told her.

"Really, that's a long way!" she replied. "I'm from Frisco. Where you headin'?"

"San Francisco," Rita replied.

"I could drive you around," the woman smiled. She paused, then said unhappily, "Oh, I can't. My loving husband will be home."

Frances sat cautiously observing as two tall black men approached.

"My sons," she said. "One's a policeman in Frisco."

Later that night, Frances sat on the cabin floor unpacking.

"Have you one of these?" Rita asked, holding out a mini torch that she'd pulled from her bag.

"No, I haven't," Frances replied.

"Might come in handy," Rita said slyly.

Frances undressed, snuggled into bed exhausted, and fell asleep.

CHAPTER
FOUR

Rita agonized over what she was going to do. She was torn between her friendship with Frances and her promise to Harold. She had the posters with Frances' photo on and the money required to seal the deal. The posters were malicious, designed to have Frances stalked and psychologically abused. The poster read, "She is cold, aloof, and withholds affection. All she thinks about is work, doing overtime. I have to get my own meals. She is slovenly around the house. Her cigarettes are laced with cocaine. Please lace her food with cocaine." Finally, Rita decided to honour the promise she made to Harold and deliver the posters tonight. She lay awake restlessly until it was time to make her rendezvous with Beavan.

Frances woke early the next morning, startled. Peering around the cabin, she saw Rita standing at the window. She was looking out through half open curtains and flashing her torch. Mystified, she lay calmly and watched as Rita silently went to the cabin door, slipped outside, and closed the door quietly behind her.

Frances crept to the window. The moon cast an eerie light on the grounds. She recoiled as she saw Rita walk slowly along the bushy path. She appeared to be signalling as her torch flashed off and on. Answering flashes soon came through at the end of the path.

Bizarre, Frances thought, climbing back into her bed where she felt safe and drifted back to sleep.

After Frances went back to bed Rita continued along the bushy path until she came to cabin number seven. Beavan was waiting for her. He had blonde hair and a ponytail tied at the back.

"Hello," he said. "Have you got the posters of Frances for me to pass around and the money?"

"Yes," she said. "Make sure you do it."

"I will. Don't you worry about that".

Frances woke later that morning at 10 a.m. to the shrill of an alarm eerie noise that filled the air as the alarm went off. She heard footsteps too, tramping past her cabin. She felt her bed move. It shook, rattled, and moved all around as she pulled the blankets over her head confused and petrified.

"Did your bed shake? Did you hear that siren last night, Rita?" Frances asked Rita.

"No," she replied. "It must have been a dream."

Why do I feel this way? Frances asked herself as she dressed.

The day was bright and sunny as they strolled to the café

for an early breakfast. As they neared a crowd of people near a woodland garden, the people raised their hands over their eyes and peered upwards at the rocky wall. They both looked up at the wall and saw climbers scaling it everywhere.

That morning they roamed lazily through wilderness trails amongst the trees. They saw squirrels amongst the wildflowers that flourished underneath the Sequoia trees. They caught the shuttle to the waterfall and watched the water as it flowed downwards, the mist gently blowing into the valley below.

Later Frances saw a man, sitting on a low fence staring at her. He appeared to be signalling to her as she stamped out her butt. His actions disturbed her. He was waving his hands around then put two fingers up to his mouth to signal he was smoking a cigarette, then he threw this hand down and stomped on the make-believe cigarette to put it out. It's my cigarette, she thought as she froze. His actions aroused memories, but why? Were her cigarettes laced with something? Was that why she felt hazy? It must be but how could that happen. She crumpled her packet, threw it away, and brought a different brand from the store. Her mind reached into more pages. Ben at work had asked her for a cigarette, and she had lit it for him. He was an engineer in the maintenance section of work, tall and scruffy with grey hair and a brown beard. He took one long drag then paused and looked at her intently. He said he would finish it later.

Eva's talk of the cigarette rep she knew and a detective. Audrey was the debtor's clerk with fair, curly hair and quite attractive. Audrey asked her to purchase a packet of cigarettes at the dairy along the North Road not far from work then Frances changed her brand, too, as they were cheaper. God, smokes were expensive at $10 a pack.

Had Eva arranged with the cigarette rep to lace cigarettes

at the reps work for that dairy and duty-free shop? Eva was the wages clerk who was five foot four inches with short brown hair. It was noon as she glanced at her watch, and they caught the shuttle to the restaurant where they had lunch.

"I'll have that package," Frances indicated to a scrumptious sandwich pack.

"Oh no, not that one," the assistant replied. "I'll get another one, a fresh one."

The assistant went to the kitchen to make another sandwich. He glanced around the kitchen to make sure no one was there. He slowly pulled out the poster of Frances, a plastic bag of cocaine, and some money. He checked the photo on the poster to make sure it was Frances, then he started on the sandwich. When the first slice of bread was ready, he sprinkled the cocaine on it and then finished the sandwich. He then pocketed the money from the countertop that he was paid.

"Here you are, ma'am," he said as he handed her the pack of sandwiches.

Funny, what's wrong with the one in the cabinet? she wondered.

In her confusion, she pushed aside her half-eaten sandwich. The taste was bitter and not like what a sandwich should taste. What did he put in that? Was she stupefied? She felt hazy and her mind was fuzzy.

I will not eat anything unsealed; she thought as her anxiety increased.

An older woman with grey hair walked alongside their table. She paused, moving her hand as though gesturing to Rita, then walked off.

"I'm going to the bathroom," Rita said as she stood up.

Frances eyed Rita as she walked to the door and caught sight of that woman as they both disappeared through the bathroom door. She thought of following but remained seated, puzzled.

When Rita got to the bath room, she met Fiona. She had short, grey, wavy hair and was five foot three inches tall. Rita gave her some posters of Frances and some money "That should do," Fiona said.

After lunch, they walked in the woods. Rita was indicating with her hand the direction they take. Frances followed meekly as though in a trance.

"Want a drink?" Rita asked her as she stood by a fountain.

Frances walked over to where Rita stood. She was stunned. The fountain was disgusting and scummy with mould.

"Why do you think I will drink from that filth Rita, it is disgusting," Frances said.

What is Rita playing at, suggesting I drink from that filth? she fumed to herself and stormed back to their cabin.

"I'm taking a shower" Rita called out later. "You can have one after me."

"Yeah, fine" Frances replied.

Frances had forgotten her soap and borrowed some from Rita, then ambled to the ablution block. The toilet had just been cleaned, so she sat rather than squatted. The water beat down, soothing her weary body as she soaped and showered, her fears disappearing like the water gushing down the drain. She dried and dressed quickly, then went to the basin and cleaned her teeth.

Later that night, she went to the mini market for bottled

water and packaged food. She brought bottled water and two ham and cheese sandwiches which were sealed.

"Fifteen dollars," the assistant said after she switched to another till.

As she pondered her predicament, she decided to ring Harold and went looking for a phone. She used her calling card as she dialled the number. There was neither dial tone nor ring.

"That call is not valid," said the voice from the receiver as she glared at the phone. She dialled the number again carefully with the same response.

As tears welled up and her face contorted with fear, she marched briskly back to the cabin. They had booked the valley tour for the next afternoon, so they retired early that night so they could have a good sleep. She lay on her bed and was deep in thought when Rita went out early the next morning. Rita arrived back after two hours.

"I made new friends," she said. "Elvis fans just like me."

As the tour departed that afternoon, they were seated several seats back from the front of the open-air bus. A peculiar feeling came over Frances, she was light headed, had a hazy feeling, and she felt fearful. She hid the loose strands of hair underneath her straw hat. The guide rambled on in a monotonous tone. Suddenly she became alert to his words.

"Sometimes you wonder what is going on in their head," he said.

Perhaps it was something to do with her hat, she mused as she lowered herself into her seat. When they stopped to view the valley, the guide passed around chilled water in paper cups. Frances sipped hers warily. When Rita offered her another cup, she refused. Then Frances remembered whenever she bought something from the shops, the assistants swapped tills all the time. She thought that was odd.

That night she made a decision to fly home the next day because she felt hazy, and her mind was fuzzy. She had an overwhelming thought about going home early; it was a frightful feeling. She felt irritable and her appetite decreased, and she felt high. She hurried to the office and gave them the key.

"Please stay with me," Rita continually pleaded with her the next morning.

"Ok," she replied wearily. "I'll need to get my key back."

The desk clerk grinned slyly as she asked for her key. He went out the back and she heard that terrible grinding noise again. It was like someone cutting a key. He appeared again and gave her the key. She fingered it as she walked to the cabin. There was an inscription on it: *Beware of copies, make sure you have an original. People found with copies will be prosecuted.* Baffled, she put the key in her pocket and went back to the cabin.

"Here," Rita said as she passed a parcel to Frances. "I brought these for you in Memphis."

Frances unwrapped the parcel which was wrapped in a brown paper bag. There was a bottle of Coke with Elvis and a red guitar on the side. It had been issued for Elvis Presley's twentieth anniversary of his death. There was also a tea towel and a pen with Elvis printed onto it.

"Gee, that's nice," Frances said to Rita as she tucked them away in her luggage.

Before they left the cabin later that day, Frances tucked the gifts that Rita gave her under one of the beds in the cabin. She wanted no part of Rita. "She led me to that scummy fountain and expected me to drink from it. I could have caught giardia" she thought.

When they left the cabin to travel to Fresno, Rita and Frances dragged their luggage from their cabin to the clearing and across the lush grass to the roadway. Frances sat with the luggage while Rita went back to collect another bag and hand in the keys.

The sound of an engine softly purring echoed in the valley as the bus wound its way up the tree-studded road.

The driver pulled into the kerb, opened the door, and stepped down. He unlocked the compartment at the side of the bus and packed the suitcases inside.

Rita and Frances each chose a window seat, and they placed their parcels in the string racks above their seat.

The driver drew away from the kerb slowly. The bus glided silently along, gathering speed, as he drove out onto the Fresno highway.

A tall woman around forty, slightly dumpy, wearing a casual blue skirt and white blouse with low-heeled shoes, walked slowly down the aisle. She paused at each seat and issued a ticket as she collected the $20 fare, clipping each bill onto her clipboard.

Frances tried to relax as the bus trundled on. Frances eyed the woman warily as she paid over her fare. She sat stiffly as she brushed her hand through her hair. She turned her head slightly and watched the woman pass her bill to a strange man seated at the rear of the bus.

Why did she do that? she puzzled.

The traffic became thicker and noisier as they drove into Fresno to the railway station.

Frances watched silently as Rita left the bus without so much as a backward glance. She watched from inside the bus as Rita joined a young, blonde-haired German man wearing an Elvis t-shirt with Germany written on it. He helped with her luggage as they walked up the ramp of the white rough cast building to the train station.

It seemed they had planned that, she puzzled to herself.

The bus drew away from the curb and swung out onto the roadway. The driver reached an almost deserted street. He swung a right and turned into the car park of the deserted coach terminal and parked headfirst in front of the building.

Frances collected her luggage and went inside. A solitary figure sat idly inside as she searched for the reservation desk.

"Name please, ma'am," the assistant asked. "Age?"

"Why do you need my age?" Frances asked her as she paid her fare.

"We need it for the ticket I am going to issue" the woman replied.

"Departs at eleven-thirty sharp," the assistant said, handing her the ticket.

Soon the coach with its engine roaring rumbled off along the road for the two hundred twenty-one-mile trip to Los Angeles.

Frances was worn out. She sat dozing as the coach travelled on. She woke when she felt the coach slow down and looked out the window. They had arrived at the Bakersfield terminal for a refreshment stop. Rita would be well on her way to San Francisco by now.

Stiff from sitting, she stretched in the aisle. Then she went off to the café for a can of Coke. She glanced at her watch. It was 4 p.m. She had slept for most of the journey.

Rita will be in San Francisco now as she had travelled there by train.

She coughed as she leaned against the side of the building sipping her Coke and having a puff. She eyed the black sweeper as he cleaned the area then replaced the bag from the garbage can. He signalled to Frances to put her Coke can into the new bag.

In her confusion, he loomed larger than life, and she felt the tension rising as she crumpled the empty can and put it inside her bag. Her mind was muddled, and she felt uneasy. Did her stalkers want her fingerprints? She was hazy and her mind confused.

A coach pulled up as she stood there and watched. A tall, young black man with black, frizzy hair stepped down. He wore blue jeans, black sneakers, and a white t-shirt with bold black letters that said *I didn't do anything*.

"Excuse me, ma'am, could I have a light?" asked a young man as he approached her.

"Sure," she said and offered her lighter. As she cupped her left hand around the flame, she flicked it on for him.

"Thanks, ma'am," he said as he sauntered away.

Frances walked over to the rail at the end of the platform and leaned on it, with both hands dangling over the side. Horrified, she stared in disbelief. There were tiny globules of red blood oozing out of her index finger on her left hand. She had not felt a needle prick when she lit his cigarette. She licked away the blood and saw tiny pin pricks as she inspected her finger closely. *This was evil.* Distressed, she screamed and ran after the man. "You stabbed me!" she yelled at him. "With a needle!" Tears welled up in her eyes.

"No, I never," he replied calmly and showed her his palms.

"Can I have your ID?" she asked, calmer now.

The man pulled his ID out of his wallet and handed it to her. She eyed it suspiciously, noted his name and that he was a local. Then she handed it back to him.

The coach terminals are dangerous. You can catch AIDS at the terminal—the words came tumbling into her mind as she recalled a conversation months ago with Anne, her catty friend. Anne said that to her many months ago.

A slim, blonde woman wearing a light green sun frock stepped forward to comfort Frances. Her blue eyes peered through her fashionable, green-framed sunshades. The woman produced a grubby tissue and gently rubbed the wound. Then she produced a plaster from her purse and applied it to Frances' finger.

Frances was terrified and felt she was losing her mind.

She was tense as she sat in her seat for the last leg to Los Angeles. Her mind was befuddled and fuzzy as the coach accelerated along the road. She dozed a while then woke as the darkness of the night overtook them, and she gazed out the window as the coach whizzed past the woods beside the highway.

It had been a long day, but the coach finally arrived at the LA terminal at seven p.m. Outside the coach, people were pushing and shoving as they tried to find their luggage while the driver unloaded the compartment. Frances located her luggage and struggled inside.

The building was huge, and she found it difficult to move through the crowds thronging around inside as she found the information desk.

"Taxi stand that way," the woman said, pointing behind her.

Frances struggled with her luggage through the door. A man wearing a chauffeur uniform approached her immediately as she stepped out. He appeared to be waiting for her.

"Taxi, ma'am?" he asked.

"Yes please," she said.

"Follow me," he said as he escorted her towards a taxi.

"LAX," he told her driver, then he turned and walked away.

Frances was dumbfounded. How did he know she wanted to go to the airport?

At the airport, a woman around forty wearing the familiar colours of Aotea Airlines approached Frances as she reached the start of the roped off walkway. The woman appeared to be waiting for her, too.

"Do you need help?" she asked Frances.

"Yes, I'd like a flight for tonight to Auckland," Frances said.

"Come this way," she replied and directed Frances to the check-in desk. "I am certain we can help."

When they reached a ticket desk, she told the blonde assistant behind it, "This woman would like a flight tonight." The woman tapped away at the keyboard and the printer whirred as it spat out a boarding pass.

"I would like to check your bags," the first woman said to Frances as they waited for her pass to be processed.

"Why are you doing that?" Frances asked her.

The woman unzipped her bags, swiftly lifted the piles of neatly packed clothing, and looked underneath them as Frances stood silently watching"

"It is standard procedure," the woman told Frances.

"What are you doing?" the blonde assistant asked her.

"Believe me, I know what I am doing. Trust me," she replied.

"I'll help with your luggage to x-ray," the woman offered as she zipped up the bags.

The woman leaned forward, pulled a trolley towards her, and lifted the luggage onto it.

"Follow me," she said to Frances as she wheeled the trolley towards the x-ray area. The woman turned her head and glanced around in all directions just before they got there.

"That will teach you a lesson, for the way you went about it," she said to Frances as she left the trolley and walked away.

Frances was stunned and stood there bewildered. She approached the information desk.

"Where are the telephones?" Frances enquired.

Frances walked over, pulled some coins from her wallet,

and dialled her home number. Harold acted surprised when she said she would be home the next morning.

"Flight AA1 now boarding at gate 25," the softly spoken female voice said over the hustle and bustle of the terminal.

Frances followed the arrows along the long corridor to the gate. She passed cafés, bars, and gift shops that lined the route. At the gate, she joined the queue of passengers ready to board. The queue moved swiftly, and she soon flopped into her seat at the rear of the plane. Frances was fatigued. A good sleep was the only thing on her mind.

By the time she awoke, arrival was imminent, and Frances busied herself preparing to disembark. She was hot and flustered. The heat at the back of the plane seemed higher than normal. She felt sticky and sweaty as she sucked on the barley sugar sweet handed out by a cute young woman. With a quick spray of perfume, the pleasant smell wafted around her.

"You'll feel like a new woman," said the woman seated beside her.

The woman glared at Frances.

and notified the home number. Harold agreed and asked when she said she would be home the next morning.

"Flight AA now boarding at gate 25," the loudspeaker ...

CHAPTER
FIVE

Frances was confused as she walked briskly down the corridor to the duty-free shop and made her way to the counter. She handed the receipt from the purchase she had made five days earlier to the young male assistant, who immediately dashed out the back to collect her purchases. A warning bell rang inside her. As she watched, his demeanour unsettled her. The young man raced back to the counter with a big plastic bag in his hand. He was the same man who served her when she had first departed. He told her the arrival date did not matter, as anything can happen on holiday. She cringed.

It was 6 a.m. and she grabbed a trolley, loaded her shopping, and went to pick up her luggage on the way to the customs hall. She was amazed—the hall was deserted, and a solitary customs officer was waiting for her. He glanced quickly at her declaration then remarked on her carton of cigarettes and let her through the gate.

Outside, Harold was slouched leaning against the wall waiting for her. Frances was so pleased to see him she hurried over and gave him a big hug, then burst out crying.

Harold drove home using a long route. He stopped at

garage sales on the way while Frances sat waiting in the van. "Next stop the supermarket, then my book shop," he said as he drove away from the last stop. Harold parked outside the supermarket a short distance from his bookshop. Harold had a second-hand bookshop and let Frances get out of the van to go to the supermarket.

"Why don't you park outside your shop?" she asked, concerned and puzzled. "It will be easier for you."

"I'll be fine," he said as he hopped out of the van and headed towards his shop with his lopsided gait.

As Frances strolled casually around for groceries in the supermarket, she caught a fleeting glimpse of a woman she thought she recognised and then that tall dark-haired woman came into her view. *That woman was at Charlene's that night just before my trip*, she thought. The woman stared at Frances without a flicker of recognition as she walked past her. Frances stepped out into the grey murky weather and struggled with her shopping in the white plastic bag. As she neared Harold's van, she passed a blue Laser she recognised parked by the kerb. When she turned back, she saw Charlene seated in the front of the car peering at her.

Charlene used to work with Frances. She was in her forties, a spinster who had light grey hair that was wavy.

That man at Charlene's party who asked if he could take a photo of me, she remembered as she dumped her shopping in the van. Frances walked to the shop and noticed Harold was talking on the phone as she approached. While she watched, he hung up, emerged from his shop, and locked up.

"Look at that car. It has personalised plates," Harold remarked, laughing, and pointing at the long, green limousine in front of them as he pulled out onto the road. Frances was alarmed as she read the license plate: I WON.

After they arrived home, Harold backed into the garage and unlocked the van.

"I've been learning to type while you were away," he said as he walked through the door at the back of the garage to his den. "I want to show you what I have learnt." Frances followed behind him and watched as he switched on the computer. Two walls were lined with shelving filled with books. Harold had made a small desk with extra shelving on the wall behind the door. Underneath the desk was the book *Mind Over Body*. Frances pulled the book out and read the title.

Harold sat down and tapped away at the keyboard. He pulled up a file of a story he was writing. At the top of the screen Frances saw the title "Truth and Lies." He showed her the typing tests he had been practising and the speed he had reached.

"Your turn now," he said when he'd finished. "See what speed you can do." Frances started tapping away on the keyboard, aware of the plaster on her finger. She paused and glanced up at Harold while he stood staring at her finger, and she saw that gleam in his eyes. On the shelf beside her, the book *The Crimes of Minnie Dean* glared back at her.

"I have to unpack and put the groceries away," she said nervously as she jumped up. She grabbed the groceries and walked through the house to the kitchen. She pondered her predicament as she quickly put the groceries away inside the pantry.

She pondered what had happened on her trip to the US. She couldn't comprehend all the incidents.

How did all those incidents happen? she thought.

The telephone rang, shattering nerves.

When she answered, she heard her friend Anne speaking in a spiteful voice: "Oh, I didn't expect you to answer, why are you home so early?" Anne was Richard's partner, a friend of Harold's, and she was a jealous and spiteful person.

Frances cut her short and abruptly ended the call.

A moment later, the telephone rang again. She picked up the receiver. It was Sam, another bookshop owner whom Harold had worked for before opening his own shop. He sounded surprised as he explained he thought he had rung Harold at the shop. He apologized and said he'd call there.

The telephone rang a third time, which jangled her nerves. It was her friend Josie. She was married to David, who used to work with Harold years ago.

"Why are you home so soon?" she asked in surprise. Then she added, "I thought I had rung the shop." Frances settled the receiver into its cradle after cutting her short. *Strange all these calls*, she thought to herself. It was all too much for her. She had had enough. She walked down to the bedroom and lay down on the bed for a much-needed rest.

CHAPTER
SIX

For Frances, the days slipped easily into nights. Physically and emotionally drained, she struggled through each day confused. She felt if she took to her bed, she would be safer. She could not take another battering.

She often stared into space as her mind wandered back through the years. The slights and comments she had endured over the years tumbled through her mind, and her sensitivity did not help either.

"You're stressed," Harold said one night. "I'll get a masseuse to come. I know one. She works with elderly people."

"Sounds nice, yes."

"My present for you," he said. "I'll have one too."

Two nights later Frances eyed Freda as she stepped into the lounge and watched as she unfolded her massage table and set it on the floor. Freda was a pleasant indigenous Maori woman, with dark olive skin, long black wavy hair, brown eyes, and a solid build. She wore a white smock and flat brown shoes.

"You go first," Harold said to Frances.

Frances was hesitant and shy. She took off her pink dressing gown climbed onto the table and lay face down.

Soft hands rubbed and soothed her weary body as she felt the stress released from within. Then the pressure intensified as those hands began kneading and pummelling on her muscles and along her spine.

"Tell me if I hurt. I'll stop," Freda said softly.

When Frances climbed down from the table an hour later, she felt a warm glow over her body and face. She watched as Harold had his massage.

"Thank you so much," Frances told Freda. "I feel so much better."

"You're welcome. You deserve it," Freda replied.

The next morning when Frances woke, she felt a terrible pain in her lower back and legs. She slid out of bed to find she could barely walk. The pain was a sharp stabbing one and it was excruciating.

Frances knew that Harold had arranged that with Freda and didn't want to let Harold know that she was in severe pain.

Frances tried vainly to stand normally. She was afraid to show her pain because she did not want Harold to know what Freda had done. She fought back her tears and struggled through the week as the pain subsided more each day.

While reading their medical dictionary she read that the plexus is connected to the sciatic nerves, which control the legs. "Appearances are deceiving," she whispered now that she knew what Freda had done. She had pressed so hard on her lower spine, and Harold had shown no remorse.

Harold had watched Frances walk and knew by the way she walked that Freda had done what he asked her to do.

Later in the afternoon as she tidied the house, she found a

scrap of paper Harold had left for her. Turn the lights off on the deck at night, it read.

Frances still received those cutting telephone calls almost daily.

"How has life been treating you lately?" Sheryl asked, her voice dripping in sarcasm. The remark cut deep into Frances's sensitivity, and she hung up.

Sheryl was a friend from the rock 'n' roll club. She stood at five foot two, had short straight hair and was very attractive.

One cold and wet Sunday, Harold was at the club for the annual Trivial Pursuit event. He also played at other clubs. She was never allowed to go.

"Walter's sick, dying," Harold said as he loped into the kitchen that night.

"What?" she said, shocked.

"Yes, that's right," he said. "Cancer."

Frances thought Harold was playing another one of his games. She thought he was kidding. She found it hard to comprehend, as Walter was a strong, strapping fellow, tall with blonde hair and blue eyes. His wife Doreen was over - weight and frumpy but jolly with a sharp cutting wit.

"We should visit them," she said, concerned for their friends.

"No," he relied sharply. "I don't want to."

"Why not? They'll need support at a time like this."

"No!" he yelled. "I don't want to see him like that."

"Callous," she said. "That's what you are."

"I don't care."

The week passed as she tried to cajole Harold into visiting them.

"Nothing on this weekend," Frances said as Harold appeared in the lounge and sat down beside her.

"No," he replied.

"We should visit Doreen and Walter."

"I do not want to," he said gruffly.

"How would you feel," she said softly, "if it were you and no one came to visit?"

"Wouldn't worry me," he replied grumpily.

"Well, we're going. They need our support, regardless of our feelings when we see him like that. I will stop cooking your meals if you don't go." Frances was pleased with herself when Harold went.

———

On Sunday, Doreen and Walter were happy to see them. Walter sat with a stunned look on his face as he spoke of his illness.

"No point now, is there?" he said sullenly as they talked about football.

Doreen piped up breaking the silence in the room.

"Why do they put fences around cemeteries?" she joked.

Dumbfounded, they all turned and stared at her.

"People are dying to get in!" she laughed nervously.

Her mind still hazy, Frances stood up and went down the hall to the bathroom. She knew Harold was stupefying her somehow because her mind was hazy, muddled, and she felt as though she lived in a fog.

Frances crept silently to the door after washing her hands. She pulled the door open slowly and paused to listen to them talking in the lounge.

"How has she taken it?" she heard Doreen ask Harold.

"Seems ok," he replied.

"Does she know you did it all?" Doreen asked.

"No," he replied.

Frances composed herself as she stepped loudly into the hall and walked back to the lounge.

"Did you see the toothbrushes?" Doreen asked as she sat down.

"Didn't take much notice," she replied.

"Our cats jump on the toothbrushes," Doreen said. "They do funny things with them, rub against them too," she laughed slyly.

That night as she lay in her bed, she thought of the strange conversations.

"I'll take you shopping," Harold said the next afternoon as he dropped the receiver of the phone into its cradle. "Perhaps we should go to the supermarket first," he said as he glanced at his watch.

Frances found it difficult to shop without her glasses, and as they rounded the end of the aisle, she paused and peered as Maureen from her last job was walking towards her. It was too late to avoid her as Maureen came over to talk to her.

As they spoke Harold piped up, "I wheel the trolley while Frances looks at the prices."

It soon became apparent to Frances that Harold had set her up. To brag and show the damage he had done to her. Frances cut her short and they left, as she was not into light hearted banter these days.

Back home, Frances unpacked the groceries and put them away. Then she rushed to the bathroom and looked in the mirror.

She was appalled as she stared at her face. There was no longer a happy, smiling face beaming back at her. In its place was a very solemn face with blank, staring eyes. Her reflection was old and haggard. Her face had fallen through loss of weight, and the lines around her mouth were even more pronounced. She was alarmed and concerned. How could she have changed so much?

Frances slowly began to realize that Harold was behind all the hurts and humiliation over the years. He had deliberately set out to destroy her. He was obsessed with keeping her all to himself.

Why had she been so blind?

How long would her nightmare continue?

That night she lay in bed unable to sleep. She worried over her predicament. "I will tackle him tomorrow night," she whispered to herself.

The next night Frances heard the garage door close as Harold parked his van. She stood in the kitchen waiting nervously.

Harold stumbled into the kitchen. She looked deliberately into his eyes.

"What the hell do you think you're doing to me?" she yelled at him.

"Hee hee," he giggled. "I did it all," he said arrogantly. "Work, too. Would you like me to plot revenge against Horrible Harry?" "No, I do not," she yelled shakily. "You know I am not like that!"

With the mention of her old boss, he tossed an envelope at her. "I rang Horrible Harry and got him to organize the staff to abuse you so you would leave work." He chuckled again.

Frances worked at Auckland Maintenance and was a systems administrator. The staff used psychological abuse on Frances and made it hard for her to do her job.

She opened it and pulled out a single sheet from inside. The letter was from a worker's union. It was addressed to

Harold as he had rung the union to get the letter sent out to him.

"I've found out where he and his wife live," he gloated.

"Do your employees know they are about to get the sack? How to get rid of employees without them even knowing," glared back at her as she read the letter that was inside the envelope.

At work they called her boss "Horrible Harry" behind his back. Frances never joined in. She was loyal and trustworthy, with no time for slights against people. She never had.

<hr>

"Gill Parkinson, the airlines engineer, he organized all that trip for me," he goaded her. Gill was an acquaintance of Harold's.

So that's what the air hostess at Los Angeles Airport meant when she said that to me, Frances thought.

"You're very loyal," he said. "Not a bad cook either."

"Loyalty—you do not know the meaning of the word!" she screamed and stormed off out of the room to her bedroom.

Frances felt the soft breeze gently touch her as she lay on the bed whimpering as memories came floating back to haunt her.

Robert came as if it were yesterday. He had been Harold's friend years ago. They had the same type of business, a tool-sharpening business for construction builders. Then things turned sour. Robert accused Harold of plotting against him and his business. Harold had told her about it. She believed him, as he was her husband. She thought that Harold would never do that. Now she knew the truth.

Then came her sister Nellie. She'd had that car accident with Harold's van. The other man was at fault. Nellie told Harold the other driver abused her. Infuriated, Harold demanded the driver's business card from Nellie which Nellie had kept for the insurance claim. Nothing happened until months later.

"That man you had the accident with," Harold said one day to Nellie and Frances, "I paid him back. I rang the man's company. Left a message. Told the receptionist that his interview for that job he had applied for was the next day." He laughed heartily.

Harold went on. "I found his home address. Rang his wife when I knew he was at work. "Can I take a message?" she asked. "Yes" I said, "tell your husband to keep away from my wife." Nellie and Frances had both looked at him in disbelief.

Oh yes, how clever, and cunning Harold was as he built his ego even higher with the plots he dreamed up. He felt no remorse for his victims at all.

Over the next few months, Frances continued to visit Walter and Doreen to support them through the tragic time they were enduring. It saddened Frances to see this wonderful man was gradually wasting away. Harold came sometimes when she forced him to.

Frances would never forget the last time she saw Walter, his thin frame lying on the bed face down and his stick-like arm trying to wave as she left. Frances knew then that it would be the last time she would see him alive. Walter died a week later, and they both attended the funeral.

"Hello," she said when she picked up the telephone the next morning.

"It's Jim, can I bring an agreement around?" he said. "I have an offer on your rental unit. Harold has already signed it at the shop." Jim was the land agent employed to sell their rental unit.

Later Frances eyed the two men warily as they stepped into the dining room. Jim had brought another land agent with him.

Jim gave the agreement to Frances, which she perused carefully. She was confused and her mind hazy. She wanted to be sure before she signed the document. Harold had destroyed her faith and trust in everyone.

"With the approval of our solicitor," she requested Jim to write into the agreement as she pointed to the document.

Nervously she picked her cigarettes up and lit one as Jim shuffled through his pockets.

"Could I have a cigarette?" he asked. "I've left mine in the car."

Frances gave him a cigarette. She held the lighter for him while he took a puff. He paused and looked at it curiously as they departed.

On Sunday as she lay on the bed, the telephone rang sharply. Frances went from the bedroom and picked up the receiver as Harold sat idly at the table. It was Doreen, Walter's widow, inviting Frances and Harold out for dinner.

"No, I'm sorry, we can't afford to go," Frances replied.

"What did you say that for?" Harold snapped as she hung up. "Are we poor now?"

"Yes," she replied sharply. "Of course, we are, you bloody prick, and you are to blame."

"I'm allowed to make mistakes," he said.

Harold had an unrealistic idea of the cost of living, especially in light of their future with his health problems and hers, too. Frances was not one to complain and suffered her back pain in silence. She always had to be the strong one in their family.

God, she thought, *I was only seventeen and this is how I am repaid.*

In addition to their joint account, Frances, and Harold each had their own bank account to do with what they liked. Harold put a small portion of his meagre wage into the joint account towards paying the bills and the rest of his money was all for himself.

Years ago, when Frances broached the subject of a retirement fund, he said he did not need one. He left it all to her, so she saved hard over the years for their future together. When Frances was made redundant, they used the money for a deposit on a rental property in both their names. The income from that paid its mortgage. She also put money in monthly to reduce the mortgage quicker. Frances planned to retire by early 1999 at the latest and to leave the vicious work force she had faced daily all these years. For the last few years, they had worked antique and collectable markets occasionally to gain experience for future income when she retired. The income was negligible; the learning valuable. What did he expect now as he systematically destroyed everything she had worked for?

That night she lay silently in the dark after being woken by a noise. Then she heard the light touch of a hand on her bedroom door followed by a persistent rattle of the door knob.

Frances heard Harold creep to the kitchen, then the ashtray grinding on the bench as he moved it around. She was petrified and prayed that noise would stop.

She consoled herself he would soon go back to bed. Oh, oh that grinding the same as all those other nights when Harold had done this before.

It was silent at last. Frances crept to the dining room and stood very still as she quietly opened the window that looked out over the deck. She was afraid to make a noise as her dark memories smouldered. Harold was now in bed.

Frances lit a cigarette to calm her nerves and cringed as she remembered her terrifying ordeals. She remembered her trip to the USA and the abuse she had suffered. She threw her butt over the edge of the deck and slowly closed the window and turned back into the room.

Suddenly she started spinning around the room. She was horrified, as she could not stop or help herself as she propelled round and round. She stopped as suddenly as she started, puzzled at what had happened and stood for a moment before she crept back to her bed.

How long is this torture going to continue? she thought as she wept into her pillow.

"I'll have cornflakes today," Harold grumbled as he dismissed the newly opened packet of his favourite cereal the next morning.

Puzzled by his refusal, she continued to enjoy her cereal, orange juice, and coffee.

That night she dashed to the bathroom after she woke feeling ill. She got there just in time as she had severe vomiting and diarrhoea. She was exhausted as she crept back to her bed.

"Were you sick last night?" Harold enquired as she set the breakfast table the next morning.

When she pulled the new packet of cereal out of the pantry, she was shocked to find the packet full of ants. Mystified, she searched the pantry. They had never had ants in the house before. *Where did they come from?*

When Harold left for the shop, she reached for the fly spray and sprayed inside the packet. Then instinct told her to take some samples of the cereal, which she carefully wrapped in tin foil. Then she hid the small parcel and threw out the packet of cereal.

It was to be three whole years before this episode became much clearer to her. Frances then grabbed her carton of cigarettes from the pantry and tore them to shreds. She carried them down to the incinerator and burnt them to dispose of the drugs Harold had planted in them.

As Frances returned to the house through the garage, she picked up a note left by Harold. *Turn the lights off*, she read. When she stepped into the rumpus room, she found another note on top of some books that were in his space: *Please remove by 30th April deadline.*

When Harold arrived home late that night, he was talkative for a change.

"I had trouble today," he said, "Ants in my shop, even in the sugar."

I'm not surprised, Frances thought.

As Frances dare not go out anywhere, she busied herself at home and contented herself with reading and watching TV.

When Frances washed her hair that morning, she was puzzled. There was no sign of the permanent wave and high lights she had three weeks ago. Harold's comments over the years rushed through her mind: *What is that stupid hairdo. It looks bloody ridiculous.* She decided to write a letter to her hairdresser to inform them, as she suspected that Harold was behind this problem by asking the hairdresser to pretend to do the perm and colour job in her hair.

"Dear Patty," she wrote to the hairdresser. "When I had my hair permed and coloured three weeks ago you did not do it, you just pretended to do it, now three weeks later there is no sign of the perm and colour. I would like you to refund my money or I will have no option but to report you to the Consumer Affairs department." She mailed the letter that day.

Slap went the newspaper as Harold flung it at her that night. She warily eyed the article he meant her to read. "Read this!" he screamed at her.

When the coke wears off, screamed the headlines. After a quick read about smoking crack cocaine, she screwed the paper up and tossed it aside.

So, he did lace my cigarettes with cocaine. She thought.

Three days later, she sat idly watching the Oprah Winfrey show. She wasn't paying much attention, then suddenly she was alert as Oprah began discussing a book called Emotional Blackmail, by Doctor Susan Forward. *That is what he has been doing to me all these years.*

Emotional Blackmail is when the people in your life use fear, obligation and guilt to manipulate you.

Frances was amazed by the discussion as the show progressed. She realized the meaning of emotional blackmail. She had perused the book in shops and discarded it. No, that was not what she needed, not what was going on in her life. While there was a commercial break, she rang her friend Rita. She lied to her. Told her to watch TV as Elvis was on.

So that is what Harold has been doing to me all these years, she thought as she grabbed her keys. She drove directly to the local bookshop and brought the book. He has masked it for so long, well hidden, she thought. She was completely unaware of what Harold had been doing to her.

On her way home she called into the hairdresser. She had not received a reply from her letter.

"I've come to collect my refund," she told Patty the hairdresser.

"I've got to see the boss," she replied as she walked out the back.

After a few minutes, Patty walked back to the counter, opened the till, and gave her the refund without even looking at her hair.

Frances slapped the book Emotional Blackmail on the counter so Patty could read the title, then she picked the book up to take home.

"A great book to read," Frances said as she walked out of the shop as Patty stood there stunned.

When Frances drove out of the shopping centre, she had to stop for some people at the pedestrian crossing. She spied two of her old work mates and abusers in front of her. She opened the car window and yelled at them, "What does it feel like to be a marriage wrecker?" Then she drove off.

That night when Harold arrived home, his face was white as he walked straight to the coffee table and picked up the book. Frances knew immediately that Rita had rung him about the book.

"Is this about me?" he asked.

"Yes," she said. "That's you in that book. What you have been doing to me all these years."

"Gee, you must hate me."

"No, I do not hate you. I pity you. You are like your parents rolled into one. Worse. What a despicable creature you are. After all these years, I do not even know you. I never have. It was always my fault." She wept as the words tumbled out.

Over the years, he had found her hot spots. He knew which buttons to press as his controlling influence gradually crept over her. He had moulded her until finally he thought she was under his control. He did not care about her emotions. He had groomed and created her.

Her eyes wandered restlessly around the room as she

realized the real Harold. Not the one she thought she knew. She knew then how he had treated her. What he had done not only to her but also both of them.

Harold's dark side had finally emerged. He was a skilled manipulator, and he had built up his ego over the years at her expense. He had systematically attacked her very being, making her self-esteem very fragile. He always had this need to know where she was and what she was doing. He used to open her personal letters, which she put a stop to years ago. He could not tolerate Frances having close friends. He always found fault with them. He would not socialize with them. He had to win arguments, too. If he lost, he would storm off sulking or get into a tantrum and be icy and aloof for days on end.

She was grief-stricken and horrified as she realized the truth. His attitude toward her was always negative, which caused tension between them. He was a passive type. He denied emotion as he withheld affection from her and always treated her like his personal servant.

She realized the enormous damage that he had done to them. Win or lose, he had set out to systematically destroy her.

There had been a rigid observance of her role despite her being the primary breadwinner. He never helped around the house while she was out working, even though he had plenty of time to spare, time that he selfishly spent on himself. Frances had been aware of this, and yet she indulged his every whim.

Harold was obsessed with her. His words more than a decade ago, said jokingly to her, flew through her mind: *No one will ever have you.*

Frances pondered whether she should leave Harold. She investigated how much it would cost to rent a small house and found it too expensive. She needed two weeks' rent and four weeks' bond, there was the weekly rent, power, and phone to pay for. She could not afford that on her meagre wage; she only worked part time on call so she could not rely on that. She worked for a survey company calling up clients asking about their power usage. It was a one-off job, then she would be unemployed again. She decided against leaving Harold as her income from eBay was sporadic and the market income only paid her living expenses, she was not capable of working full-time. Harold had destroyed their financial situation.

"I remember you," Denise from Ace Computers said as Frances introduced herself on the telephone. "You came into our shop to look at computers yesterday. How can I help you?"

"I would like more information regarding your computers," Frances said.

Frances had investigated buying a computer to start a business at Harold's suggestion. He had demanded that she start a business working from home. He had no thought as to how they would survive.

Frances knew where she stood. He had made that clear after he made a list of what he would allow her to do. He gave her the list that night. "A list for you" Harold said, "You are to abide by my rules and do as I say," he continued. She called it his "Control Freak List;" it had become obvious that his jealously was difficult for him to keep in check. "You are not allowed to see your friends, not even Rita. You do not need money, because you are not allowed to go out anywhere. You will do what I tell you." It was typed on his computer.

"Who do you think you are giving me a list like this. Stuff you and your Control Freak List"

What kind of life would that be, conforming to his wishes constantly?

As she had gathered the information during the past six weeks, she had found it fascinating but daunting. Setting up the computer while still deeply affected by the traumas in her life which proved to be a mammoth task.

When she got the computer home, she unpacked it and set it up. She started using it to set up Harold's business. She had not used these files before when she was employed. She created a stock list, invoicing, and the general ledger to track Harold's invoices. After that she created files for her business.

After enrolling in courses, she enjoyed learning Word, Excel, Windows, and the internet. Although she was continually tired and her mind fuzzy, she tried her best while coming to terms with what he had done to her.

"A typing service would be good," Harold suggested as he loped into the office and slapped a book down on the white computer trolley.

Intent on improving her skills, Frances ignored him as she concentrated on the course manual open at the keyboard functions page. She paused, dumfounded as she glanced at the book. The title leapt out at her: *Transferable Skills: How to Get the Job You Want*.

"Yeah, with hundreds of others," she replied as she pushed the book away. "Besides, I'm not a typist. Never will be."

Over the years she had become a yes person to him and to everyone as she tried hard to please people but was never allowed to be herself.

As she struggled vainly, she found it was hopeless, spending hours typing just one resume. It was not worth the effort, and dejectedly she gave up and decided to do markets and sell books on the web. This gave her the incentive to pull herself together and get on with her life.

"Nonfiction more interesting than fiction," she whispered to herself as she used her knowledge of Front Page to create a website. She was pleased with the result. Frances was doing a course on setting up a web page.

At home she was intent on uploading her book catalogue when she finished the file. She set it up on the internet and uploaded her catalogue. The next morning, she had five book orders from Amazon. Amazon was to be her main customer.

Meanwhile the subtle abuse continued while Harold drove her around helping to gather her stock. Almost daily something would happen that would have no meaning except she knew it related to her life and that Harold was controlling her every move. Shop keepers would show her books she was interested in even although she had never been in the shop before. It was obvious that Harold had contacted them and let them know they would be coming into the shop.

One night as she sauntered into the classroom, Betty the Asian tutor was setting up the company's home page on every screen for the internet course.

Casino—enter here, the screen glared at her as she slid into her seat.

"Douglas," Frances called to the head tutor, "I have the wrong screen. It's a casino page."

"Oh, you don't want to go there," he said, smirking. "Your husband would not like you using your credit card running up a big bill." He strolled over and changed the screen.

That afternoon she had played the pokies for an hour at the casino for something to do. She liked the odd gamble, but Harold hated her playing.

As she decided Harold needed help desperately, she thought Masie from the Maintenance union from her last job might help, as she was still paying her union fees. She tapped out a letter on her computer:

She printed it out and mailed it that afternoon.

As the weeks went by, she withdrew further inside herself. She became sullen and could not communicate with anyone.

In the doctor's waiting room one day, Frances stood idly eyeing the brochures in the rack on the wall when a pamphlet on cocaine caught her eye. She furtively sneaked a copy into her handbag.

That evening at home, she sat down at the kitchen table with the pamphlet. "Crack cocaine," she read, "is not safe to use in cigarettes. It is a dangerous substance and acts very quickly when mixed with water."

When she finished the pamphlet, she turned to the internet. "Cocaine has an immediate effect and creates an intense high." As she read on, she knew she had experienced most of those symptoms.

It was fascinating and horrifying as she continued reading. "Anxiety sets in, and users are suspicious and are often confused. They also have short tempers, and their thinking is impaired. They suffer loss of appetite and insomnia."

She was appalled as she read about erratic and paranoid behaviour and periods of extreme depression.

"A user could suffer diminished vision, insomnia, and

weight loss, as well irritable, confused thinking, and suicidal despair. Withdrawal symptoms are fatigue and depression."

Frances was mortified. It must have been at least a year since her trip. No wonder she was cranky and did not know what she was doing. All her anger, shouting, and not eating. She then realized that everyone knew because Harold had told them.

Harold had rolled all of their faults into one and told everyone they were hers. So, people thought they knew all about her. He certainly had no respect for her after she had devoted all her life to him.

For Christmas of 1997, Frances and Harold's daughter Cindy and Cindy's three daughters—Sheryn, Kirsty, and Robin—came for a visit. It was hard for Frances to enjoy Christmas day, but she put on a brave face and tried to overcome her problems.

As they all sat on the patio around the wrought-iron table, covered with a green, lacey tablecloth, sipping wine in the heat of the sun, Harold passed Frances an envelope. Frances opened it slowly and read the card.

"To my loving wife," Harold had written. "I hope next year is better for you. From your loving husband." She hastily closed it and put it aside, stunned.

How could I be "loving" after all of this? she thought. *Not with what I have been through.*

Two weeks later Frances was browsing the situations vacant in the local paper when an advertisement caught her eye: "Person wanted to help deliver gifts on a casual basis."

Frances rang Julie who did the advertisement.

"Hello Julie, I would like to apply for the job of delivering gifts for people."

"Yes, you can come around now for an interview" Julie said.

Frances arrived at Julies for the interview.

"Hello Frances" Julie said.

"I need someone with a van so they can deliver the gifts, have you got suitable transport.

"Yes, I can use my husband's van" Francis said.

"Can you start on Monday Valentine's Day" Julie asked Francis.

"Yes, that's no problem" Frances said.

After the interview, she decided to try it. It would get her active on those special occasions, such as Mother's Day, Father's Day, and Valentine's Day.

Valentine's Day was her first day on the job, and she was delighted to deliver elegant gifts to the surprised recipients, despite the humidity and heat of that February day.

He never gives me gifts; she mused as she drove around doing deliveries. As she loaded her second delivery, she was dismayed at her boss Julie's attitude.

"If you put your smoke down you could go faster," she said to Frances. Frances drove off with a roar, thinking, *how dare she? I am entitled to a break.*

Later that night, Julie arrived uninvited to enquire how her day had been.

"I pissed my pants all over the car seat," Frances said with a giggle as Harold looked on in horror. I couldn't find a toilet."

"Yes, that can be a problem when you are out and about delivering gifts" Julie said.

"Why did you say that? It is not you," Harold said after Julie left.

"I have found my bloody tongue after all these years," she replied harshly. "And I will use it. Fuck you."

"Stop that language," Harold said, appalled. "You never use that word."

"*Fuck fuck fuck!*" she screamed at him. "*You hear me? I do now!*"

On Monday morning, Frances was surprised and pleased to receive a reply from Masie, the union rep. She had arranged an interview in two weeks' time with a unit manager at her last job named Selwyn. This gave her time to type a document for the meeting.

As she still worried about the power of attorney that Harold had made her sign before she went to America, Frances drove to the shore to see her new solicitor. After parking her car, she browsed the shops and glanced around occasionally to ensure no one was following her. There were two Asian men waiting at the traffic lights. They were staring at her as she nervously pushed the door open and walked into the building.

"I remember you," the receptionist said as Frances approached the desk. "Take a seat. He will not be long. Would you like a coffee?"

"No, thank you," Frances replied as she thought, *There's a bug in my car. He knows I am here.*

Frances's solicitor rang her family lawyer, who assured her that the power of attorney had been revoked. He would put that in writing, too. Frances was relieved.

"Hello, Frances," Judith said when Frances answered the phone that night. "I have not heard from you for years. Frances I am ringing about the family tree." She rambled on and Frances could not get a word in edgeways.

Judith was a distant relative who was doing the family tree just like Frances. She had short straight mousey brown hair and was five foot two.

"How are your books going on the web Frances?" Judith asked as Frances banged down the receiver and cut her off.

How could she know I sold books on the web? I haven't heard from her in years. Harold must have rung and told her about Frances' books on the internet. Frances had a web site with Abebooks.com. It was easy to manage, uploading a new catalogue every week. Most of her sales came through Amazon.

Frances brought her books from second-hand book shops, second-hand shops and auctions.

Harold had made sure that everyone who ever touched her life knew about her, and the stalking pattern had been created.

Flustered, Frances sat down on the computer chair. She was puzzled as fleeting glimpses of the past crept in. There was that other solicitor she had tried locally; she knew he knew who she was when he had asked all those questions in a sarcastic tone: Was she on drugs? Could she be committed? She had hardly uttered a word. Harold was ensuring he had control over her with the enduring power of attorney. However, she was not aware that he knew she had revoked it.

These people were playing mind games with her.

Masie rang Frances to meet outside in the street before the meeting with Selwyn. She had made it quite clear that she was not interested in a private discussion beforehand.

When they met, Frances gave Masie a copy of her memo before they entered reception. "This is to let you know what they did to me."

Masie stood in the sunshine on the sidewalk and skimmed the pages. "I will see what I can do," she said.

In her confusion, Frances felt fragile. She was aware of her ill-fitting clothes, loose through weight loss after not eating much in the USA which was five months ago. Selwyn quickly ushered them into his office as Masie handed him a copy of the memo which they both read carefully while Frances sat silently waiting.

"No," Selwyn lied, grinning slyly while his grey eyes twinkled. "We never did anything. There's nothing I can do to help you. I work for my grandchildren."

Harold had told Horrible Harry that she worked for her grandchildren.

"It's a wonder you never saw it coming," Selwyn added with a smirk.

Selwyn had a positive attitude. He raised his eyebrows and was devoid of emotion as he flatly denied the abuse. Frances was appalled at Selwyn's attitude. He was admitting in a roundabout way that he knew what they had done to Frances. His attitude told her that as he moved around in his seat and his facial expression told her that he knew too. He was void of any emotion as he lied to Frances and Masie.

So, it was a smoke screen to hide the emotional blackmail, Frances thought.

"But Selwyn," Maisie interrupted, "the staff fed her cocaine."

"So?" he said dismissively.

"The people involved have left the company," Frances said as they ended the meeting abruptly.

Masie gathered the memos and gave them back to Frances to ensure Selwyn never kept a copy.

"Would you like a coffee?" Masie asked. "There's a café down the road, I will pay."

As they sat at a dirty white plastic table on the sidewalk, they sipped their freshly percolated coffee while the strong aroma drifted in the air. It was twenty degrees, and the sun was shining in a clear blue sky.

"What do you think of Selwyn's integrity?" Masie enquired.

"Certainly not one hundred percent for a person of his responsibility," Frances replied as she tried to make sense of the meeting. Her mind was muddled, confused, and she was unable to comprehend properly. It had taken Frances a long time to get over the cocaine and abuse.

"I don't mind paying. All those union fees you paid," Masie said as she departed. Frances left at the same time to go to her car and drive home pondering the meeting.

Over a year ago Horrible Harry upset her, and she had cried for hours at work in her office. Raymond, a supervisor, and Lindsay, the tough union rep, found her upset.

"Harry gave me this big pile of work to do and said I have to finish it today, which is impossible," she told them.

"You need to join the union," Lindsay said. "I will go to the wages clerk with you and get them to start deductions from your pay on the next pay day." So, he bullied her and forced her to join the union.

Months later, there were many union meetings because the company was going to break away from the parent company and become a stand-alone unit. Gary, her union rep, was supposed to find out the details of her job description. Frances reminded him before each meeting. He said he would do it but never did.

This continued for months. No one was interested in helping her. She was annoyed and resigned from the union. However, months later, with the abuse in full swing, Horrible Harry came to her office one day.

"Are you in the union?" he screamed at her as he thumped a union notice on her desk. He knew that she had joined the maintenance union and was upset about it.

Frances was terrified and reviewed her situation. She re-joined the union and requested them not to advise the company.

Frances realized now that during that stressful time, she was stupefied with cocaine, and her thinking was impaired. She had become anxious and suspicious, her temper a quick fuse, and she had experienced extreme obsessive-compulsive behaviour.

Audrey had come into her office and found her crying profusely.

"What's wrong with me?" she sobbed "Why do I feel like this? Why are they treating me this way?"

"Go to the doctor," Audrey advised.

"What can he do?" she had replied, and she never went to the doctor.

Now she wished she had.

Masie had never spoken to her privately, and Frances had wondered why she had never forced the issue. Instead, Masie joined forces with the company and would not help Frances at all. Had Masie spoken to her, she would have learned the truth.

More memories floated around, crueller than ever.

"Gee, that's sad," a colleague named Ricky said when she told him she was leaving on that last day at work.

There was also Andrew, the private consultant who pointed her out to his boss Paul. He was hired by the company to organize the business into shape. Andrew was trying to improve the staff image by employing younger staff. He felt that Frances was now too old for the company. He continually said to her during the last few weeks at work, "You need a lawyer." And on another occasion, "We need to lift the image of the staff."

A temporary accountant named James told her, "It's hard to get a job after fifty." When she mentioned her problems to him, he said, "Let me know where you are going" and "Selwyn knows what he is doing." Frances found those remarks strange as she was not going anywhere.

"Have you decided what you are going to do after you leave here?" an engineer named Fred asked. She was puzzled at that, as she remembered James remark from the day before.

Ben, whom she liked and respected, started saying strange things to her, too. She felt it was like he was talking about her life, but his conversation had never clicked in her mind. Harold was in pain all the time because of his stroke, and he had tried suicide twice. The first time he took an overdose of pills when he had been collecting the pills over a long period of time. He also took an overdose the second time he tried suicide when he was put on life support,

"Being in pain all the time. Someone dying," he had said.

"What do you do here all alone?" he asked a surprised Frances.

Peter, who was usually friendly, avoided her and looked at her strangely. She was puzzled even more when he said, "My wife has the number of the radio station set on her phone at work. She listens to the competitions on the radio. She hits redial to enter the competitions." That was a strange coincidence because Harold did that all the time.

Horrible Harry was being made redundant because he was incompetent, and all the staff knew it.

"Better off dead, he should not try suicide," Horrible Harry said after he entered her office after she had told him about Harold's suicide bid. "That is why I had the week off work to care for him."

"Harold," she said. "Suicide attempt. The second time. I was home caring for him."

"Did you know that he tried suicide when you rang in and said you would be off work for a week?" he asked her.

"Yes," she said simply.

She did not tell him on the phone because Harold might hear, and he would not like that.

Frances had never spoken to anyone except her best friend Christine about his first attempt, as she wanted to spare Harold's feelings. The first time she had rung Christine, who came to the hospital and comforted her. Frances was numb. She could not cry, and she had a headache.

"Take some Panadol when you get home," Christine said.

"I can't," she replied. "He has eaten them all." She laughed lightly to relieve the tension within.

As Harry walked towards her, she was shocked at his words as he rambled on about his father's illness. She possibly looked relieved as she did not know what was wrong with Harold. He never told her anything. He would never talk about his health problems, and she worried silently. After all, you cannot help someone if they will not talk to you. As it turned out, he was too busy talking to other people and slandering her to make her look bad than be bothered talking to her his wife.

One day as Frances was sitting outside with other staff, Ben walked past, and Frances remarked to him about stopping smoking. Both of them were trying to stop smoking. Suddenly Eva screamed sarcastically to Frances, "Gee, you are nasty." Frances was stunned and did not know where to look. She sat quietly waiting to escape.

Many times, her office door opened quickly, and when she turned to look there was no one in sight even after she looked out the window. She never heard footsteps on the gravel outside her office.

"I treat people the way I would like to be treated," Selwyn said with a smile on a very rare occasion that he sat with the staff.

One day Audrey came rushing into Frances's office with a folder in her hand. "The list is out," she said, and showed Frances the staff flow sheet for their department. Audrey was listed under Frances's name, and Frances was listed as Audrey's supervisor. Frances was appalled. She did not want to supervise Audrey, who bucked the system all the time. She spent a long-time outside smoking and talking to whoever came along.

The next day Ben came into her office. He said the staff flow chart was on the wall in their office. He wanted to show it to her. Frances went with him to his office and found that Frances's job as systems administrator was vacant. Frances was listed as a debtor's clerk. She was horrified. They were playing games with her.

Management appeared unconcerned regarding her constant memos about when testing should start for the new computer system. Frances was concerned about her responsibilities and the stress it would involve. God, she would be pleased with a new system. This one was crap and had never worked properly.

When Auckland Maintenance opened, they were lean and mean with permanent staff and used casual temporary staff where each one interpreted the system differently. The management never believed in staff training. She had experienced that herself. When Frances started, the system has been a shambles, and they severely abused her for all her hard work over the years.

One day a casual remark forced her into action. When she searched the root directory of the computer, she found a file that indicated testing of the new system had started two months before without her knowledge. This was the last straw for Frances. She hurriedly wrote out her resignation and handed it to Andrew the consultant. Andrew had been employed as CEO until the business changed to a stand -alone unit. He pretended to be upset by this and said he would investigate Horrible Harry and let her know the next day. When Frances went to see Andrew the next day, he said they could not let Horrible Harry go just yet, they needed him. Frances handed in her two-week notice but only had to work two days because she was going on holiday to the USA two days later. She had saved enough money from her good wages to go on the trip.

David, a very quiet storeman, had laughed loudly and

heartily right in her face when she told him she was leaving. Frances was extremely hurt and stunned at his response.

"What happened to Harold at Christmas?" Audrey had asked. She knew that Audrey was talking about Harold's suicide attempt. So Horrible Harry had told the staff about it.

She pieced the conversation together and recalled the sheer horror of it all.

They were to go on a cruise with Rita and Rita's husband Kerry in December 1996, on a boat they owned, for a couple of nights. Harold did not want to go, even after inspecting his sleeping quarters. He never wanted to go anywhere with her. She now knew it was all part of his plot.

"The break will do us good," she cajoled him.

"You go. I'll be alright," he had said.

"No, I want you to come too. It will be good for you."

The conversation continued back and forth as she tried desperately to include him.in going on the boat.

"I promise I won't do anything stupid," he said. "You go and enjoy yourself."

In the end, Frances went by herself with Rita and Kerry. But she never enjoyed herself, as she constantly worried about Harold. She rang him continually and wished she had stayed at home with him. Now she knew Harold had planned all this to let people see how selfish she was.

"Mrs. rich bitch," Audrey had said to her once.

Frances never replied after all no one knew her circumstances, did they. They would never be rich, only comfortable.

Horrible Harry came to her office and Frances told him, "Audrey's work habits are bad. She talks and smokes outside all the time. She needs to be spoken to about that. She holds me up, and I cannot do month-end on a timely basis."

"She has a heart of gold," Harry said to her.

"That's not good work ethics," Frances said to Harry.

Did Horrible Harry expect this of employees rather than good honest hard work and loyalty to the company, she wondered.

Frances was generous, too, but it was hidden because of the mind control tactics Harold had used on her for over three decades.

Her memory wandered forward and back to her job. She remembered the hassles that continued with her job. She still had other people's work to do so she could complete month-end on a timely basis. Yes, she thought, that was all deliberate to stress her out.

One day she found her neat and tidy piles of work in disarray. Someone has searched my office, she thought. What were they looking for? Then eventually for their final and evil event they sent her to Coventry. The staff isolated her from them and left her on her own, they would not socialize with her,

The female staff members went out to lunch. She was not invited, although they talked freely about it in front of her.

Am I paranoid with all these happenings? she had asked herself as she tried to comprehend why they were treating her this way.

They were corrupt. They did not care what happened to her. Frances had always tried to be fair, even if it almost killed her in the process.

She felt she was losing her mind. And who could blame her? Did anyone not think there's got to be something wrong with this man?

Frances was upset with Horrible Harry. He had questioned her closely one day over a decade ago regarding their new house plans. Due to the conditioning treatment, she'd received from Harold, she never thought anything of it. Her thought processes were damaged even then.

"Did you do the plans and everything?" he had asked.

Not knowing why, he was questioning her nor even wondering how he knew, she simply said yes.

Her mind wandered back even further over a decade, remembering their house they had built. Now she thought she should have said 'yes, I worked out what we would like in the house and Harold agreed. He'd even gone over the measurements of the house at Frances's request to make sure they were fine and said they were great. Harold had agreed all the way through, knowing the house would be inadequate once it was completed.

She knew that Harold had told everyone that they were "her house plans" because of all the remarks that were made to her and the people he brought around to have a look. Frances clearly remembered one day they arrived at the house and Harold was placing marks on the walls with nails high up for the builders. He never told her what they were for, and she never thought to ask.

When the house was completed, the electrical switches were all in the wrong places, well in from the edge of the walls, and the telephone jacks were all up high, so the phone cords hung down and looked ugly. Frances had managed to disguise one with a wall hanging, but the dining room was bloody ridiculous.

Frances was alarmed at other mistakes in the house, and when Harold built the bar for the rumpus room, he deliberately scratched all the formica. At the time it happened, she could not understand why he had done such a thing after all she trusted him implicitly.

She found it was now amazing she never twigged, but as the experts say, these fanatics disguise their intent well.

On her last day at work, just before Selwyn presented her with a bouquet of flowers, Bev pushed her through the doorway and said, "Don't cry."

After the presentation, Selwyn asked the staff lining the walls of the grubby canteen if they had anything to say to Frances.

"What hotel are you staying in?" Peter asked her with a grin.

"Ooh, too rich for me," he smirked after she replied.

"I never picked it," Frances replied. "Rita did. It's not expensive."

"Going to gamble?" someone asked.

"No, we are not, we are going to see the shows," she replied.

"I hope Frances and her husband are very happy" Selwyn said at the end of the meeting.

This was her last day at work, and she went around to say good-bye to her co-workers. Each woman stood in the doorway of their office. Then one by one they hugged Frances and wished her luck.

As she left, she felt like ramming the bouquet into the rubbish tin but didn't have the guts.

The telephone rang loudly, interrupting her train of thought. When she picked up the receiver, no one spoke.

A few minutes after she put it back down, it rang again. She picked it up again and still no one was there. She stared at it, puzzled.

She leafed through the phone book to ring Bell's fault number. Bells checked the line and found there was no fault.

"The phone's bugged," she told Harold with disbelief that night.

"Where did it come from?" he asked.

"The PI," she said.

"It came from a garage sale," Harold said.

"No, it never." She instantly regretted her reply as her mind flashed back more than a decade.

After being made redundant from her work, Frances obtained new work. Later, however, Danny her boss went bankrupt. Frances was loyal to him during those hard times after the receivers moved in. Danny had repaid her by finding a job for her with his friend Robert, a private detective. The PI and his company were moving offices, and during the shift,

Robert walked over to Frances through the muddle of boxes and spare telephones on the floor.

"Frances," he said, "would you like a telephone?"

"Yes," she replied. "We could do with another one at home." Robert picked up a nice, clean phone and passed it to her.

"I want that one," Phillipa piped up "it's the best one" she added. Phillipa had been with the company for five years and was entitled to the best phone.

"No, this one is for Frances," Robert said sternly, glaring at Phillipa.

A few weeks after the company moved to the new premises, Harold rang Frances at work early one morning.

"Danny just rang me," he said. "Robert is going to sack you today."

"What?" she replied, stunned.

"Danny thought it might be better if you resigned," Harold said.

"No way," she replied, puzzling over why Danny would ring Harold and not her.

Frances sat all day working and waiting. Each time she went into Robert's office, she noticed he was smoking heavily. Then later all the other staff were sent home early, and Robert strolled over to see her.

"Your three months is up," Robert told her. "You're fired. Come into my office and collect your final pay. I will give you two weeks in lieu of notice." That was it. Out of a job.

Frances had been employed for a three -month trial and then she was sacked. She went quietly to Robert's office and collected her pay.

As she mused over this, she recalled other happenings and knew that Harold was behind her redundancy, too. When this period of layoffs occurred, there was Pat who kept telling her she only needed a part-time job. These comments from someone who did not know her circumstances baffled her completely.

A few months after Frances was made redundant from the Auckland Star, she and Harold had a stall at Blockhouse Bay Community Centre Antique market and Pat appeared.

"Are you happy?" she asked Frances as Harold sat quietly. He was white in the face.

"No," she replied simply.

They did not have much income at that time because she was unemployed. Frances never thought about why she felt unhappy. She never realized it was what Harold was doing to her that made her feel that way.

When the layoffs affected her department, Frances had every right to fight for her job as the criteria was "last on, first off." She knew her friend Charlene would lose her job if she fought. Frances chose friendship against income, as she felt she would have a better chance of a job than her friend would. Boy, she thought, look how she repaid me.

Instantly *she earns more than me flew into her mind*. Harold had shouted out this in a restaurant in 1977.

Harold said something she never heard and startled her as she came back to the present.

"We will replace this one," Harold said, pointing to the phone. "On Sunday."

The next day after Harold went to work, she was stunned when she found the telephone was missing from the dining room. She searched the book shop the best way she could amongst the muddle, especially in the back room. It was not there either. Where had he hidden it?

On the Sunday as they viewed the new telephones on the shelf at the electrical shop, Harold picked one off the shelf as Frances stood watching, still hazy and confused.

"We will have this one," Harold told the assistant.

Yes, she mused, *now that was set up already bugged again when they brought it.*

When Frances drove home after shopping on Monday, she caught a fleeting glimpse on their street of a vanity license plate on a car parked in their street. DEVIOUS, it read. Was that one of his plots?

Harold went around to see Robert's wife Pam. They lived close by, in Glen Eden. Pam was five foot three, tall with long straight hair.

"There is an antique market on Sunday at Blockhouse Bay, and I would like you to ask Frances if our marriage is over," he said.

"Sure thing. But won't she be suspicious since I don't go to the markets?" Pam said.

"Yes, she probably will. But I have to know if there is any hope for our marriage."

"Ok, I will do it."

There was the market in Blockhouse Bay in May, and Frances booked a stall for the antique market as it was close to home. She felt emotionally vulnerable as she faced the world trying to get her life on track. She was astonished to see Pam walking towards her. She thought it was strange, as the markets were not Pam's scene.

"Hello," Pam cooed. "How are you?"

"Not too bad, considering I have been psychologically abused for the last thirty-four years," she replied as she burst into tears.

As Pam went on talking, Frances cringed behind her stall and cried profusely as Pam continued to speak to her.

"Is your marriage over?" Pam enquired.

"Yes," Frances said.

Another stall holder named Sharon came over to her and asked Frances if she was alright. Frances took a few deep breaths and began to get control of herself again.

One night before Harold shut his shop, he rang her. "Could you put the aerial down on my van, so I don't forget when I park it in the garage tonight?" he asked.

So that is how the phone is bugged, through the aerial of his van?

The van was parked on the grass between the two units until he sold his old one.

There was a tradesman coming this morning, and Frances quickly tidied the house, then she opened the garage door to let him in.

Beware mice—the sign leapt out at her. This was a note that Harold had stuck on his den door.

When she entered the den, she found a huge mound of bird shit and feathers all over the floor. Harold had emptied the birdcage to attract mice to make out she was a dirty housekeeper.

Before tearing down the sign, she took a photograph of his loopy behaviour and hid the note for evidence against him.

Frances needed bubble wrap for her parcels. Harold suggested she try the post office. The next day she went to the post office.

"There is none in stock. I will look out the back," the clerk said. She left the counter and reappeared a few minutes later with a huge sheet of bubble wrap.

"We received a parcel with this wrapping. You can have our rubbish if you like," the woman said as she offered it to Frances.

As the tension rose, she felt her muscles screw tightly into little knots around her shoulders. she tried hard to relax. The mere thought of the bubble wrap upset her - she did not want the Post Offices' rubbish.

At the end of the next antique market day in Pakuranga, an Auckland suburb, Harold arrived to drive her home. When he loped into the hall, his face was white as a sheet, and he looked right at her. He wandered around talking to other stallholders as she struggled with her boxes and loaded the van. Then they drove home in silence. Frances drove her car when Harold wasn't going with her.

What was he up to while I was packing up? she wondered.

Back at home, Harold continued with his typing. He was determined to master the skill. He was still working on "Truth and Lies." One night when she walked into his den to get a new pen, he was tapping away at it. As she was leaving, he turned to face her.

"I am allowed to make mistakes," he said. She glared at his white face. "I made a mistake when I plotted against you. I don't want to destroy our lives. I lied about you to everyone." His face was whiter than white, and she stormed out. There was no apology for what he had done.

Frances went back to Harold's den half an hour later. "Not

with my life you can't. You do not care about my feelings, and you are throwing me into a terrifying nightmare. You want to possess me, no matter what. You have enlisted others who thought they were helping you. You are tormenting me with your emotional turmoil, and you are slowly destroying me. You are driving a wedge between us with your actions, and you don't recognise your actions as abusive."

She paused. Harold glared at her, his face white as a ghost.

"I am a very private person," she continued, "and I have never expressed my fears to anyone. I worry about your health and what we will face in the future. I was willing to help and support you, but now you have destroyed our lives.

"I have worked hard for over thirty years to ensure we would have no money problems in our retirement years. You have betrayed me and destroyed our lives. This is your dark side, the one I never knew existed. You were rejected by your parents when you were young. Your fear of abandonment terrifies you.

"You were five when your parents abandoned you, their first child. You lived with your aged grandmother in a home which lacked warmth and affection. You never recovered from this trauma and the intimacy.

"Your father was openly abusive. However, you cleverly hid your controlling and abusive behaviour for over three decades. You cunningly set out to dominate me and keep me in my place while you ensured all the time your public image did not suffer. You are very plausible, as you hid your anguish and self-loathing.

"'Be thankful that I'm not like my dad,' you said to me often over the years. You have inherited the traits of both your parents. Your father was icy, moody, intolerant, cruel, destructive, and sarcastic, and you have the morbid jealousy of your father as you have practised power and control on me over the years.

"Your mother is very demanding, spoiled, jealous, and child-like, and she has no empathy towards sick people. 'You don't keep sick people at home,' your mother said to me years ago. 'You put them in hospital, give them to someone else to care for them. That's what nurses are for."

Frances was sitting in the dining room, her face contorted with rage as she spoke to Harold.

"I'm not like that Frances" Harold said.

"Yes, you are" she replied. "You cannot accept how your life has been and now you take it out on me I can't stand any more abuse from you" Frances said.

"I want to support you financially, so you don't have to work," he said.

"Support me! On your income? Ten thousand dollars—that's all you earn. We can't live on that. Your shop is only a toy to play with. You never earned enough to support us!"

"I didn't know that," he said.

"No, because you let me pay all the bills," she said and stormed out.

"You have let me pay the bills and shown no remorse."

"We can build a new life together" Harold said.

"No, we can't you have gone too far with your abuse" she said.

Harold just sat there contemplating what she had said. He knew what she said was true and now he was lost for words. He finally got up off the chair and went to his den.

Harold sat at his desk contemplating his life. He knew he shouldn't treat Frances like that. But he had been doing it for thirty-four years, and she only just found out. His morbid jealousy got the better of him. It wasn't her fault he had a stroke, and he couldn't shake this feeling of self-loathing. He was trapped in his paralyzed body, and he hated it. Frances always treated him well, yet he continued to treat her badly. He was contemptible. He was obsessed with her and wanted her all to himself. He knew he was a psychopath.

CHAPTER
ELEVEN

The lift was out of order, and Frances was apprehensive as she climbed the stairs slowly. It was her first day of her part-time job at Data Entry Services, where she would be doing data entry and general office work. She never told Harold where she was working.

When she reached the landing on the first floor, she glanced around. She saw four doors leading left and right with brass nameplates attached. She turned left, approached the door, and knocked softly. There was no answer, so she turned the handle and pushed the door open and stepped cautiously inside as she nervously ran her fingers through her hair. She gently smoothed her skirt and clutched her handbag tightly to her side. One woman was talking on the phone.

The larger office, the one she stood in, had workstations set up opposite her against the wall. There were computer terminals set on four of the desks. After the dark-haired woman hung up the receiver, she stood up and walked towards Frances.

"You must be Frances. Welcome to the company," she beamed and offered her hand.

"Yes, I am," Frances said as they shook hands.

"My name is Margaret. I'm the supervisor. Would you like a coffee while we wait for the others to arrive?" she asked. "There's a lot to learn. I will show everyone together." She walked to the kitchenette and made the coffee.

Three other women—Mary, Annette, and Sharon—arrived soon after, and they began learning their work. They learned how to code the stock forms and check the prices before entering the data on the computer. Just before five, a tall woman with light brown hair strode in. She was smartly dressed, and the round rims of her fashionable glasses framed her grey eyes. Maureen was the boss. She had introduced herself to the new group earlier in the day and told them that staff were hand-picked and that they were the best staff on the market.

"How did they go today, Margaret?" she asked.

"Very well," Margaret said with a smile. "They learned a lot, especially the coding of the stock forms. They are ready for data input tomorrow."

"Goodnight, girls," Maureen said as they disappeared through the doorway.

That night Frances was exhausted. There was so much to learn before they could begin to process the forms.

Harold started to lay the table. "I will do the dishes after, too," he told Frances.

"What are you doing that for? You never helped around the house when I was working hard," she said.

Harold dumped the cutlery on the table and stormed to his den, his face contorted with rage.

Frances followed him.

"Why are you treating me this way?" she asked him. "Were you jealous of my income?"

"Yes, you were earning more than me. I was jealous of that," he said.

"Well, one of us had to make a decent living. You don't earn enough to support us. The shop is only a toy to play with, and you get hundred dollars a week. It's pocket money."

"We have four hundred dollars a week from rent. We can live on that," Harold said.

"If we do, who is going to pay the mortgages, rates, and insurance?" Frances said.

"I didn't know that," he said.

"No, because you did not want to know," she said.

———

Two weeks flew by as they learned the ropes. There was a lot to learn. It was not monotonous; there was plenty of variety, and Frances enjoyed the company, too.

Seated at the table during the morning break, Margaret started the conversation after Harold had loopy Ed contact her about Frances the previous day. He paid her five hundred dollars to abuse Frances during work hours. Margaret was grateful for the money as she had some pressing bills to pay.

"I heard about a terribly jealous man last night," she said. "He went to great lengths to control his wife. So extreme it was not funny," she said gleefully.

Frances, who was seated at the end of the table opposite Margaret, quietly recalled the title of the book, *Emotional Blackmail.* She was completely unaware that Margaret was talking about her.

Arriving home that night, Frances busied herself packing her stock for the market that she and Harold were attending the following Sunday. They had stalls booked next to each other so they could help each other with customers.

The week flew by, and on Saturday night they loaded Harold's van to get an early start the next morning.

After a quick breakfast, they left early.

"You don't have to take your own cup, do you?" Harold asked just before they left.

"I can't remember" she replied. "I will not take one today."

They went down the hallway to the garage and climbed into Harold's van.

It took half an hour to reach the hall and park the van. The hall was huge. Trestle tables lined the walls, two chairs behind each table. Stallholders were busy arranging their stock to catch the buyer's eye. The hall was alive with noise as they introduced themselves to their neighbours and idly viewed their stock.

After they carted their stock into the hall, they set up their stalls. Frances went for a coffee before the public was admitted at 10 a.m., and the woman from the next stall chatted with her as they strolled to the café.

At mid-morning, a small boy walked around with a tray in his hand, collecting cups to wash. It was then Frances remembered that they used crockery cups. Harold had set her up again—he had told them to give her a paper cup.

An older grey-haired woman approached Frances as she sat behind her stall.

"Is there a market for royalty books?" she enquired.

"Yes, there is, but not in New Zealand," Frances replied.

"Can I have your phone number? I will ring you," the lady said. "I have boxes of books everywhere. I keep tripping over them."

So do we, Frances thought.

Frances had seen Harold talking to the woman earlier and was sure she was sent to her by Harold because she sold books on the internet.

"I do not want to come here again," Harold said as they packed up their stock at the end of the day.

No, I bet you do not. Just like all the other times when you have approached other stallholders to abuse me, she thought.

Frances was unable to ask him why as she had closed down because of the abuse.

You never return to a place once you have contacted them about me, Frances thought.

"Shall we call into McDonald's?" Harold as they drove out the entrance onto the road. "I have some coupons to use up."

"Ok," she replied wearily. *What is going to happen there?* she thought.

As they sat in McDonald's eating their hamburgers, a woman came in.

"Hi," Olive said as she approached their table. She was also a stall holder at the market. "500 - 600 hundred dollars for a day stall, 1000 - 1500 for a weekend one," she continued. "That is good money. I was lucky and had a good teacher."

"We did not do too bad," Frances replied.

Lucky you. We never make anywhere near that, Frances thought.

"I must order now. See you later," Olive said as she turned towards the counter.

"Who was that?" Harold enquired.

"Olive. She works for Bream Auctions."

"Never seen her before."

"You must know her. She is there all the time."

"She cannot have been on duty when I have been there."

They finished their meal and left. As they walked to the van, Frances tried to put on a brave face as she opened the door and stepped inside. She was upset. She had a right to be, as she fought her tears in vain.

Driving home in almost silence, she tried to keep the conversation going. But she was unsuccessful. Harold would not budge when he was like this. He pretended to be nice to her and then he coerced others into insulting and abusing her. Making a fool of her in front of all those people. Telling her not to bring a cup and that woman saying about the boxes of books she had at home—he coerced them to do that.

I have feelings, she wept to herself.

The next day at work was a cold, miserable May Day.

"It is my in-laws' 35th wedding anniversary," Mary said. "I have left some special food in the fridge for them to enjoy."

It is our wedding anniversary. too. Thirty-six years, Frances thought.

Later Maureen strode into the room and approached Frances.

"I am doing an internet course Jun 10th," she said.

"Coincidence. So am I," Frances replied. "Perhaps it is the same course."

I think I have been stalked for some time.

After a while, Margaret approached Frances.

"I would like you and Mary to spy on Sue," Margaret said to her. "She is taking far too long with her work. Keep an eye on her."

Sue was a staff member who helped occasionally in busy periods. She was an extremely large woman with long dark hair, and tall which made her appear larger.

Nothing to do with me, Frances thought. You can do your own dirty work. That is what supervisors are paid for.

"I would like you to find out where she works. That other company, too," Margaret said. "She answers without a company name when I ring. Maureen and I have had no luck. She will not tell us. Sounds like a funny outfit.""I will try and find out," Frances replied just to keep her happy. She was not a pimp and had no intention of spying and did not like staff who liked to score brownie points.

Margaret handed out 25 forms to everyone to edit in

preparation for data input.

"Maureen just told me we only need to write up 25 percent of the forms," Margaret said as she walked briskly to the table. "How many have you done?" she queried, glaring at Frances.

"Ten, Margaret," replied Frances.

"Twelve," said Sue and Annette in unison.

"Thirteen," replied Sharon.

Frances was astounded and she found it hard to believe Sharon had done more than she had, as she was a slow worker.

"Ok, finish the quota," Margaret said as she walked off happily,

Frances worked flat out, faster than she had in a long time, determined to catch up. *They will not show me up,* she thought.

Later Margaret approached and glanced at the documents stacked high on the table. Frances's pile was higher than all the others put together. Margaret had done that deliberately to show Frances up and work harder than the rest of the staff. She was humiliated.

Harold has found out where I work and rung them to coerce them into abusing me, it is the same as my last job, Frances thought.

If only I could support myself financially, I would leave Harold and divorce him she thought. *I'm not capable of working full-time. I've tried the police; they don't believe me* she thought with despair.

"Look at that, Frances," Sue said as she handed her a form.

It's none of your business, she read what was written on the form, startled. Frances was annoyed. She had been set up again for pretending to spy on Sue.

Frances found the stock form later to check it and found it was incomplete.

"Should we keep the forms in their branch areas?" Mary asked Margaret.

"No, it does not matter," Margaret replied.

"Margaret are the forms in branches?" Maureen asked as she strolled into the room later.

"No," she replied. "Sorry my fault."

Spontaneously Frances said, "Someone mentioned that earlier."

"Come to my office," Maureen said sternly.

Suddenly Margaret burst out of Maureen's office and yelled at Frances as she stormed into the room.

"Frances, you just got me in the shit for not putting the forms in branches!" she screamed.

"Sorry, Margaret," she said. "I did not mean to." She continued sorting the forms.

Oh yes, she sighed to herself. Margaret is always hard on me and not the others.

"We will run out of work soon," Margaret informed them. "Who would like to go home early?"

"I would," Frances volunteered, eager to leave after a humiliating day.

"Relax when you get home Frances," Margaret said as she left. "You run around too much, always so busy."

The telephone rang not long after she arrived home. It was Ian. She worked for him selling advertising part-time. He knew she was working all day, yet he always rang not long after she arrived home.

After she turned on the computer, she logged onto the internet to check her emails. Astounded, she read, "I have just received a book in a unique shipping container, a pizza carton." Anna one of her customers had written. It was obvious to Frances that Harold had someone tamper with her emails.

They'd had pizza last night, and the empty box still sat on the kitchen bench as her mind wandered back to the previous evening. After she had parked the car in the garage, she entered the house through the internal entrance and heard a noise that sounded like the ranch slider closing. Harold limped down the hall towards her.

"That boarder of Don's has a laptop. You can go on the internet too," he had said.

Don was the tenant in their home unit in front of their home. He is in his seventies and has short white hair.

Immediately it became obvious Harold had asked the boarder to log onto her computer, tamper with her emails, maybe even copy email addresses.

Thursday night she had severe stomach ache and diarrhoea. In the morning, she was still running back and forth to the bathroom, so she called off work.

"Have you been gallivanting the last couple of days?" Linda enquired when she arrived at work on Monday.

"No, I have been sick," she replied.

"Could you do the dishes today?"

"Yeah, sure," Frances replied.

"Any fairs this weekend?" Margaret asked.

"Yes, just to browse," Frances answered.

"I need a dolls fair. I need a new dress for my porcelain doll," Margaret said.

Frances had had new hair put on her childhood doll. Paula, a work mate, organized it for her. For weeks after, Harold kept putting Frances' doll on their bed. In the end she inspected the doll, as she was curious. The legs had been switched with badly patched legs.

As she prepared dinner at the kitchen bench, the telephone rang. She dropped the potato she was peeling and picked up the receiver. It was Ian.

"How was your day?" he said. "Horrible, I suppose." Then, before she could reply, he added, "Been there, done that."

Stunned, Frances hung up abruptly.

By early June, she had had enough of the emotional abuse. It had escalated at an alarming rate. Now she was able to ascertain what was going on.

I have got to get proof, she thought as she left work one afternoon. She stopped in an electrical store not far from work. She viewed the mini tape recorders. At the counter as she waited to be served, she became uneasy as she noticed the punk boy with bright yellow, spiky hair watching her every move.

He cannot be watching me, she said to herself dismissing the thought.

In the carpark at work the next morning, she slid out of her car, then hesitated. She peered around, put the tape recorder in her pocket, and then secured the opening of her pocket with a small gold safety pin.

Frances almost bumped into a woman coming out of the bathroom as she walked in. She checked her device and adjusted the pin slightly, then went into the office.

"What is that book you are reading, Mary?" Frances asked as she walked into the office. Mary did not reply. Frances was upset that Mary did not reply.

Later Frances peeked at the book. *Cruel Legacy*, by Penny Jordan. She glanced at the inside flap. The book was about a girl who married young and through tragedy in her life became the breadwinner.

Coincidence? No way. Frances thought.

As she sorted the documents on the table, she glanced down at her long-sleeved cream blouse. There was a red spot on it. She thought it was blood.

A piece of paper floated across towards her. She picked it

up, and it too had a red blotch. Startled, she thought it was ball pen then blood. What was going on?

"How did you do that?" Mary enquired. "Did you prick yourself with a pin?"

Frances was astounded and continued with her work as she saw the red spot on her blouse sleeve.

Her mind wandered as she drove home that night.

Oh yes, they all knew about the tape recorder.

It was difficult to react to Harold these days. She never knew what mood he would be in. That night she had hidden the tape recorder inside the kitchen drawer with the microphone hanging outside beneath a tea towel. She tried to discuss the abuse he was having her subjected to. He refused and walked in a huff to Don's.

Harold went to David's house to ask a favour. "Next time Frances is at your house can you call this phone number for TV 10" as he gave David the slip of paper. "Ask for Bob, tell him you are to make the announcement that day about joint property if a couple split. He knows what to do and you have to watch TV to be ready for the announcement."

"Right, I will do that" David said.

"They will say that ten minutes before the announcement, special announcement coming up. Make sure you have the TV on" Harold said.

"Sure, I will" David replied.

Frances went to visit her friends Josie and David. David sat idly watching TV and playing with the remote control. Josie was average height with short blonde curly hair. David, who was stocky, stood at five foot ten. He used to work with Harold.

"Special announcement," he yelled to them. "On TV 10 soon."

Moments later, the words SPECIAL ANNOUNCEMENT glared back at them from the screen.

"All matrimonial property is to be divided equally. Property not applicable are inheritances and other money that has not been put into joint names," the announcer said.

So, Frances thought, Harold got someone in TV 10 to make that announcement, that was to tell me I could not claim my redundancy money if we divorced because I put it in joint names.

After that, they discussed the birthday party Josie was having for her mother Adel the next Saturday.

That night Harold got mad when Frances tried to discuss the party. She had hidden the tape recorder underneath some cushions on the lounge suite.

"I am not going," he yelled at her.

"Are you sure you don't want to go?" she asked again.

"No, I am not and that is that," he said grumpily. "you told Josie about my suicide attempts. I did not follow or trace you to work either."

Why would he say that, Frances thought?

"Maybe not, but someone did," she said. "Did you get loopy Ed to ring them?"

"Yes, I did," he replied with a laugh.

The harder she tried to save her marriage, she believed that her marriage could be saved if Harold behaved himself. The more pig-headed he became it was obvious he did not want to discuss anything. He thought he was right all the time. She was to do what he told her to do.

On Saturday night, Josie greeted Frances at the party and David asked how she was, so she told him about her problems with Harold.

"You can get mini tape recorders," he said. "Hide them on the body with a tiny microphone. Why don't you get one of those to tape Harold?" he said. Therefore, Harold had told them about her microphone, too.

F rances turned on the computer after Harold left for his shop that Tuesday. She began typing.

Dear Detective Watson,

I am writing about the severe psychological and emotional abuse my husband is subjecting me to. He has a fertile imagination and delights in plotting, stalking, and psychological abusing me. He is a control freak and tries to control my life. He has embarked on a reign of terror against me.

He brags to me about what he has done to me. He tampers with my car so I can't go out. He won't let me see my friends. He has destroyed some of my possessions.

I found out through the book Emotional Blackmail by Doctor Susan Forward that he has been psychologically abusing and controlling me for the last 34 years.

He tried to get me to change my occupation. Nine years ago, after I worked for a private investigator, I found out that he had a bugged telephone planted on me before I left the company.

He has contacted two companies that I worked for and coerced them to abuse me until it got so bad I had to resign.

He has tampered with my emails and coerced the recipients to abuse me by email.

He arranged for me to be stalked and psychologically abused while I was on holiday in the US. I was stabbed by a man with a needle and stupefied with cocaine. I cut my holiday short because of this.

He is continually using put downs and sarcastic remarks to me. He delights in doing this to me.

He is jealous, insecure, and controlling.

I fear for my safety.

Please help me.

She had read about Detective Watson who was involved in another abusive relationship and she thought he could help her.

As she drove towards the post office, she took a left here, right there. She wove around the streets and noted cars behind her, constantly glancing in the rear vision mirror. There did not appear to be anyone following her.

Despite her nerves, she strolled casually along the street and browsed the shop windows as the Post Office loomed in front of her. She hesitated while glancing around, she didn't want anyone to see her mail the letter as she was certain she had been followed. She was extremely paranoid about being followed. She was hyper vigilant, then she noticed a man who stood on the footpath. He was watching her.

She watched as the man walked away slowly then pulled a cell phone out of his pocket as he climbed into a black car parked at the curb. There was a small brown child sitting in the front seat.

Frances darted to the slot in the wall, shoved in her letter, and went back to her car. When she drove out of the car park, she took a little side street, took a left and a right, then drove on as she anxiously peered in the rear vision mirror. She was dismayed when she spotted the black car with the driver and child following behind her. She drove faster left, right, and onwards as the man followed while talking on his cell phone. She finally lost him as she drove home.

After parking her car in the garage, she went inside and flopped onto her bed where she lay deep in thought about the morning's events.

Strange that guy—did he follow me?

They use cell phones as they track me. So easy to divert suspicion, which explains all those other strange occurrences too.

She went into the kitchen for a coffee and lit a cigarette as she pondered what she should do. She thought she would ring Harold to see if she could get his vibes now that she recognised his mood. She settled down by the telephone with her coffee and ashtray and dialled the number of Harold's bookshop.

"Hi." She paused as she puffed nervously on her cigarette.

"I don't want to talk to you" Harold said, he was aloof so she hung up abruptly.

Harold knew that she was followed that morning. He also knew that she knew too. She only had to study him and now she could tell. This time she had hit the nail on the head. Harold's response was enough.

———————

Frances eagerly cleared the mailbox daily and kept hoping. But she knew deep down inside her there would not be a reply from Detective Watson.

She decided a direct approach was necessary. She drove to the Henderson Police Station three weeks later, taking a copy of her letter with her.

She felt uneasy as she peered out her rear vision mirror, sure that the blue car with the woman driver was following her and had been for some time. She continually turned left and then right down the side streets, but still that car tailed her. Frances became flustered and anxious, so she drove directly to the police station, unable to shake that car from her tail.

There was a desk sergeant seated at a table on the left of the counter as she casually stepped inside.

"Can I help you?" the elderly desk sergeant enquired.

"I would like to see a policeman," she replied softly.

"Over at that counter, they will help you," he said as he pointed to the right.

A policeman wearing his blue uniform entered from the room behind the counter as she approached.

"I would like to see someone privately," she whispered to him.

"Speak louder, I cannot hear you," he asked her gruffly.

She repeated it louder and received the same response, then he repeatedly asked her to speak louder until she was yelling at him.

His requests puzzled her, as she knew that her voice was loud anyway.

"Wait there, Miss. I will go and get someone," he finally replied.

As she wandered away from the counter and waited, Frances saw a woman smiling at her as she stepped slowly down the staircase towards her. It was Paula, an acquaintance of theirs. Without a flicker of recognition, Paula continued past Frances, still smiling as she disappeared into the room behind the counter.

After a few minutes, a young police officer in his thirties, tall with dark coloured hair, strode towards her.

"Can I help, Madam?" he asked.

"I mailed this letter to Detective Watson some time go," she said as she handed him the letter. "I have had no response"

The officer grabbed the letter as he ushered her into an anteroom, which also housed the Victim Support Team. He asked her some questions as he read the lengthy letter.

"There is no criminal charge," he advised her. "None whatsoever. However, I will pass this on to Detective Watson. The incidents are only coincidental," he continued. "We cannot afford to investigate. We have not got the funds. Why don't you leave him?"

"That lady," Frances said. "She knows me. I do not want my husband to know I came here."

"Did she recognise you?" he asked.

"I don't know, she was smiling as she walked down the staircase."

Frances finally realized that her mission was hopeless.

As she drove home, she played the conversation repeatedly in her mind and was confounded as she realized they would do nothing.

So, stupefying someone with cocaine nor jabbing someone

with a needle is not a crime. Of course, they are not crimes. How could they be? That officer told me so. It is strange that other people are sentenced for far less crimes.

She rang Ian the next morning about getting more work. He said he would call in to see her that afternoon. Ian was short with dark hair and blue eyes.

"How are things going?" Ian said as he handed her a book and some papers when he arrived. She was startled as she casually put the items down on the table and saw that one of them was a book called *Home and Safety Crime Prevention.*

After Ian left, she leafed through the book, astounded as she read a chapter called "Violence in the Home: Living in a Violent Relationship." "The police and women's refuge can help," she read. "No one has to put up with violent behaviour. Seek help if the violence is severe enough for you to fear for your safety."

Frances was horrified as she continued reading. "Violent behaviour includes making you do things against your will, stopping you from having a job, treating you like a servant, laying downs rules for your behaviour, making you feel bad, humiliating you, putting you down, and insulting you." She could not help reading further, and she found it fascinating. It described her life completely. "Not allowing you to have friends, limiting your activities, controlling what you do, and coercing others to increase the abuse."

Yes, she sighed as she lay down on her bed. That is what Harold has been doing to her all these years.

The next day she was back at work at Data Entry Services and pleased to be busy.

"Percolated coffee, anyone?" enquired Margaret at morning tea.

"Yes, thanks," Frances said as she left the office for a smoke.

There was no percolated coffee left when she arrived back, so she started making instant coffee.

"There is some percolated coffee for you," Margaret said, pushing the plunger and revealing the dregs in the bottom. "You like yours weak," she added, laughing.

There was only half a cup after Frances poured the dregs, so she added more water and sat silently sipping her coffee, feeling humiliated again. How could Margaret be so cruel?

After they finished their morning tea, Sharon came up to Frances and consoled her. "People will forget what your husband is doing to you," she said.

"Nearly time to go home," Linda said later as she looked at her watch. "No work tomorrow."

Frances was thankful there was no work the next day. When she arrived home, she was exhausted and lay on her bed for a rest. She was dismayed that she could not stop the abuse she was being subjected to.

As Frances searched Harold's den for a pen the next morning, she pulled out a clear plastic grocery bag she spied behind some books. She was alarmed and amazed when she opened it and looked inside. There were thousands of dollars all neatly folded in twenty-dollar notes. She hastily put the bag back without even counting it.

Where did all that money come from?

Back at work the next day, Mary was doing her usual tricks and annoying the hell out of Frances. Mary had been a schoolteacher. She was very demanding, abrupt, and far too bossy.

Linda called out as she walked into the room, "We have to start the creditors ledgers, debtors' ledgers, and general ledgers data entry today, so we need to learn how to code them."

Margaret gave them some more questionnaires to do.

"We will do the job together," Mary said to Frances as she peered over her shoulder before she sat down.

"What is the answer to this?" Frances asked Margaret. Before Margaret could answer, Mary jumped up and stood over Frances in a threatening manner.

"Do it this way," Mary demanded.

"I only asked a question," Frances snapped. "I am quite capable of doing my job."

Mary kept rabbiting on, and then Frances lost her concentration. She jumped up and hurled the papers at Mary.

"Do the lot!" she yelled as she gathered her belongings. "Stuff the bloody job!" She headed out the door.

"What about your contract?" Margaret yelled after her.

"Fuckin' stuff that, too!"

Thank God I have not signed the contract, she thought.

Maureen was very conveniently waiting outside the door.

"I think we should talk," she said to Frances.

"What about—"

"Calm down," Maureen said. "Let's go downstairs. You can smoke while we chat.

Is your husband still having you abused?" Maureen asked her.

Yes, he is and I can't take any more abuse" Frances told Maureen.

As they chatted for a while, Frances told her about some more of her problems with Harold.

"Go home. Do something for yourself today," Maureen said as they departed.

Frances was sick of their stupidity and antics. This insidious abuse had stuffed her brain. She couldn't think clearly, and it made her confused. She had enough to contend with at home without this terrible abuse at work, too.

There was a reply from Detective Watson when she arrived

home. He reiterated there was no criminal offences against Harold, even although she was drugged with cocaine and a needle stuck in her. They aren't crimes, because he said so.

She looked at the date of the letter and realized the reply was written on the day she went to Henderson Police Station. The reply was from Papakura Police Station. She did not doubt that her letter had been faxed to the front desk boys—have them answer it to get her off their backs.

He desperately needs help, she thought with dismay. I will have to try another angle. But what?

I need help to let the police look into this abuse which Harold is inflicting on me. I also need help for me to get over this abuse, he is hurting me all the time. She thought.

"You can take a longer break today," Margaret said to the staff before lunchtime the next day. "I need to export the data."

"Good," Frances said. "I need extra time to shop."

Frances arrived back after one hour and a quarter.

"It's not ready yet," Margaret said. "Take some more time."

Frances took off for another half an hour.

"Gee, that was a long break," Margaret said nastily when she arrived back.

Frances continued to work part-time; she was pleased to get out of the house despite the continual abuse they subjected her to. She tried hard to ignore it and kept to herself.

That way I will be safe.

"People forget quickly about your husband's abuse," Annette said to her one day during a break after she had been severely abused. That was two people who had said that—Sharon and Annette.

Did they believe the lies Harold had spread? Or were they sympathetic to her plight? They might forget, but how could she ever after all these years of betrayal? Not only that—they did not know she was a moving target, stalked and abused in all facets of her life.

Annette and Sharon had never participated in her mistreatment unless Margaret forced them to, she was aware of that. With her mind constantly confused, they slowly nibbled away at her piece by piece as the harassment continued.

The 10th of June was the day for the internet course that Frances and Maureen were to attend.

When Frances walked into the room, she found there was only one seat left. She seated herself in front of Maureen.

"I would like to sell a book on the internet," a woman told Gary, the tutor, as she turned around and smirked at Frances who sat behind her.

"You will need to go to a chat room," he replied.

That was no coincidence, Frances thought. She knows I sold books on the internet.

The next morning, as she sat sipping her coffee, the telephone rang shrilly and she snatched the receiver up quickly.

"Good morning, Frances," Margaret said. "I am afraid that your work is not up to scratch. Maureen told me of your problems. There is not much work, so you can have the rest of the week off. I will ring next week when there is more work."

"Ok Margaret that's fine with me, I need a break from work" Frances told Margaret.

How dare Maureen discuss her problems with Margaret!

CHAPTER
THIRTEEN

A week later Frances woke to the shrill sound of the telephone.

"My name is Priscilla," the voice said to her. "Margaret has left Data Entry Services, and I am the new supervisor."

"Oh," Frances said, relieved. She had not expected to hear from them again.

"Could you come into work this week?" Priscilla asked.

"What days and hours?" Frances asked. "I need time to organize myself. I just cannot work at short notice."

"Will Wednesday be suitable?"

"Yes, fine. See you at nine o'clock."

Priscilla greeted her when she arrived at work. Not long after, Maureen appeared suddenly behind Frances and spoke to Priscilla while she worked.

Priscilla was tall and slim. She had a pleasant face with deep piercing eyes and a crinkled smile that touched her lips.

Frances was thankful that Margaret had resigned from the company, as she was pregnant and at least she did not have to suffer her stupid antics and abuse anymore as it screws your brain up.

There was a market in Whangarei at the weekend, and

Frances had decided to attend to escape the abuse from Harold's torments at home. It was a quiet weekend and there was no sign of stalking, so she sat at her stall and relaxed. Then she drove home.

The abuse towards her had become a vicious cycle. She was a nervous wreck, and she was not able to focus on her work or anything.

One day as she walked down the hallway towards the kitchen, she noticed that Harold's bed had been removed from the bedroom. She was astounded and wondered where his bed was.

As she walked into the kitchen, Harold was sitting with his arms resting on the table. In one hand, he tightly gripped a white envelope. She dropped her bag on the floor and went to the computer to check her emails.

"This is for you," Harold said as he loped into the room and dropped the envelope on the desk.

She sat and watched him as he struggled off then she saw his white face when he half turned back. He was fighting back tears. She felt a twinge of pity welling up inside as he reached the garage door. Then she opened the envelope when she heard him drive off

"My client has informed me that you have both agreed to separate," she read the letter from Harold's solicitor. "It is advisable you contact a solicitor so that proceedings can begin."

Stunned, she stared around her at nothing in particular.

Oh god, how hard she had tried to get Harold to talk to her. He would not budge; it was not her fault.

She thought of the note Harold had left her weeks ago:

"Can I have our joint savings account? There is eighty thousand dollars in there the profit from the sale of the rental unit. My share is five thousand. I understand that you will dispute this."

Frances did not intend to dispute anything. She was far too weary and confused to bother. She just wanted to get on with her life and become abuse-free. She just agreed with whatever Harold told her in his notes he left her and in conjunction with a consultation with her solicitor.

She felt relieved that he had moved out at last. '*I am free from him now*' she thought.

'*I can't get help for him so it's best we separate and then divorce.*'

The telephone rang breaking the silence around her.

"Hello," she whispered as her shaky hands held the telephone.

"Mum," her daughter Cindy said. "It's me. Dad just rung. I wanted to know if you are alright."

Cindy lived in Hamilton, so they rarely got to see each other. They chatted frequently on the phone.

"I am fine. Stunned I suppose. He has got no one to blame but himself."

"Mum, you do not have to stay in an abusive relationship," Cindy told her.

Cindy was a social worker who dealt with these problems all the time. She knew what she was talking about when she told her mum.

That night Frances lay in bed unable to sleep. Her mind wandered back over the years. Harold had subtly undermined her confidence and dominated her all of those years. She had become a possession, a property he thought he could control. He had developed a formidable need of her, one that was so great it had demolished his ability to see her as a person. There was neither remorse nor an apology when he walked out of her life fourteen months after her trip to the USA.

The next morning, Francis called in sick. Her mind was fuzzy as she pondered her problems.

She used to lovingly give Harold surprise birthday parties, ones that he delighted in humiliating her as his way of thanks. One of his favourites was placing his hand over one of her breasts and looking gleefully into the camera when photos were taken. Every time she would protest at his behaviour, but he would continue to harass her in front of the guests.

The last surprise party was his fortieth birthday 18 years ago. Frances had organized a group of twelve guests to celebrate at the Theatre Restaurant, a popular place in Auckland City and had included his interfering sister Marilyn and her partner.

She had told Harold that they were having dinner with Josie and David. As they walked through the aisles to their table, past all the invited guests that Harold did not see, Frances saw Marilyn's twisted and deformed hand grab at Harold as he walked past her. Her action spoiled the surprise as Harold looked at all the guests waiting for him.

Frances hid her annoyance at this intrusion when she sat down. That night Harold was cheerful and gleefully happy all night. However, his attitude felt different, Frances felt.

Marilyn his sister insisted on knowing the hint about Cindy their daughter whom Harold had spoken of in a letter to his mum. Marilyn was persistent, about knowing something about Cindy as Frances kept her mouth closed and told Harold this was not the place for that delicate discussion. Cindy was not married and to get pregnant at this time was not heard of.

As the liquor that Frances had paid for slowly ran out, one of the guests proposed a toast to Harold.

"Ah," he replied maliciously with glee, "I have a big surprise for Frances, too. Frances is to be a grandma. Cindy is pregnant!"

Everyone knew that Cindy was not married, and in those times, it was unheard of to make such an announcement, especially in public. The announcement killed the party when the embarrassed guests departed soon after, disgusted with his behaviour and treatment of Frances.

That night they drove home in silence. Frances felt humiliated. She was stunned and hurting inside very badly.

The next day Frances went to visit her friend Christine. She had dark brown hair and blue eyes.

"I'm disgusted with Harold," Christine said as she tried to console and comfort her. "He had no right to do that. What was he thinking?" Frances told her she did not want to go home ever. She felt betrayed and the pleasure she had felt in giving Harold the party had been destroyed.

As she came back to the present, she suddenly realized that in all the thirty-six years they had been married, he had never once given her a party.

The next day after work, she had an appointment with a new hairdresser.

"How about a shorter cut?" Pat enquired as she wrapped the pink fabric cape around her and tied it behind her neck. "It will frame your face better."

"Fine, I will leave it up to you," Frances said, offering her standard reply.

"Terry will wash your hair," Pat said as she led Frances to the basin.

While she leaned back, she was uncomfortable, her feet dangling in mid-air as she tried to relax as Terry washed her hair. She was aware of the pain in her muscles as she held her head lightly against the basin and felt fingers scrunching, rubbing, and massaging her scalp.

As Pat was snipping away at her hair a customer walked in for a chat.

"Hi, Pat," the woman said.

"Hi. Did you know that Jenny has a caravan now, doing it up?" Pat said.

"Has she? She will be able to go on holidays now," the woman replied.

"Yes, the caravan needs new curtains and some painting inside," Pat told her as she finished cutting Frances's hair.

"So, Harold walked out," Pat said to Frances as she pulled the hair dryer from the wall and started to blow dry her hair. "My mother used a note my father wrote about their finances, what each one should get." Used it to gain more money."

Frances did discuss with her solicitor about five thousand dollars she had in investments. Frances felt she needed the money to have some enhancement done to her face to repair the damage that Harold had caused. She had hoped this treatment would help her feel better, as she had felt so empty inside for years, despite the fact that she had loved Harold so much. Harold had caused her face to be lined with wrinkles. There were deep lines, and her mouth had dropped down because of the psychological abuse he inflicted on her.

Frances withdrew that money from her bank. Her solicitor never advised her to declare it in the divorce settlement, so she kept the money hidden then invested it in stock in the hope of eventually having her face repaired. After all, Harold had that stash of money she had found that he never declared.

Then she thought of the previous afternoon when she had driven into the city and had idly played the pokies at the casino. She had called into Doreen's on her way home to see how she was coping after Walter's death.

"I went to the casino yesterday," Doreen said. "I put in two dollars seventy cents."

"You could put a caravan in our yard" Doreen said. "To sleep in oh no, you cannot, my son tried that and kept falling out of bed, the site is on a slope" Doreen laughed.

Frances was upset because the caravan and casino was part of her abuse. Her stalkers, abusers would think of a theme and it would follow her around. It screwed up your brain.

Later that day, after Frances arrived home, she was startled by rapping on the ranch slider door. Don, the tenant, had come to pay his rent. Then he stood chatting away. She could not get rid of him unless she was rude.

"I would put caravans between these units," he said seriously. "Make use of the space."

Eventually she cut him short and went back inside, as she remembered Lesley's repeated phone calls talking about the caravan she lived in, then finally Lesley told her she lived in a caravan park. *Another theme to distort my mind*, she thought. *So, caravans are going to follow me around.*

All of these people hardly knew her, yet they knew everything about her—or rather the lies Harold had told them. All these people without any connection between them and their talk of caravans. They were trying to coerce her into making her feel bad, guilty, or screw up her head.

Harold had previously been under the care of Mental Health twice - a hospital unit in Henderson for his suicide attempts - which came back to haunt her. She decided he needed more psychiatric help. It was obvious he had never resolved his problems before.

As she sat at the computer tapping away on the keyboard, typing a letter to Mental Health, the memory of Harold's second suicide attempt three years previously haunted her.

It was the first week in December. The night before he had stood by the fridge eating an ice cream soda he had made.

"Yummy. This is good," he had said to her gleefully and with a sparkle in his eye as he ate.

The next morning he was rushed to hospital unconscious. After examinations and a scan, the hospital put him on a life support machine. They did not know what was wrong; they thought it may have been a stroke.

Rita had arrived as the ambulance was taking Harold to hospital. The three of them were to have taken part in a car rally that day. Rita drove Frances to the hospital and stayed with her until they had scanned Harold.

Francis had sat huddled and worried, talking to him in the hope he would respond to her voice. At 11 p.m., the nurses had told her to go home and get some sleep. Then just before she left, a doctor made a chance remark about a drug overdose which she pondered as she drove home.

When she arrived home, Frances searched the house and

found nothing until she emptied a rubbish bin in Harold's den. There she found hidden in the bottom a small sticky ball of chemist's prescriptions, which she carefully unfolded as she sat at the table.

With the tattered pieces in front of her she managed to delve into the story behind this and found that Harold over a period of weeks had collected these prescriptions and obviously hid them until he thought there was enough for his plan.

She immediately rang the hospital and told them of her find. They were delighted she was able to help as he was now in a critical condition. It was a different hospital that he was admitted to and they never thought to do a blood test for an overdose of pills.

When Frances arrived at the hospital the next day, she found Harold sitting in a wheelchair waiting to be transferred to an open ward.

"I failed again," he said as Frances stood numb in front of him.

Harold stayed in the ward for several days. Frances became alarmed as he appeared preoccupied with opening the windows. She felt he might try to jump. When she reported this to the sister in charge, she was relieved to hear that the windows only opened a little.

A psychiatrist attended Harold over these days. On the final day, Frances wanted to speak to the psychiatrist again before Harold was discharged. She felt another talk with him would help Harold. But she had to feed the parking meter and told Harold that she wanted to see the psychiatrist when he visited the ward.

When Frances arrived back a short time later after feeding the meter, she found that Harold had already seen the psychiatrist. Then he'd asked for his discharge without telling the psychiatrist that she wished to speak to him too. Frances was stunned and hurt.

Their life went on normally, without any guideline with which she could help him. Harold, she now realized, had used the horrifying emotional blackmail. It was a cry for help that he would deny and refuse to discuss.

Frances's sister Nellie came around to visit a couple of days later. She was in Auckland on holiday from Australia, where she lived.

Now the pieces of Harold's devious plot fell into place. Nellie had arrived for Sunday lunch and found no one home. A next door neighbour told her that Harold was in hospital with a possible stroke.

Harold had known that Nellie was coming but never told Frances and depending on how that nightmare progressed with Harold in hospital, Frances found she had no supplies ready for the Chinese meal Harold had promised her. There would certainly have been no time to defrost any food to prepare for the meal.

Alone in the lounge while Harold was in his den, Nellie questioned Frances about his stay in hospital and the life support unit. She lied to her sister to save Harold's feelings and his dignity. However, she told Nellie they thought it was a mini stroke, as one of his arms was paralyzed during that time.

She now felt this was a ploy for Nellie to see her reaction and that Harold had already told Nellie his truth for what it was. That time in Sydney, Nellie had danced around and sung something to Frances which she never understood and she asked Nellie to repeat which she refused.

She wants him dead Nellie had said as the garbled words flew clearly through her mind now. Then she was mortified as she recalled other conversations about death of which Harold seemed preoccupied with.

Frances knew then, as she sat at the computer completing her letter to the local psychiatric unit, that Harold had been lying to everyone to gain sympathy and alienate her by saying she wanted him dead. She also noticed he did not use the walking stick that he had used for the past two years. That was part of his ploy to gain sympathy and ensure that Frances was maligned wherever she went. Wherever did he get that thought? she wondered.

With her letter completed and tucked into an envelope, she rushed out and mailed it immediately.

———————————

Harold and loopy Ed drove to South Auckland with a mission in mind in June 1998. He was going to Olden Times antique and collectables shop to see Diana. He took a poster he had made on his computer.

Diana had an antique shop in South Auckland. She was tall with short blonde hair and was quite attractive. She also did antique markets the same as Frances. She is an extremely astute business woman.

When they went into the shop, Harold asked the assistant if she was Diana.

"Yes, I am Diana," she said. "What can I do for you?" She had short, straight hair and was attractive.

Harold gave her the posters.

"I want you to deliver these posters around the antique and collectables markets to teach my wife a lesson," he said. "Here is five hundred dollars for your cooperation."

Diana took the posters and money. She was amazed at what she read. Frances's name appeared in big letters across the top, then a photo of her in a fancy barmaid costume, taken just before her trip to the US. Below that was written:

Frances says she is an astute business woman but she rips you stallholders off when she buys antiques and collectables from you. She sells them on eBay for over double the price more than what she buys them from you. Sometimes it is three times the price. The US exchange rate is favourable against the NZ dollar. She brags about it.

She is a dirty housewife, and the toilet is filthy.

She has a gambling problem and drinks too much alcohol.

She can't cook decent meals.

She wants her husband dead.

"Yes, I will deliver these posters on Sunday before the market opens. It is in Papakura," Diana said.

"Thank you," Harold said. "I hope they abuse her because of these posters."

"I will make sure they do," Diana said.

On the Sunday she went for a drive and called into the local market for a browse. She came upon Jacinta sitting at her stall selling jewellery. Frances sometimes shared a stall at the markets with her. Jacinta was blonde with blue eyes and was dressed neatly. Frances stopped to chat.

"There is a poster with your photo and details on it," Jacinta said to Frances. She laughed loudly at Frances.

"Don't be stupid. That's ridiculous." Frances giggled with disbelief.

After browsing the rest of the stalls there was nothing that interested her, so she went home. On the way home, she pondered the remark by Jacinta about a poster and details but dismissed it. It was too weird to be true.

She picked up the telephone when it rang the next morning.

"This is Graham from Mental Health," the voice said. "We have made an appointment for you for tomorrow 2 p.m."

"I will be there," Frances said.

Still time to get help for Harold and maybe save our marriage, she thought eagerly as she navigated the maze of corridors to the reception desk the next day.

At a few minutes after 2 o'clock, two men approached her in the waiting room and ushered her into the interview room.

"I'm Doctor Ward," the tall, thin man said. "This is Geoff, a support worker."

They discussed various parts of her letter and chattered about other things, too.

"TCB," Geoff said. "The clever boy."

"Yes," she replied. "He has used that for years. I know now it was when he had set me up, to make me look bad. He would say 'TCB' and laugh at me in front of people. Harold has been under your care twice. It is obvious he never got the care he needed."

"Elvis Presley's motto was TCB, taking care of business. Harold had an Elvis jacket with the motto on. He translated that to 'the clever boy.' He would use TCB when he had set me up to make me look bad.

She slowly began to realize where this conversation was leading.

"Does the television talk to you, tell you to buy things?" Doctor Ward asked. "The radio too?"

"No, definitely not," she replied. "I am not schizophrenic. Are you going to help my husband?" she pleaded. "He desperately needs help."

"I think it best if we give you some medication," Doctor Ward said, "to take in the meantime. I would also like you to have a brain scan. Meanwhile, Geoff will keep in touch and support you."

As she stormed out of the building, she was furious. *They think I am the one who is nuts, not him*, she fumed to herself as she settled into her car. Fancy asking me if the radio and TV tell me to buy things.

The telephone rang as she arrived home. It was her friend Adele.

"Would you like to come to dinner tomorrow night?" she asked. "We could have Chinese."

"I will pay," Frances offered, knowing that Adele was extremely poor, always in debt and short of money.

"No, I will. I am flush at present," she laughed. "Can you pick me up and take me?"

When she picked Adele up, they drove to the takeaway around the corner. Frances was astonished when Adele presented a fifty dollar note in payment, and she saw other large notes poking out of her wallet too.

"I will pop next door to get a bottle of whisky," Adele said as she disappeared out the door.

"I've got a thousand dollars in the bank at present," Adele said as they drove home.

Where did all that money come from? Frances mused.

"I am frightened," she confided to Adele on the way back. "Harold frightens the hell out of me. There's always something unusual happening."

As they walked into Adele's kitchen, Adele grabbed a personal alarm from the table and handed it to Frances.

"Here take this. It was for Barbara, but you many need it more than her. " You are having so much trouble with Harold."

They finished their meal in silence. After the dishes were washed, Frances went home to ponder on the money that Adele had. She had no obvious means of money at all.

In the meantime, Frances planned for her future, should her attempts at psychiatric help for Harold failed.

Not uttering a word to anyone Frances faxed a letter to Internal Affairs Department and enquired about changing her name by deed poll should the need arise.

Later, as she was outside doing some gardening, the telephone rang. She dashed inside to answer it. It was a man; she did not catch his name when he started speaking.

"I am from Mental Health," his deep voice boomed through the receiver.

"Hello. I hope you are able to help Harold," she said.

"If your husband is going to the lengths you have described, he would need the finance to do so. Someone is putting up the money for it," he said.

"That wasn't an angle I thought of. I think the telephone is bugged too," she said. "There is the possibility this conversation is being listened to."

"We should have a meeting," the man said. "Next Friday, one p.m. Does that suit you?"

"Yes," replied Frances, jotting down the details.

When there was a knock at the door later that day, she opened it to see Don standing there with his rent book and money.

"I decided to pay the rent today," Don said.

He was quite talkative and went to great lengths to keep her talking while her mind was elsewhere.

"People change their names by deed poll," he said. His words jolted her back to the present. "I know someone who did a few years ago." He grinned at her slyly. "I'm lucky I don't have to work. I worked hard and managed to put some savings aside." He reached into his pocket and pulled out a document.

"See this," he said offering her his bank statement as he pointed to a very large sum of money.

Startled, she thrust it back at him and abruptly went inside as more pieces of her puzzle fell into place.

She remembered the last time she collected the rent. He'd gone to great pains to show her he no longer had a telephone connected and showed her the caller display unit sitting on the coffee table.

He was the financier, she knew that now because he showed her his bank statement, but who was controlling her telephone and fax?

Don was a bitter old man. He hated women. He was sixty-five, short, bald, and talked crudely at times. Harold had told Frances that Don had been sucked into marriage by a foreign woman half his age and she had a young son. After they married, she had cajoled Don into adopting her son. Then when the adoption papers were signed, the woman fled with her child to Australia, and he was forced to pay for their support.

Brenda her neighbour called out as Frances basked in the sun on the deck overlooking the short valley below, so she went over to the fence to talk to her.

"We have the internet now," Brenda said. "It works okay even although our lines are split," she laughed.

Is that how the phone is bugged? Frances thought. *We are always having trouble because of there being two connections on the one line split in two.* Was he listening to her conversations on the phone?

At work the next day, a new receptionist named Kelly had started. She was pleasant, tall, and wiry, and Frances warmed to her when she joined her outside for a ciggie.

"When is your next market?" Kelly enquired.

"Next weekend. Down south," Frances said, amazed that she knew about the markets.

"How did you know I did markets Kelly" Frances added.

"Maureen told me that you did antique and book markets" Kelly said.

"Where did Kelly come from? How did they employ her?" Frances asked Sharon suspiciously that afternoon.

"Maureen's partner Peter, a friend of his," she replied.

A few days later Frances cried profusely during the appointment with her solicitor. She went to her to start proceedings for their divorce.

"You need time," Alison said to her. "I will write and tell his solicitor."

Two days later, she received a note from Harold: "I ask you one more time to finalize our settlement."

She rang Alison her solicitor and told her as she crumpled up the note.

"I've sent my letter," she told Frances.

The next week, she received a letter from Alison, saying that Harold's solicitor had replied to her letter. "They want action immediately," she read. "They want to know why you haven't brought a new car with the seventeen thousand dollars you withdrew from the joint account. Harold can't afford to pay any more money into your account. You are receiving the rent to live on it."

Furiously, Frances barged to the computer and started typing her reply.

You know my present physical and mental state. I haven't bought a car because I don't think I am capable of making the right decision. He purchased a new van. Am I not entitled to buy one too? I do not use the rent money to live on. It is run as a business. All rents go into a separate bank account to pay all costs. There is nothing much left after paying rates, the mortgage, insurances, interest, and what is left goes towards the tax. Furthermore, if Harold had taken an interest in our finances, he would realize that. He chose to live in a vacuum, oblivious to the cost of living. He played at making a living with his toy businesses he had, using me as a slave to do everything, including his accounts. I was stupid. I indulged and spoiled him. Now look at the thanks I got.

The next day Maureen, who lived not far from Frances, drove her home while her car was being repaired.

"I received a letter from my solicitor," she said to Maureen. "He's complaining about the seventeen thousand dollars I withdrew for a new car."

"Well, he's entitled to half," Maureen said curtly, without bothering to question her.

Frances was going to the Matakohe market at the weekend. Lizzie greeted Frances with a big hug as she parked her car outside the hall. *A love bomb*, Frances thought furiously. *What is going to happen at this market?*

"A big buyer from Auckland rang. He's coming this weekend," she said as she helped Frances with her stock.

Frances always anticipated this market with delight. It was

nice to get out of the big city, away from Harold's antics, and have time to catch up with the other stallholders, despite the fact that some of them harassed her.

While she was browsing the stalls later that day, a woman approached her, holding out a bowl filled with slips of paper. The woman picked one out and Frances barely had time to read "I love you" as the note flicked past her eyes.

"Fortune telling," the woman said to her, offering Frances the bowl. "Take one yourself." She did not say that Harold had organized this little affair.

Without thinking, Frances delved into the bowl and picked a slip out. "Forgiveness," she read.

"No way!" Frances yelled as she stormed back to her stall.

Frances had quite a good day despite the subtle harassment she endured. Aware of the artful abuse at the markets for a long time, Frances chose to ignore it. They all thought they were helping Harold as they slowly destroyed her feelings. The longer the abuse continued, the further she withdrew into herself. The stallholders were saying horrible things to her, designed to hurt and confuse her.

Harold attended the meeting the day Gerald the land agent came to their home about selling the two units. Harold was cold and aloof to Frances.

"Could I have a key?" Gerald asked Frances before he departed.

"No, I'm sorry," she said. "It will have to be by appointment."

"Don't you trust me?"

"Sorry, I don't trust anyone," she replied as she looked at Harold's white face.

"It will make it harder to sell," Gerald said.

"That's tough," she replied. "It's not my fault I am in this predicament."

"I'll arrange for a photographer and a caravan of our salespeople," he said as he departed.

The phone rang not long after. It was Adele.

"I've been thinking you should change your solicitor," Adele said.

"Why?"

"I don't think yours is doing a good job that's all. I can give you the name of mine. I've got his phone number right here."

"I'll think about it," Frances replied warily.

"By the way, Adele, could you give me a reference? I need one for my second-hand dealer's licence."

"Yes, I will write one up for you," Adele replied.

The next day there was a note in the letter box from Harold. "I think we should both have new solicitors for the sale of the units. I would like my second-hand dealer's licence and passport too."

There was a market in Taupo the following weekend, and Frances decided to use a timeshare week and make a week of it. She felt it was time to have a few restful days after the market. Months ago, she had asked Jacinta to join her, but now she'd decided against it because of all the abuse and never mentioned it to her again.

She is just like the rest of them. She told me about the poster Harold had distributed.

The emotional abuse started subtly when she arrived at the market and was unpacking her stock. Her stall was u-shaped, with nonfiction books on two tables and collectables on the other table. There were people milling around her stall when the market opened. The stallholders used covert aggression on her, which made her confused and made her feel bad about herself and jumpy.

A man paid fifty dollars for two commemorative Coca-Cola bottles. She was pleased with her first sale. Another man brought two books from her. The day went well.

Later Diana showed her a plate. Printed in a circle around it were the words *an act of kindness is an act of love.* Debbie and several other stallholders came over and asked her if she was still going to use her timeshare. It soon became obvious that Jacinta had put them up to it, but despite all that she enjoyed the market. The man in a shop handed her a card. "Just in case you want to buy real estate. You are buying real estate aren't you," he said as she disappeared out the door. Frances contemplating what had been experienced during the weekend. She decided to dismiss it from her mind. She cut short her stay in Taupo and decided to go to Rotorua for two nights.

As Frances drove down Fenton Street in Rotorua, she came across the Spa Resort. They had a vacancy sign up, so she pulled into the car park and went into reception.

"I would like to book a room for two nights," she told the receptionist.

"Would you like a room with or without a spa," she said.

"Spa please," Frances replied.

"We have a restaurant and café," the receptionist told her. "It is open from seven a.m. until nine p.m. The spa is turned on automatically at two p.m., daily."

The spa was turned on, so she stripped off her clothing and hopped into the spa. The soft bubbles eased the tension in her back and shoulders. She stayed soaking up the peaceful atmosphere for an hour. She was relaxed.

After she dressed, she took the activities brochure to the tour desk.

"I would like to book a half-day tour tomorrow with lunch and a massage at four o'clock," she told the receptionist.

The receptionist processed her tickets and gave them to Frances. "Be in the lobby at nine-thirty."

After a delicious dinner of roast lamb and vegetables in the restaurant, she went to her room to watch the TV news and *Shortland Street*. Later she visited the spa again, then went to bed.

Frances felt rested when she woke up the next morning. She got up and had a shower, the water cascading over her body, then she got into the spa, the bubbles soothing her body.

As Frances sat in the lobby later, talking to three women tourists waiting for the tour guide, a tall man with a moustache approached them.

"Hello, I am Peter," he said to them. "Are you waiting for the Whaka tour?"

"Yes," they replied in unison.

"Come with me," he said.

When they were seated in the minibus with the other tourists, Peter stood in the stairwell of the bus and addressed them.

"Welcome to the Whakarewarewa Living Maori Village tour," he said. "When you are in the village you must stay on the pathway. If you stray off them, you could get scalded by the boiling water or the bubbling mud pools."

"The area is part of Rotorua City and had thousands of visitors each year" Peter said.

When they arrived at Whaka, Frances was amazed at the entrance.

"What a lovely archway with Maori figures carved in it," Frances said to Peter.

The group walked along the pathways among houses and Wharenuis (meeting houses) and native bush. The hot pools of water vented clouds of steam into the air and mud pools bubbled away. As they came to a bubbling hot pool of water with steam boxes in it, Peter stopped the group.

"These boxes are used to cook the Maori's food. They also use the water to bathe in and heat their homes," he said. "The steam vents along the way show where the hot geothermal ground is."

They came to the Pohutu geyser.

"If we wait a few minutes, the geyser will erupt. It is about thirty meters tall," Peter said.

Then there was a rush of hot water cascading into the air. It was magnificent.

"That is amazing," said Frances.

At the end of the tour, it was time to drive to the Skyline Complex, with its gondola rides to the restaurant at the top of the hill. The view was fantastic, with panoramic views of Rotorua and the sparkling lake.

They were seated at a table and helped themselves to the scrumptious buffet meal.

"This is delicious, the roast ham and vegetables and there was a good selection of salads. Pavlova desert which is a New Zealand delicacy was devine" Frances told the group, they all agreed.

"Yes, it's one of the best in Rotorua," Peter said.

After lunch, Peter drove them back to their accommodation.

As Frances lay on her bed, she felt restful and waited for her massage. At four p.m., Frances entered the massage room. There was a massage bed and a cabinet that held oils and lotions.

"Hello, Frances," Amanda the masseuse said as she entered

the room. "Please strip down to your panties and lay face down on the bed."

Amanda started massaging Frances's back and poured lavender oil on her. The stress dissolved under the gentle hands that rubbed and kneaded her body. Then the massage intensified by applying stronger pressure and pummelling her body before she finished.

"Thank you, Amanda, that was great," Frances said.

Then Frances went back to her room and lay on her bed.

The next morning after breakfast, Frances packed her bag and drove the three hours to Auckland. She was glad to be home.

The day after she arrived home, Frances opened the door to Don's loud knock.

"I want to give you two weeks' notice," he said, holding a sheet of paper out in his hand. "I am going to move somewhere else. May I have a reference please? I've outlined roughly what to say."

Frances glanced over the sheet, noting that he'd included the phrase "no wild parties" in his notes.

"You've been a good tenant," she told him. "No wild parties at all!" she added with a smile.

"I have to ask you, as I don't know how to contact Harold. I would like you to give this to him." He held out an envelope. "I don't know Harold at all."

Memories came floating back from two years ago when Harold took charge to find a new tenant. Ordinarily, they both saw potential tenants and agreed before signing an agreement. In this case, Don had signed the contract with Harold at his shop, and Harold had informed Frances when the deal was complete. She remembered her annoyance at the process. Harold had never done that before. So, Don was planted on her for a reason, no doubt about that.

A few days after they had listed the two units for sale, Gerald arrived with prospective buyers. Frances went with him over to Don's to inspect the unit.

"I got this unit from Harold because I knew him," Don told Gerald as they inspected the unit.

The next day Harold came around to get something from the garage.

Over the next few days, the garage door made strange noises each time she opened or closed it, then finally the chain came apart. *So that's what Harold did when he went into the garage*, she thought. *He pulled the chain on the door so it would break.*

She located a repair company in the yellow pages and rang for a person to repair the door.

"Mr. Hohepa will be there this afternoon," the receptionist told her.

To her surprise a Pakeha man arrived to fix the door; with a name like Hohepa, she was expecting a Maori. Then she was puzzled, as she was sure she had seen this man somewhere before.

After he fixed the door and Frances had paid him, he said, "Why don't you have a wild party before you shift out?"

Gerald the land agent rang not long after. He had some clients who wanted to view the property, and they agreed on a time later that day. Gerald arrived before the client and went to view the storage area under the house. He found the lock jammed and could not even get the key in the lock, so he jemmied the lock off.

Two days later Don came down to pay his final rent. He waffled on and mentioned super glue as Frances was away with the fairies, deep in thought.

Ah, that's what happened to the lock. Harold shoved the glue into the lock.

Harold had told her years ago that if someone pissed him off, he would super glue their locks. He had to hurt them. He just had to win.

Don came over to see Frances about nothing in particular. Just before he left, he said, "What comes around."

Frances knew then there was another round of abuse and stalking to start.

I am going to set Adele up. I have suspected her in the past that she has had something to do with the abuse, Frances thought as she drove around to her place.

"I just found out Harold used super glue on that lock," she told Adele as she settled down on the couch.

"Did he?" Adele asked.

"Yeah. You know what? I still have his fancy machinery, and I am going to glue the lock. It is worth hundreds," Frances said.

It did not take long for Adele to pass on the discussion. The phone rang just after she arrived home from Adele's.

"Bill speaking," the voice said. "Could you mention to Harold I'd like to buy his machinery."

Frances suddenly remembered that the man who repaired the garage door was a friend of Harold's.

"I'll tell him," She replied curtly.

As she stood in the dining room, she knew now that Harold still had her under surveillance. He was controlling her every move while he wallowed in bitterness over his failure to keep her, and then he organized this barrage of abuse to be hurled at her everywhere she went.

All through their marriage, he never had the ability to see her as a person with feelings, and losing her was his worst nightmare.

CHAPTER SIXTEEN

Early in December 1998, as Frances was working at home for Maureen, the telephone rang.

It was her solicitor Mrs. Wilkinson who was processing their divorce. "I've just had a call from Harold's solicitor," she said. "Harold is very ill. He opened his shop and collapsed on the counter. Customers could not wake him. He was unconscious, so they rang for an ambulance and he was taken to hospital."

"What do you expect me to do?" Frances asked, well aware of the games he played. She felt terrible when her solicitor insisted she visit Harold.

"Well," she said, shocked, "go and see him."

"I'll ring the kids. They can do that," she replied briskly as she clicked the button. She only paused a moment before she picked it up again and dialled. When the receptionist answered, she asked for Maureen.

"Hello, Frances," Maureen said when she picked up.

"I cannot do this work at home. I will drop it back tomorrow," she said in despair. "Harold's in hospital." She was upset that Harold was in hospital but there was no way she would visit him in hospital.

She received a quick response after an urgent call to Cindy her daughter, who was at work, and she arrived later that day.

"Give these to your father," she said to Cindy as she handed her a parcel of his favourite snacks. "I'm not coming. I would only give in to his stupid games. I can't for my health's sake."

Later that night, when Cindy came home, they discussed Harold's illness.

"It's a kidney infection," Cindy said.

"Yeah, I thought as much," she replied. "There is no way he would get in that state unless it was deliberate. He never took his pills, made sure he was ill, then he drove to the shop to make sure everyone would see him. It's all part of his game to make people see what a bad person I am."

"Yeah, Mum," Cindy replied. "I thought that too."

Then Frances told Cindy she needed to take some documents back to work. She grabbed her car keys and said, "I won't be long."

When she arrived at work, Maureen greeted her.

"Sorry about Harold," she said. "What's wrong with him?"

Frances told her what had happened and that he was disabled and prone to kidney infections.

"Can you tell by looking at him?" Maureen asked.

"No, not really," she said. She didn't want to talk about it with Maureen.

"Mum," Cindy said when she arrived home, "would you like to go for Christmas dinner at a hotel this year?"

"That sounds great," she said. "How much will it cost?"

"One hundred dollars each adult," Cindy said.

"I'll give you a cheque now. I may not have that much later." She wrote out a cheque and gave it to Cindy before she left to travel home.

Cindy called later that week.

"Would you mind if Dad comes with us on Christmas day?" she said.

"No, I suppose I can suffer him one more day," she replied suspiciously. She suspected it was to be a reconciliation with Harold.

I will show you what you are missing, she thought gleefully as she travelled to the best and one of the most expensive apparel shops in Auckland. She purchased a two-piece, dark red flocked, slim-fitting, sleeveless dress with a sleeved jacket.

As she eyed herself in the mirror, she was pleased with the result. *My divorce dress.*

On Christmas day, it quickly became obvious that this was a try at reconciliation. Cindy and the girls left the table and went outside to leave Harold and Frances on their own. But Frances enjoyed herself with Cindy and her three granddaughters. Cindy was divorced from her husband Peter. She worked hard for a government agency to support herself and her children. Frances felt great in her new outfit, and she ignored Harold's sly looks. See what you are missing, she thought.

"You are a lucky fellow," the man at the next table said to Harold. "All these beautiful ladies with you."

Frances held her tongue as she thought, *I'm the ex-wife, sonny.*

After dinner they went to Cindy's to contend with the presents. Frances had brought one for Harold, uncertain whether she should. It was just as well that she had, as Harold presented her a card with a voucher to buy perfume from a chemist shop. Then he left not long afterwards while Frances slept the night and went home the next day.

Gerald the land agent rang later in January to say he had a contract on the units. Could he come around for her to sign it? Frances was thankful that it looked like the units would sell quickly.

When Gerald arrived, he explained the contract and offer to her, which she accepted.

The offer was well below what they expected, but she was well past caring, and she would no longer have to put up with the stream of traffic through her house. Some of these people were obviously sent by Harold, who had the audacity to ask where she was moving to.

As Frances packed her belongings, she did so logically, room by room. But by the time the removal van arrived, there was still the garage to pack. Harold did not want anything. He had written her a letter and told her to dump everything into a skip. He left everything to her, including his rubbish. However, when the units were put on the market, she made him take some furniture to make the unit look more spacious.

After the contract was signed, Cindy pressured Frances into buying another house.

"Mum, you will have to buy one soon," Cindy said.

After the settlement there would just be enough to buy a house, but not in Auckland—the prices were too high.

Frances and Cindy viewed houses together until they finally found one that fit the price she was looking for. The land agent informed her the vendor would not go any lower, though she found out later it was overpriced.

There were two houses on her final list at Wa Kawai a small coastal settlement on the west coast west of Hamilton. One had garish carpets and a grotty kitchen, but the price was higher and she could not afford the renovations as well. So, she settled on the other that needed complete renovations inside, which she could afford.

For the last week in her unit, Frances was ill with the flu and her mind constantly clouded as she tried desperately to pack up. In her confusion, she allowed the removal company to pack everything that wasn't packed. They put everything into storage in Hamilton while the house she purchased was being renovated. She had purchased a shell of a house; everything inside needed replacing, including the kitchen, though she left the bathroom for later. She spent thousands on renovations to make her new home liveable and presentable.

The renovator did a good job. When she stopped by one day to check the progress, he asked for a progress payment. She offered him a cheque, which he refused.

"I need cash," he told her. "To pay my boys."

Frances still had the travellers' cheques, which she had kept hidden for the last couple of years, so she cashed them and paid the renovator fifteen hundred dollars to settle his bill. Then she went to the bank and withdrew the balance of his account. He refused her a receipt, and there was still a small area to finish after she decided what to do with the kitchen.

Finally, she moved into her new home on a back section in Wa Kawai. Unpacking was a mammoth task. She placed all unwanted boxes in her garage.

When Frances changed her phone number, she made it an unlisted number so Harold could not find her.

As she checked her mailbox the next morning, she heard a door open from the house in front of her. She spun around and saw a woman dressed all in white walking down from the steps towards her.

"I am Anita," she said, smiling pleasantly. "I hope you will be very happy here in Wa Kawai."

"Thank you, pleased to meet you. I'm Frances. I'm sure I will be very happy," she replied.

Anita was around seventy-five years old, with long, grey-streaked hair tied into a bun. She had brown eyes and olive skin.

Several months later, Frances decided to try to get back into the work force. More than three months had passed since she had worked. Also, Data Entry Services had not contacted her, although they had assured her and Waitakere Mental Health that they would take her back. Because of the medication she was on, she was lethargic and did not feel inclined to work. The mental hospital had given her Risperidone for a paranoid delusional disorder. She was adamant that she was suffering from Post -Traumatic -Stress - Disorder but they did not believe her. The symptoms are the same. But as she struggled through each day with her befuddled brain, she knew that if she did not try, she would never work again.

One advertisement caught her eye when she perused the situations vacant column of the local newspaper. Data Entry Services required temporary data entry clerks on call in Hamilton. It was a branch of the Auckland Data Entry Services. When she went for the interview, there were two sets of tables with eight computers on each set and a large filing cabinet; otherwise it was sparsely furnished.

The criteria were strict. Security and police checks, forms

to complete. But she tried hard to work, toiling on diligently while her mind was still muddled and despite the fact that she felt inadequate. She was not worried about the checks; she had no criminal record of any sort except for the odd speeding ticket. And she had worked for the Auckland branch.

There were quite a few temporary workers gathered in the large boardroom as Susan the team leader went over their induction. She was tall with dark brown hair. Her bright hazel eyes hid the hardness caused by her occupation, and she was always smartly dressed in a light-coloured corporate suit.

"If there is anything you wish to disclose, you must do it now. If we find out later," she continued, "you will not be able to work for us." She repeated the point several times and Frances was sure she looked directly at her.

Over the following days, Frances found herself wondering how Susan could always remember her name with so many people to keep track of. And a bit more oddly, she also had apparently checked Frances's file and made note of her address, since she asked Frances how she liked living at Wa Kawai.

Frances found it hard to concentrate as she learned all the requirements of the job. Those first few weeks were a big trial as she worked hard to clear her muddled mind. She was unsure of herself, reserved, and kept apart from other staff members as she tried vainly to gain some normality in her life.

"Frances, phone for you," Susan called one day.

Frances went to the phone and picked it up. "Have you lived in Hamilton or Otara at all?" Josie enquired. "I am checking your application for the data entry job and I have found someone with the same name."

"No, I have never lived in either of those areas," Frances replied.

"Thank you," the woman replied. "I will check it out and get back to you"

Susan asked Frances and Justine if they would like to work in files after they completed the work earlier than expected. "You will be scanning all documents," she told them.

When they both reported to Jeanette, the supervisor in files, a woman gave them instructions on the work. Frances found it mindless, tedious, and boring work. But at least it was work, she thought, as she waved the hand-held scanner over the documents in front of her.

The next week a letter arrived from her new solicitor, Karl Harrison, who had received a letter from Harold's solicitor requesting their separation date be brought forward six months. Karl was a lean young man in his early thirties, with dark curly hair and a short goatee beard. They had only been separated for eighteen months and had to be separated for two years before divorce proceedings could begin. Harold expected her to lie so he could marry the new woman he had met. It certainly had not taken him long to latch onto his next victim, she mused.

In her reply, Frances wrote that she had no intention of committing perjury for anyone and that she also felt it would be an entrapment from Harold as he set her up for a serious crime with a conviction for perjury.

As Christmas approached and she found she felt much better mentally, she decided it was time to make new friends with local women. She advertised in the personal column of a Hamilton newspaper. When she dialled her allocated number after her first advertisement, she was delighted to find she had one reply with a contact phone number. She hung up the phone, then picked it up again and dialled the number immediately.

"Hello," Frances said. "Are you Natalie? I am Frances. You answered my advertisement."

"Yes, that's right," Natalie said as Frances could not get a word in edgeways as Natalie kept talking.

"All those men want is food and sex. I have a millionaire friend, he's overseas at the moment, don't think I will see him again. He's impotent. He did not think it fair on me. Perhaps we could meet for some fish 'n' chips. Have a chat. Must go now. I have a massage to do. Will give you a buzz next week."

What a weird conversation, Frances thought as she placed the receiver into its cradle.

She received two more replies the following week. Frances rang Tricia, and they arranged to meet at a café at Centre Place Mall on Saturday afternoon.

As Frances waited at the spot they'd agreed to meet on Saturday, it seemed at first that Tricia was not going to show up. Frances anxiously eyed the people milling around the entrance to the mall. Suddenly she felt a tap on her shoulder. When she turned around, there was a tall, large woman behind her. She had short brown hair and brown eyes.

"I'm Tricia. Are you Frances?" the woman enquired.

"Yes, I am. Let's go and get some coffee."

As they walked to the café, she noticed that Tricia walked slowly and awkwardly. She explained she had just had operations on her knees.

"My legs just about kill me sometimes," she said. "I'm still off work. I hope to be back soon. Do you work, Frances?"

"Yes, I work part time for Data Entry Services."

"Oh, opposite the service station, is it?"

"Yes."

"How many answered your advertisement?" Tricia asked.

"Three so far. I'll wait until the advert expires," Frances replied. "Then I will arrange a dinner so everyone can meet. It's too close to Christmas to do much now with everyone so busy." Frances was pleased with the replies to her advertisement. She would contact the ladies in the new year to arrange a night out for dinner.

On the way home, Frances drove to Cindy's house. She ignored the white station wagon parked outside and walked inside the house.

Inside, she found Harold seated on the couch in Cindy's living room. Beside him was a woman. She was Harold's new partner. She had short grey hair and was dressed in a suit, Startled Frances whirled around and started to leave but not before she saw the gleam in Harold's eyes.

"Can I have my mail, Cindy?" she called out puzzled.

"Have you just finished work? We're doing the Christmas thing," Cindy whispered as she handed her the mail after she danced bizarrely into the room.

"I'll call next week" Frances replied hastily as she departed.

Harold was ecstatic seeing Frances.

"Where does your mother work?" he asked Cindy after Frances left.

She told him.

Ahhh, now I can ring the company and coerce the staff into psychologically abusing Frances, just like the other companies. I could also get them to arrange the stalking and abuse where she lives, Harold thought. I am glad I was at Cindy's when she called in.

Frances rang Phillipa when she got home. Phillipa was one of the ladies from her advertisement, she had dark wiry hair and stood at 5 foot 2. Phillipa was too busy to talk but agreed to meet for dinner at a Hamilton restaurant the following Saturday. Frances offered to pick her up on the way from Wa Kawai, as she lived on the main road going into Hamilton.

On Monday morning Susan walked around handing out the acceptance letters for those who had passed the criteria required for Data Entry Services. She kept walking back to Frances and hovered at her desk.

"Is there one for me?" Frances asked.

"No, not yet," she replied.

"Admin rang me last week and queried two addresses I might have lived at," she told Susan.

"You should have said yes. They might be rich," Susan replied.

"There must be people with the same name, and they might be criminals" Frances replied dumbfounded.

New Year's Eve Day finally approached, and Frances packed her car for the market at Wa Kawai she was attending that weekend. As she humped out her boxes of stock and loaded them into her car, Frances's neighbour Anita stood in Frances's driveway and stared as she packed the car.

"That box is very heavy, isn't it?" Anita said as she walked right around to the back of her station wagon and pointed to the box in the middle.

It's not her business or anyone else's, for that matter, what I do or where I go, Frances thought as she quickly closed the hatch back-door and ignored Anita's question.

It was a slow weekend. The abuse emerged, and she tried to ignore it, enjoy herself, and have a reasonably nice break away from her nosey neighbour. She felt she was a moving target wherever she went.

Back at work after the new year break, Susan gave Frances the confirmation letter that cleared her to work. That same day, Frances received a nasty email from Harold's new partner.

"I'm his spokesperson now," she wrote. Sounds like he has met his match, Frances thought. "Please leave Harold alone. I am the boss now, and you will do what I tell you."

Frances replied to her. "Harold is lazy," she wrote, "and never once helped me around the house while I was out working. I was his slave while he sat around watching TV and videos all day or otherwise indulged in extramarital affairs when he had no work to do. He is selfish and ignorant, always ready with his snide remarks deliberately designed to hurt. I even processed his accounts for him and received no thanks at all."

On the 8th January, there was an official opening of an Elvis memorial at a park in West Auckland. Her friend Mary talked her into attending.

When Frances arrived at the park early, she was upset and tearful. She did not feel like joining the crowd that had already gathered, so she sat on a low, white fence at the edge of the park. Mary's husband Brendan spotted her there. He was five foot eight inches tall, with white, curly hair. He strolled over and talked her into joining them at their table. She was uneasy, nervous, and felt self-conscious. She had not socialized in over a year. An acquaintance of Frances from the Elvis Presley Fan Club named Noreen approached after she sat down at the table. She was five foot two inches tall, with dark curly hair. She was dressed in Elvis memorabilia.

"Hi! How are you?" she asked as she gave Frances a big hug.

Another love bomb and the start of a new round of abuse, Frances thought to herself.

"Fine," she replied quietly, not wanting to encourage a conversation.

When the unveiling ceremony was finished, Frances stepped forward for a closer look at the memorial and was astonished as her eyes fell upon another of the people gathered there.

That shirt. I know the colours, the silk fabric. It was Harold, leaning over the back of a wheelchair talking to the person seated in the chair.

Appalled, she sneaked back to her seat, where she watched and waited to see what he did next.

Rita came over to speak to her for a short time, but Frances was barely aware of what she said before she went back to sit with her friends.

How dare he attend? He did not like Elvis nor attend many club functions when we were married.

Then she picked up her handbag and strode off when it was safe. She bumped into Mary on her way out as she looked around, but could not see his new partner with him.

"I'm going home. Look who is over there," she said to Mary as she stumbled away crying.

Her tyres squealed on asphalt as she drove home.

How dare he spoil my day. I drove all this way just to go home again. He knew I would be there. He did this deliberately.

When she got home, she checked her contact box for the final day of her advertisement and found she had one more reply. A woman named April. So, she rang her and arranged to meet her the following Monday.

April arrived early at Centre Place Mall. She wanted to suss Frances out before she met her. She had seen the poster of Frances at her son's antique shop, and a friend of hers at the *Waikato Times* had alerted her about the advertisement.

She intended to give Frances a fright, let her know who she was and give her a scare about where she lived. She was a short blonde woman who appeared shorter than her five feet two and approached Frances as she waited at the entrance to Centre Place Mall. April was dumpy, wore blue jeans with a pink blouse that made her appear larger as she tried to hide her flabby stomach, and appeared to be in her early sixties.

"Frances, pleased to meet you," the woman said as she gave Frances a big hug. "I'm April."

April made a big display of a hundred dollar note as she offered payment for her coffee. "Oh, I'll have to change this," she said as she slowly pulled the note out and showed it to Frances.

As they sat at the crowded café sipping their cappuccinos with fluffy marshmallows floating on top, April dominated the conversation, jumping from topic to topic.

"I'm living on my redundancy money. My son and daughter-in-law switched roles. She went back to work; he became a house husband. He's into collectables. I help out once a week."

"We broke up four months ago, he just up and moved out," Frances said.

"I'm a justice of the peace," April added proudly.

Deja vu, Frances thought as she sat watching and listened to April intently and with suspicion. She could not get a word in edgeways and felt there were too many similarities in her life that were hard to comprehend. The big hug routine had been used in the past as the next round of stalking started.

Despite her bulk, April was attractive, her deep blue eyes smiled prettily, her short hair elegantly styled.

"I notice you are wearing your rings," Frances butted in as she indicated to April's left hand.

"I don't want to lose them," she said.

"Mine are at home, a friend who deals in jewellery offered to buy them, but I want to keep them for my children."

"Did you have a power of attorney?" April asked. "For selling the house, my husband signed one."

"Get much from your settlement?" she slyly asked Frances.

"My ex didn't want anything. I tried to give him things. He took a few things. Whether he kept them I do not know. He left me to pack up everything, the accumulated junk over the years. I've got a garage full of boxes to sort," Frances said despairingly.

"You should have a garage sale," April said.

"No, I can't be bothered. I will give a lot to charity as I sort through the stuff."

"Where do you work?" April enquired.

"Data Entry Services," she replied.

"Must be boring," April said.

"No, there is plenty of variety in the forms," Frances said.

"We must get together, go for fish and chips somewhere," April said. "Any health problems?"

"Only emotional ones and a hip problem," Frances replied.

"No one can hide in New Zealand," April said as she stood up from the table to go. "You should sell your story to a woman's magazine."

How could she be so nasty, vindictive, and hurtful? Frances thought as she walked away. *A law-abiding citizen I have never met before.*

Frances was astounded. How did she know she had a story to sell, she hadn't said anything to her about Harold? *How did she know it was my advertisement in the paper, how did she know I am in hiding?*

"Not just a woman's magazine," Francis whispered to herself as she walked away. "I am writing a fuckin' book and gathering the plot as time goes by."

As Frances drove home, she felt anxiety slowly creep over her as she thought about April. There was no coincidence in her comments about being in hiding and selling her story to a woman's magazine, that was for sure.

April helped her son with antiques and collectables, so she must know about the poster that Harold had distributed. She also seemed to know about the power of attorney, so maybe that is on the poster as well.

By the time Frances arrived home, she had thought out her plot. She grabbed the telephone and rang the women to arrange for them to meet for dinner at a Hamilton restaurant Saturday week.

The women arranged to meet outside the restaurant. But as Frances approached her, April pretended that she didn't remember her. Natalie, who was coming from Morrinsville twenty kilometres away, was late, so they went inside to be seated. Almost three quarters of an hour later, Natalie still had not arrived, so Frances went outside to look for her. But she never appeared.

Fifteen minutes later, Frances walked in at the end of a conversation and was puzzled about what they had been talking about.

"You can compete with another woman, however not another man," April was saying as Frances reached the table.

They chatted freely as they enjoyed their dinner. But Frances was aware of what was going on around her as she tucked this information into the pages of her mind to record in her diary the next day. *April is certainly one to watch out for, because she knows about me*, Frances thought.

They continued chatting away.

"I'm going to Morrinsville tomorrow," April told them as Frances realized Natalie was a hoax.

"I enjoy garage sales and rummaging through second-hand shops," Phillipa piped up.

Frances was not sure if that was a dig at her, as that is what she did too.

By the end of the evening, Frances was amazed. She stored all her information for future reference.

The next morning Frances sat recording the conversations of the night before. How had April found out about her? That was a mystery.

On Monday at work, Brenda approached Frances, seated at her desk as she flicked through documents.

"Slogging your guts out to make a dollar," Brenda said, her voice dripping with sarcasm.

Frances became alarmed as she thought about that strange remark. She had made the same comment to Harold recently by email.

Everywhere I go these peculiar incidents happen as though these people know me and what I do. If I can piece everything together, I can logically examine what Harold has done. These people were stalking her, that was for sure. *It needs to be stopped so I can have a life.*

She searched through her diary and found the day in June of 1988 when Harold had told her that he and loopy Ed had visited Diana's Antique and Collectables shop in South Auckland. She faxed a short note to Diana and asked her about that day. She was sure that was the day that the stalking and harassment started. Diana had a shop and also did the markets with her husband Peter.

An hour later Diana rang her.

"Yes, I remember that day well," Diana told her. "Harold came in with a man with a gammy leg, I looked up my diary," she explained without denial. "I need a prod, what do you want to know?"

"I am sorry, my solicitor told me not to discuss it," Frances lied to her. "You know exactly why they came. It was to deliver that poster. I want to know what they said about me that day."

"I'm sorry, I don't remember anything at all," Diana said.

Frances closed the conversation and hung up. It was hopeless to pursue this line any further. Then her mind grabbed yet another memory. Jacinta, the woman with whom Frances occasionally shared stalls at the market, had said to her three months ago. "There's a poster with your photo and details on it." At the time, Frances had laughed, because it was preposterous.

Ah yes, she mused. *That can be the only way that anyone could recognise me, that is for sure*

Where are you going to run to? Words that her friend Rita had drummed into her many years ago.

"Did you get kicked out of Wa Kawai?" a surprised Marilyn piped up nastily as Frances arrived early for work the next day.

While she enjoyed her morning tea break, she sat in the sun smoking a cigarette. Pania, a supervisor, strolled over to Frances and sat down beside her.

"Has your ex-husband ever contacted any companies you worked for?" she asked.

"Yes," Frances replied, startled, "Every company I worked for since 1976." Frances was uncomfortable as she idly shifted her left foot to rest over her right leg. "I never knew at the time, but I do now because of what had happened to me all these years."

Frances did not fully comprehend the implications of that conversation as she brushed it aside and went back to work. Due to her emotional state, she was not into casual conversations. Abused people close down; they will not talk about anything.

There was no work on Friday, so she drove at a leisurely pace to Tirau and parked her car outside the shopping centre. She strolled inside the collectors' shop and viewed the stock with an appreciative eye.

A short, dumpy figure suddenly loomed ahead of Frances in one of the aisles and startled her. She peered closer and recognised April, who told her she could sell her story.

Frances then stood and waited silently behind a large oak chest. She crept slowly out the door when April moved out of her vision.

As she drove home, she pieced incidents together and concluded April knew Maria and Jacinta. Maria had brought a book from her at a market and paid with a $100 note. Jacinta, that time when Frances had stayed with her, had run around her house like a looney as she pretended to look for a $100 note. *Another piece of the puzzle*, Frances mused. *That is why April knew so much about me. She knows some of those people from the markets.*

In February there was a reshuffle of supervisors within Data Entry Services. Anne, the new supervisor for Frances' department, stood at five-five with long auburn hair neatly tied back with a red ribbon.

Later in March, several temporary workers, including Frances, were called to a meeting with Lisa, the supervisor from the agency.

"Data Entry Services require more full-time staff," Lisa explained. "They call them core temps. They work full-time, providing there is work available. You lucky people have been chosen for the opportunity for this work, should you desire to do it."

Frances was eager to raise her income and was pleased to have been chosen.

Anne started reorganizing her department and rearranging the work stations to suit the workflow. Frances was annoyed that most of the staff had a choice of seats, but Anne seated Frances at the head of a bank of workstations where she faced Denise and Jane on each side of her.

Denise was a talkative woman. She discussed her life at length as she worked away at her desk. But Frances never joined in; she listened as she continued to work. Denise was married and supplemented their income while she studied psychology at the local tech. She was thirty and had short, tight, curly blonde hair, blue eyes, and freckles that dotted her cheeks.

"I read some of my diary last night," Denise said to Jane one day. "It is very interesting. I must have cooked a lot. I must have been hungry."

"I'm going to have a massage tonight," Jane said to her. "I am looking forward to it to get rid of the stress."

"Sounds great. Maybe I should, too," Denise said.

"Where did you work before, Frances?" Denise enquired as she drew her into the conversation.

"Data Entry Services in Auckland" Frances replied quietly.

"I watched a tape last night and went to see a fortune teller," Denise said.

"You are not going to die young are you," Jane piped up.

"No," she answered. "No one's going to poison me or anything like that."

Not interested in their conversation, Frances tried hard to ignore them. She was much wiser now, and she found it extremely hard not to listen because there were too many incidents that related to her life. Discussions from the past came back to haunt her, discussions which had meant nothing to her at that time, but that offered, as she played them over in her mind, the picture of the slander that Harold had spread.

That woman who seemed to follow Frances always appeared during her tea break then made those ridiculous remarks to her. Frances decided to change her break time and left half an hour earlier, yet that woman still appeared not long after her.

Strange, she mused to herself as the woman sat down beside her.

"I've had calls from clients today," she said. "I don't usually, being the manager." Frances looked at her curiously, her lips pursed tightly.

So that's who she is. Heather Morris. No wonder she tries to intimidate me at times. Just sits there glaring at me, not saying a word.

After she mused on this for some time, Frances was sure that someone reported to Heather as she walked through the cafeteria for her breaks.

I will suss this out soon, she thought, remembering the day Heather had told her, "Some people get punished too much" and then walked away.

"Management will spy on you. You won't even know it. They do horrible things to people who break the rules," Brenda said to Frances as they chatted that day.

However, the subtle psychological abuse finally took its toll. Frances found it difficult to concentrate while her mind was fuzzy and not focused as she was still recovering from the stalking and abuse.

As she pondered over all of the incidents during the past few months, she made an appointment with her solicitor, Karl Harrison.

Seated with Karl at the small conference table in his office, Frances handed him her diaries.

"The abuse started after you advertised in the personal column," he said incredulously. "But how did they know it was you?"

"I don't know. But all sorts of strange things have happened. I would like you to read my diaries and advise me if I can do something legally about it. April is definitely one of my stalkers, I am not sure about the other three."

She handed him a small pile of newspaper clippings. "These are about cases similar to mine. This guy got jail."

Karl raised his eyebrows as he read the headlines in front of him.

Defence Epic Criticized as Abuse of Court.
Judge Calls Penman a Malicious Schemer and Control Freak.
Judge Sends Devious Plotter to Prison.

"Harold's worse than that man!" she cried.

"I'll get back to you when I've read your diaries," Karl said as he shook her hand.

Later when Frances picked up the phone, she realized it was dead. Another fault, she mused.

As she left through the ranch slider door, Frances passed the sweet-scented jasmine that climbed the rails of her deck. She made her way to Anita's and knocked on her glass door.

"Can I use your phone?" she asked Anita. "Mine has a fault. I need to ring Telecom."

"Sure, come in," Anita replied as she took her to the telephone near the other end of the kitchen.

Frances rang Telecom and reported the fault. They said they would come out the next day to fix it.

"Did you know that two men tried to break through my ranch slider last week?" Anita asked. "I yelled to them through the other door. I took the phone with me and told them I would ring the police. Then later a car went down your driveway. Some people got out and looked around your house. I ran out and told them to clear off."

Frances stared at her in disbelief. She noticed the telephone cord was far too short to reach that far.

In the post that day was a letter from Karl. Frances eagerly slit it open. On his office letterhead she read:

I have read the excerpts from your diary, letters to the police, and the police complaints authority. It may be possible to bring a prosecution under the Crimes Act, in the form of a psychological and emotional abuse charge.

However, in order to prove such a charge to the standard of proof required in a criminal prosecution, which is beyond reasonable doubt, evidence would need to be brought which is irrefutable, such as a report from a professional psychologist who would then be able to testify on your behalf.

She was thrilled. She immediately began searching the yellow pages for forensic psychologists. She picked one at random, called, and made an appointment for the following week.

Five days later, Frances parked her car at the top of a long driveway outside the psychologist's office in Hamilton. There were two cars parked in the carport. The office was in his home and the interview room and reception were all in the one room. There was no partition between the two areas.

Frances took in the surroundings as she sat in the chair

while she waited for Doctor Marvin Johnstone. A large mirror hung on one wall directly in front of her, and the shelving underneath the mirror was lined with reference books. To her left was a table where a tape recorder sat, and a pile of tapes sat neatly beside it. Above the table a picture of a woodlands in autumn, the gold and yellow standing out from the light blue background.

"I will not be long," Marvin said as he worked on his computer, which sat on a table cluttered with paper on the far side of the wall.

As Frances glanced over at him as he worked, she was suddenly alert. She watched him press a button underneath the desk to the right of his computer. She spun around in her chair immediately and perused the room however she saw nothing amiss.

Why did he do that?

"No one knows you are here," Doctor Johnstone said as he seated himself in front of her.

"So, you do markets?" he enquired. "Where do you get the stock from? Do you get receipts?"

"Not many people like giving receipts," she answered truthfully. "If they don't, I make a note on a piece of paper for my files. I like to keep my files accurate.

"Yes," she said to his next question without neither hearing nor understanding him as her mind wandered off.

"Hhhhhhhhhhhhhhh you must think about cross examination in court, how you would stand up to it," Marvin told her gruffly in a tone that startled her.

The interview did not progress much while Marvin asked her about family and made some notes. He then ended the interview just short of one hour.

How did he know I did markets? Why press that button? Was there someone listening or even watching? Why did I say yes to that question I didn't understand? she asked herself as she drove home. She felt extremely uneasy as she replayed the interview repeatedly in her mind.

She recalled the two cars in the carport. Yet he claimed there was no one else there, and he seemed to concentrate on her business activities more than anything else. But why?

She tried hard to logically analyse the meeting, then decided there did not appear to be any point in continuing that line of enquiry. Why spend one thousand dollars for a report that would lead nowhere?

The next day at work, Frances told Marge as they sat outside having a ciggie that she was having her hair done after work.

"Where?" she enquired.

"I know where to go, but can't remember names yet," Frances lied.

When Frances arrived at the hairdressers, located in the mall, Betty rammed the cap on her head as soon as she walked in the wide entrance. Then she seated her right at the front of the door. Betty used the hook to pull some strands of hair through the holes in the cap then left the strands all wispy and loose as she left Frances seated where passers-by could clearly see her.

"I will shift you," Betty said as she approached her again. "I wouldn't like my enemies to see me like this." She moved Frances to the back of the salon.

What's that stupid hairdo? It looks bloody ridiculous. She heard Harold's voice in her mind.

Frances drove home after the hairdressers and pondered the happenings. She was sure that Marge had something to do with the happenings at the hairdresser. She had queried Frances again before she left work, she seemed determined to find out which hairdresser Frances was going to.

Five months later, the two-year separation agreement expired and Frances received the documents for the divorce. Karl Harrison had been tardy and never notified her until three days before the court hearing. By that time, it was far too late to lodge any objections.

However, during the weekend Frances felt it was her right to lodge a memo with the courts and Harold's solicitors, as the insidious abuse continued almost daily in her life. She tapped out on her computer:

Harold is the author of his own misfortunes. He treated me like a chattel, a slave, not someone to cherish. He would never really discuss his problems, our finances, nor anything relating to our lives. He was too busy talking to everyone else as he guilefully set me up to make me look bad.

Despite all the problems, I cannot see why we just cannot walk down the aisle again. We could all dress in black and say "I do not," and then I could hand him over to his next victim.

I have filed this document in a court of law should anything serious ever happen to me. I fear for my safety. However, the corrupt police will not action my repeated complaints, as stalking and harassment are not criminal offences in New Zealand, despite the legislation passed in parliament in 1997.

Yours sincerely,
Frances Jones

When she was satisfied with her document, she printed it and faxed copies to the District Court, Harrison, and Harold's solicitors.

Harold sat at the table rereading the letter he had received from the Family Court.

Dear Harold,
I am writing to let you know that your decree nisi will be granted on the twentieth of September 2000.

Harold was ecstatic. Their divorce was being finalized. Now he could marry his new partner, Mary.

"Mary," Harold said, "the divorce will be granted in September."

"Oh, my love, that is great news. Now we can get married soon," Mary said.

They got along together, but he had to force himself from refraining the use of emotional blackmail and psychological abuse on her. He did not want to lose her. The abuse was ingrained in him, and it was difficult to keep his feelings in check. After all, he had abused Frances for thirty-four years before she found out what he had been doing to her, and that was only because she found the book *Emotional Blackmail*.

He still wanted to hurt Frances and kept a check on her abusers. He kept it hidden from Mary.

Frances snatched the receiver from its cradle. The line was dead. She angrily slammed the receiver down.

I wonder if someone's tampered with my connection. It has been dead a lot lately. Also, the internet, with those messages, no dial tone.

She approached Anita to use her telephone to ring Telecom again and reported the fault. They advised her they would attend the next day.

Anita droned on with her usual twaddle, and then Frances pricked up her ears, tried to focus her hazy mind, and listened intently.

"My husband tried to poison me," Anita said. "I looked at the plate, dipped my finger in, and tasted it. I said, 'That's rat poison.'"

"How did you know?" Frances asked.

"Because it glistened," she said.

That sample of cereal. Harold refused to eat it. I was violently ill. I have to get it analysed. The scene was firmly fixed in her mind.

Harold had told her he had a rodent problem at the shop. He had told her the day after she was ill, then he said he had ants in the shop as well.

Telecom technicians arrived the next day to check the line, and they made a couple of changes to the street connection near the fence.

The next day Jane was away from work sick, and Frances and Denise discussed their large expenses with one another.

"Yeah, I have a large solicitors bill. My ex is causing me trouble," Frances told her.

"How long were you together?" Denise asked. "Why did you separate?"

"Thirty-six years. He's a control freak. He made a list of what I could and couldn't do. It shocked me. I never realized what he had done to me all those years."

"Did you walk out?" Denise asked.

"No, he did. He found he couldn't control me anymore, when I found my tongue after all these years," Frances sighed. "He did not like the new me, the one I should have been years ago. I had become a yes, yes, and yes person to all his demands, no matter how small they were. I wasn't allowed to be me.

"I should be retired now. I worked and saved hard all these years. It was not what he wanted. He destroyed everything I worked for," she said sadly. "Now the divorce is final, and I hope I can relax.

"He poisoned me with rat poison. I still have samples. He arranged for my cigarettes to be laced with cocaine. I should get them analysed," she sighed.

"Why don't you do something about it now? Denise said.

"I am thinking about doing that" Frances replied.

"Will you get some money out if it?" Denise asked.

"I do not want money. I want justice served."

As Frances picked up the phone to call Graham, her mental health worker, she was unsteady on her feet and her hands were shaking.

"I will be out to see you today," Graham said when described her feelings.

Frances was pleased to see Graham when arrived.

"How are you?" he asked her.

"I am a bag of nerves," she said. "Look at me. I'm unsteady on my feet, my hands are shaking, I have low energy, I isolate myself from people, and I have insomnia. I am stressed, and the muscles in my shoulders are tense."

"You must continue to take your medication," he said.

"I am," she replied.

"What you are experiencing is short term. You will get better as the days go by."

He put the phonograph on the table. "You know you told me that you brought some vintage records from the Wa Kawai antique shop," he said. "This will help you as you listen to your vintage records."

"Thank you so much Graham, it will give me an interest to do something with the records. I really appreciate you loaning me the phonograph"

I will come and see you again next week," he said as he left.

That night Rita rang Frances. Rita never rang unless she wanted to quiz Frances about Harold.

"I've got some problems, Rita," Frances said. "I just found out he poisoned the cereal, the cereal he refused to eat. And the stalking has started again, too."

"Why don't you try your doctor's records," Rita advised before she hung up.

Later that night Frances remembered that day at the doctors in 1997.

Someone's poisoning or drugging me, she had said as she pointed to her dilated pupils.

"No one is doing that," the doctor had replied.

She dashed to the computer to search the internet for the

medical clinic she had attended, and then she typed them a letter to request copies of her medical records for September 1997.

Early next morning, Frances rang the clinic and asked for their fax number, then faxed the letter to them.

At work that morning Frances panicked. She needed to receive her medical report now. So, she approached Anne the supervisor and asked if she had heard about her problems. When Anne said she had not, Frances outlined some of her problems to her.

"Could I send a fax? It's urgent," she asked Anne. "I'll pay for it."

"I'll send it from this office," Anne suggested as she pointed to the fax on the table in the far corner, then she paused.

"Gee, your husband must be a powerful man," she yelled at Frances. "He must have loved you so much," she shouted as Frances sat there stunned.

"Not good to know that," Frances replied softly.

Anne had been told that by Pania the supervisor after Harold rang them.

"Perhaps it's better if I get admin to fax it," Anne said as she changed her mind and walked off holding the letter.

When Frances checked with admin later that morning, a woman gave her the letter. There was stamp indicating the date and time of faxing.

"There's been no reply," the woman said.

When Frances arrived home that night at 5 p.m., she immediately rang the clinic.

"I'm Frances Jones. I faxed your office twice today," she explained.

"No, we've never received a fax from you nor Data Entry Services," the woman replied.

"I'll do it again now," she said, upset as she settled the paper into the machine and sent it on its way.

A few days went by, and she received no reply. Then it became clear they had probably destroyed or altered her medical records.

————————

For some time now, Frances had toyed with the idea of selling up and moving away from Wa Kawai. She was absolutely sick of the narrow-minded people and emotional abuse they subjected her to everywhere she went.

As she leafed through the local newspaper, she came across Wilson's Real Estate. A photo of the owner, Barbara Wilson, beamed out at her from the advertisement. She rang and made an appointment with Barbara about putting her home on the market.

When Barbara arrived, they sat discussing the price to list and the company profile. She was a pleasant woman, a tall slim Samoan around thirty-five, casually but neatly dressed.

"What's your neighbour like? I don't know her," Barbara asked.

"Nice retired woman who lives on her own," Frances replied. She didn't want to discuss the fact that Anita was an extremely religious person, high up in her church.

"Are you getting tired and nervous?" she asked.

"Yes," Frances replied without explanation.

Frances stood by her bedroom window and watched as Barbara departed. She was surprised when she heard Anita call out to the woman.

"Are you coming in now, Barbara?" Anita called out to her.

Then Frances waited and watched as Barbara entered Anita's home.

Bull shit, she thought. *Barbara pretended she didn't know her.*

Half an hour later the telephone rang.

"My sources tell me you're selling your home." It was Shirley, the agent who had sold Frances the house.

"Yes, I have just listed it, next week for three months."

"How much?" Shirley enquired. Frances just ended the conversation. She could find out herself.

As the phone rang once more, she answered gruffly.

It was Cindy. "Is your house on the market yet, Mum?"

"Yes, next week," she replied.

"What day? Will you be at work that day?" Cindy asked her. "Who has the listing?"

"What's this? An inquisition? Why do you want to know all that?" she asked her daughter suspiciously.

"Nothing, I just wondered."

Despite her confusion, Frances had always been analytical, and she sat deep in thought as she carefully mulled over the conversation with Cindy.

Harold is coming to steal the evidence of the rat poison. That's easy. I will set a trap.

As she pulled the cereal packet from the pantry, she knocked the salt pot down and spilt the contents all over the shelf. After she cleaned that up, she carefully wrapped some cereal in tin foil, ripped off a paper towel from the rack, and screwed it up to make it look worn. Then she wrapped it around the tin foil and popped it inside a plastic bag. It looked just like the real one she had hidden in her pantry years ago.

After finding a box, she carefully wiped her fingerprints off all surfaces with a damp cloth, laid the parcel inside the box, and placed it inside the wardrobe.

I will teach you, Harold. I will get your fingerprints, too, as further proof.

The listing day came, and Frances drove off to work. She

had thought that maybe she should stay home and hide her car but decided against that idea.

When she arrived home from work that night, she anxiously scurried towards the bedroom to survey her trap.

She wasn't surprised. She had known that she was right. The parcel was too fat, and the plastic bag was scrunched at the opening and not folded flat like she had left it.

"Frances," Anita called out loudly from the door.

"Any people look at your house today" she questioned Frances.

"There are no cards on the table, so I don't think so," Frances said.

Now I have to find out where to get the sample analysed.

A cold wind rustled in the trees behind the wooden shelter where Frances and Marge sat chatting while they enjoyed their smokes during their break.

They both watched as Janet struggled with her swipe card to open the door. She burst through and sauntered over to sit with them.

"Have you been here all this time?" Janet enquired innocently.

"Yes, watching the spies," Frances joked. Let them know that I know, she thought.

"I've three part-time jobs," Marge said.

"Gee, I couldn't be bothered" Frances laughed. "You're older than me too."

"Hi, it's Adele," the voice said as Frances picked up the phone that night.

"Long time since I heard from you," Frances said. "I've got heaps to tell you." I've put my home on the market."

"Have you?" she asked, surprised. "Maybe he'll die young and leave you in peace."

"No, Harold used to talk about that," Frances said. "I went to the doctor, his talk distressed me so much. The doctor said not to worry about it, he is fine."

As Adele rattled on, Frances's mind wandered, preoccupied with her predicament. Adele's chatter instantly brought her back to the present as she heard her say, "The apple tree in the middle of the lawn, the small garden around the deck, and a small lawn to mow."

Frances realized that it was her own backyard that Adele was describing, and this astounded her. She always knew that Adele was involved in her abuse despite her denial that she knew Harold. Adele had never been to her home in Wa Kawai, so Harold must have told her when he came that first day on the market.

"Maybe he traced you on the internet or telephone or your car registration plate," Adele continued as Frances's mind went back to the events of yesterday.

The next day at work, a meeting was called for all temp staff. Lisa the supervisor was solemn as she stood by the door of the boardroom and watched as the staff filed into the room.

"Our contract with Data Entry Services is to expire at the end of April," Lisa said. "The contract is up for tender and we are concerned we may not win it for the next three-year term. We thought we should let you know, and it could also affect your rights. We will advise you as soon as we know."

One month later, the staff were advised that the agency had lost its contract.

Madeline, the supervisor before Lisa who had left the company on the pretext that she was retiring, now appeared on the scene as the proprietor of her own company. She had used the information available when she was supervisor to guarantee she would win the contract from the agency and with a full complement of workers. Lisa advised the staff, who were appalled at the treachery, but she assured them their jobs were safe.

"We are having a party Friday night. A thank you to all staff," Lisa said,

All the seats were taken when Frances arrived late for the party, so she hung back near the edge of the door. Lisa spotted her and offered her seat to Frances. She was seated next to the company's industrial rep, who bored Frances as he chatted to her.

"Have you had a holiday this year?" he enquired.

"No," she replied.

"You need a holiday in the US," he laughed. "Have you had a *holiday* this year?" he emphasized louder. He was referring to her holiday in the USA. But Frances ignored him as she picked up her drink and joined Pieta, who had just arrived.

As this mind-bending abuse continued almost everywhere she went, Frances decided it was time to investigate further. She made an appointment with Robert, a private detective.

Fear controlled her life. Even using her home telephone or one at work seemed like a risk, so she used a public telephone booth in a side street not far from work. Robert arranged an appointment for the next day. She had to ask Anne for time off work.

As Frances drove towards Robert's office the next day, she glanced in her rear vision mirror and saw a white car some way behind her. But she thought nothing of it. She was early for the appointment when she arrived, so after she parked her car outside the office, she stood on the pavement and had a ciggie. She peered along the road from where she had come and saw a white car parked some distance away with someone seated in the driver's seat.

Your minds in overdrive, she told herself. Of course you weren't followed.

Robert was five foot ten with greying, wavy hair.

Frances described to Robert the check on her references her most recent employers in Auckland. "I want you to find out if there is anything adverse being said about me from my previous employers, because they abused me, too."

"I'll have my report ready in a few days. Call back on Friday," he said. "Where does your husband live?"

"Auckland. You can find his address on the internet white pages," she replied.

At lunch time on Friday, Frances rang Robert, who said the report would be ready at four p.m.

"You can walk around Hamilton with your head held high," Robert said as he handed her the report.

"Maureen from Data Entry Services did say that your husband was a cripple," he added. "They don't know what they are doing."

She found nothing out of the ordinary as she eagerly read the report. But the remark from Maureen disturbed Frances, as at no stage had she told anyone there that her husband was disabled.

The report said that Frances was a very good worker and that they would employ her again.

Pania seated herself next to Frances the next day at work as she took an early lunch.

"How did that interview go for that job yesterday?" Pania enquired.

"Okay," murmured a stunned Frances.

"I hope you get the job," Pania wished her back.

Sheryl served Frances in the café for her afternoon break.

"Gee, you will be glad to get out of here," she remarked sarcastically as Frances departed.

While Frances drove home that night from work, tears rolled down her cheeks. She was a bag of nerves because of all this abuse. That night she flicked through the white pages, found Robert's telephone number, and dialled it.

"Sorry to bother you at home," she apologized to him. "Did you ring Data Entry Services in Hamilton as well?"

"No," he replied instantly and startled she was sure he was genuine.

"I'm sick of all this. It is too long, over three years now," she cried into the telephone as she recounted the white car that first day, she visited his office.

"If you're that worried, go to the police," he advised.

"I'll do it through my solicitor," she replied as she hung up.

Always suspicious now, Frances searched for Harold's address on the internet that night. But she could not find his telephone number. It was obviously unlisted now.

At work on Monday, Frances became aware of a shadow at the window situated in the room divider in front of her. She was startled as she looked up to find the manager staring at her. But he moved away as she stared back at him.

It was the third time in the past week she had caught him peering at her. Other times he had come around the screen, stared at her, then he moved away. She nicknamed him creeping jesus.

She frantically decided it was time for a chat with Lisa.

"It's not fair," she said to Lisa. "I am being stalked and abused everywhere I go, including work, and my telephone is bugged, and I am followed sometimes, too."

"I'll have a talk to management see if they can offer a solution," Lisa suggested.

Two days later Lisa rang her at home.

"I've had a discussion about your problem with management, and they said they will increase security to stop your husband from entering the premises," Lisa told her.

"That is no good," Frances told her "My *ex*-husband is not coming inside. He has coerced some of the staff to abuse me."

"The extra security should help," Lisa told her. "Besides, you live at Wa Kawai and there's only one road in and one road out."

The solution did not work. The stalking and abuse continued until Frances reached a state of exhaustion and severe anxiety. She offered her resignation to Lisa a month before the new agency took over.

"I'm sorry, Lisa, but I just can't cope anymore," she said. "I have too many emotional problems to cope with."

"Would you like a break, perhaps come back later?" Lisa asked.

"No. I think it's for the best if I don't come back," she replied. "Best for my mental health."

"You are a good worker, and they don't want to lose you. I have had nothing but praise about your work habits, and you always dress well," Lisa said.

Lisa was very persuasive. She talked Frances into taking a month's break and to resume work when the new agency took over next month.

One day soon after leaving her job, Frances woke early feeling pain in her hip. It throbbed through her body, and she wondered how much longer she would have to put up with the pain.

As she had closed up inside over the years, she had told no one of the pain as she silently endured it. Some people had noticed, but she casually passed it off with a comment.

"Did you trip?" Tom said to her, noticing her limp one day.

"No, it's my hip. It keeps dislocating on me and makes my left leg collapse," she replied.

She also suffered more pain in her left leg that continued to get worse.

Frances found relief by standing up from her desk and walked around to get her poor, aching body back into action again. Her body would stiffen up if she sat too long, and she found working almost unbearable, the throbbing in her back becoming continually worse. She was not into James Bond movies, but her life was shaping into a real-life thriller.

CHAPTER
TWENTY-ONE

Frances was excited as she drove towards Hamilton. She was going to pick up her new kitten from her granddaughter Kirsty, whose cat had a litter of five kittens. When she arrived at Cindy's house, she rushed inside and gave Cindy and Kirsty big hugs.

"Here you are, Nana," Kirsty said as she handed Frances the kitten she had picked out. Kirsty was five foot two inches tall, with short, straight, dark brown hair, and was very attractive. The kitten was ginger and white. From the back, he looked as though he wore ginger pants and white stockings.

"Thank you, Kirsty. I'm going to name him Honey Boo," Frances told them. She hugged and stroked Honey Boo, and he started purring.

When she arrived home, she sat down and hugged the kitten. He was hungry, so she fed him some cat food.

He slept on her bed at night. She kept him inside for two weeks, so he could get used to her home. She loved him so much.

While Frances was off work, she went to Doctor Michaels. He suggested that perhaps Mental Health should come and see her at home.

"They could help you," he said. "I will refer you to them today."

Two days later Frances sat on the settee trying to read. There was a loud knock on the ranch slider door. When she answered, there were three strangers standing there. The woman said they were from Mental Health.

"They raped my brain," Frances cried, repeatedly hugging Honey Boo as the three crisis team support workers walked into the lounge.

"Doctor Michaels contacted us," the woman in the light green, two-piece suit said gently.

"We would like you to come into our unit for an assessment," the short, dumpy man told her.

"I see you read books," the woman asked. "Can you concentrate?"

As the reality of her situation became apparent to Frances, she paused before answering.

"Yes," she lied as she tried to cover up her anxiety and her deep sense of fear as her heart thumped away. She was very afraid they would take her away.

"I will ring you later with an appointment time," the woman said as they left.

Later that day, the woman phoned Frances and gave her an appointment time with a psychiatrist for the next day.

So, the following day Frances sat in the small room her eyes wide open as she viewed her surroundings cautiously.

"I would like you to help my ex-husband," Frances asked Doctor Simpson. "He needs psychiatric treatment and is a control freak. He has tried to control me for over three decades."

"Why do you think that?" he asked her.

"He distributed a photo of me to ensure I am stalked and abused at places I frequent."

"Frances, I would like you to tell me what you have been experiencing."

"I am being followed at times," she told him. "I was working at Data Entry Services, and they abused me too. I am sure my telephone is bugged, and my neighbour monitors my movements."

"Do you think this room is bugged?" Doctor Simpson enquired.

Frances slowly turned her head as her eyes took in every detail of the room before she replied after considering the question carefully.

"No, I don't think so," she replied. But she was suspicious.

"I lied to the woman who came from Mental Health," Frances said to him. "I told her I could concentrate, and I cannot. These people are controlling my life. I do not know why they want to monitor my activities."

"I would like Doctor Michaels to change your medication. I'd like you to begin taking Amitriptyline," Doctor Simpson said. "I will arrange for the local support person to visit you."

As Frances left the building, she felt relief at the hope that she would really be free again, and over the next few weeks she started to relax as her anxiety gradually reduced. But she still suffered from fatigue, a dry mouth, and insomnia. Graham, the support person, called in on a weekly basis, and after four weeks she was ready to return to work.

———

The months passed quickly after Frances returned to work at Data Entry Services. She quickly settled in and started to enjoy her life, despite the effects of her medication as she slowly regained her confidence.

She was still wary of the other staff members, so she kept

to herself. But she was proud of her fingernails, which she had stopped biting as her stress had reduced. And she continued her part-time business at home, gathering stock on a weekly basis.

Three months later, with Honey Boo purring contentedly on her lap, Frances flicked through her psychiatric report and the reply from the head psychiatrist. She was astounded and horrified.

Frances believes that her ex-husband is a "control freak" and is using other people to harass, abuse, and control her life, even after she moved away from Auckland. She also believes that someone up there is controlling the incidents.

She is very annoyed, as she stays home most of the time when she is not working for the Data Entry Services, and she believes that someone is bugging her telephone. She denies feeling depressed, but is angry and hostile because of these activities and no one will believe her and is fed up with these people spying on her.

Frances had Amitriptyline prescribed for middle insomnia, which she says has improved her sleep pattern. She reports poor concentration and short-term memory loss. However, her energy level has improved. There were some suicidal thoughts some weeks ago, but she says she can now guarantee her safety.

Her history involved treatment in Auckland where she was diagnosed with a paranoid delusional disorder, which was treated with Stelazine. However, she believed the medication was for her anxiety. The Auckland clinic arranged a scan at the hospital, but she never received the results because the report was lost in the hospital system.

She refuses to take Stelazine because of the side effects, and there is neither forensic history nor a family history of mental illness. Her mental status examination started when she arrived promptly. She was cooperative, and she appeared relaxed, with good eye contact. Frances gave a good account of her suffering, and there is no psychomotor retardation or agitation. She dresses neatly and has a good standard of personal hygiene.

Her mood is angry subjectively, and her affect was reactive full range and her thought processes organized with no loosening of association. Paranoia was recorded in the first session; however, she denies thought broadcasting, withdrawal or insertion and any delusions of control or thought control and any passivity experience.

She denies any ideas of reference, delusions, or auditory or visual hallucinations, while her registration was intact. Her recall was three objects with one trial, as her attention and concentration were intact, and she could spell world backwards.

Her serial sevens were normal. However, she can only recall two out of three objects at five minutes. She was fully orientated in time and place and person and is in-sightless. Frances does not believe she has a problem. She feels her husband needs treatment.

My impression is that Frances has a fixed paranoid delusional system. Her psychotic symptoms resulted in some

*degree of secondary depressive symptoms, and these
symptoms have affected her life in all areas. In the absence
of other psychotic symptoms, the working diagnosis is
paranoid delusional disorder.*

*There is, however, no doubt that she is suffering from a
psychotic illness but is not considered a risk and is not
justifiable under the Mental Health Act for compulsory
treatment. I recommend the use of an antipsychotic when
she runs out of her night sedation.*

Frances was mortified, they do not believe I am suffering from Post-Traumatic Stress Disorder.

Then she read the reply to this report from the head psychiatrist, which stunned her completely. A psychiatric registrar who was of the opinion that she had developed a fixed persecutory delusional system consistent with a delusional disorder. He noted that these symptoms had produced a degree of secondary depressive symptoms which affected her life.

The registrar felt he was unable to implement compulsory assessment and treatment within the terms of the 1992 Mental Health Act. Her mental disorder, he said, is characterised by disordered thinking in the form of a complex persecutory delusional ideation. The April guidelines for compulsory treatment suggested that her symptoms would constitute an example of "serious danger."

"Her family," Frances read, "have been notified that there is ample evidence that collaborative voluntary effects at treatment have been spectacularly unsuccessful and that I suggest when the opportunity arises that she is detained under the Compulsory Mental Health Act."

Frances was mortified.

They do not believe me. I am suffering from post-traumatic stress syndrome. The symptoms are similar. They have never even interviewed me thoroughly nor asked to look at all the evidence I have gathered. How can society behave like this, as they appear to be ordinary, decent human beings, yet they believe the slander and punish someone continuously for something they never did?

I really do not believe this is happening to me. I might look like a bimbo, but I have held responsible positions with companies over the years. It is the abuse that has made me look the way I do.

Well-educated, professional psychiatrists should update their knowledge and skills with current phenomena and not sit idly behind a desk passing judgement without a thorough interview or viewing all the evidence she had gathered. The reports astounded Frances. She was mortified that they could assess her in this way, without even looking at her evidence.

Later in June as Frances was clearing her emails, her computer crashed and would only go into safe mode. So, she rang her support company to find out what she should do. They told her that her hard disks were completely wiped and said she needed a start-up disk with Windows 97, which she could get at the local computer store.One day at work, alone at her desk, Frances was concentrating on her work and ignored a voice she heard nearby, not realizing it was directed at her. Suddenly someone bent forward to make himself heard. She paused, surprised, as she looked into the man's face.

"How is the work going?" creeping jesus said kindly to her.

As she looked up at creeping jesus she said "fine" and then bent down to her work again.

At lunchtime she went to the toilet and broke down and cried. She found she could not stand it when people were nice to her, and she also cried as she drove all the way home.

Alas not long after, Frances became aware as the abuse gradually crept in on her from late September. When she sat outside alone at a table, Heather came out and sat next to her, not saying a word. It was intimidation tactics again. There had been other incidents, too, but she could not really remember them as the anxious feeling crept over her again.

Her friend Rita had come back into her life. She accepted her at face value and as Frances felt the need for a break, they arranged a week's holiday in Melbourne. First the staff were nice to her. But as the days went on, they began doing stupid, horrible things to her. But she became friendly with Margaret.

After the vacation, Frances began driving Margaret home after work, especially if the weather was poor,

Margaret borrowed Frances's umbrella one rainy day, and when she finally returned it several days later, Frances noticed it was not her umbrella. The handle and spokes were different. After that, curiously, Margaret did not want another ride home with her.

"How are you today, Frances?" Sheryl sneered as she handed her the change for her purchase at the cafeteria.

Creeping jesus still appeared at times and peered at her, which made her feel even more self-conscious. She began avoiding him as much as she could.

One night as she was clearing her emails. There was one from Debbie, who had just arrived home from Melbourne just before Frances's trip there.

"I am driving to Wa Kawai this weekend," she wrote, "and I will call in and see you. I will bring some cookies for afternoon tea." Frances emailed her to say she was off to Melbourne herself.

As Frances left late for her drive to Auckland, she stopped at Huntly to collect some Australian cash, as she had already purchased her traveller's cheques. The ANZ bank had no Australian cash, so she withdrew five hundred dollars and went to the bank down the road to change it.

Frances then drove to Rita's in Pakuranga, Auckland, to be ready for departure to Melbourne the next day. Rita was overjoyed to see Frances.

"How was the drive up?" Rita asked.

"It was good. There was not much traffic."

While Frances had enjoyed the trip, she became very aware of just how tight Rita was with her money, despite being wealthy. Rita's husband had died a few months before and left her millions of dollars. Kerry created a business designing and manufacturing TV parts. But you would never have known it to look at her, and she was a miser, as Frances found out in Melbourne.

While they ate lunch in a Melbourne café, Rita refused to pay three dollars to put her food on a plate, so she kept her food that she had brought until they left the café. While Frances ate her lunch, the assistant kept watching to make sure that Rita never ate her food in the café.

As Frances paid for a further purchase, Rita ducked out of the café, Frances felt mischievous for once in her life.

"You wouldn't think she was a millionaire, would you?" Frances remarked to the assistant as she handed over the money.

"Is she?" the surprised woman asked her.

"Yes," Frances replied with a smile. "Don't you know? That is how they make millions—because they are mean and miserly."

As the day passed, Frances tried to coerce Rita into going back to the café for take-home food. But Rita was too embarrassed and refused to go back. This had dashed Frances's plans for paying her back.

Back home at the bank one afternoon, the teller screwed up some paper and threw it over her shoulder and onto the floor.

"Oops," the teller remarked. "I wouldn't do that at home."

"Aren't you going to pick it up?" Frances enquired, surprised.

"No, the cleaner can," she replied.

After Frances arrived home that night, she felt an eerie feeling creeping over her as she thought of that spooky incident at the bank. Quite often at night as she sat on the couch, she would read junk mail and the newspaper when the commercials were on TV. When she had read them, she screwed up the junk mail and tossed that and the newspaper over her shoulder behind the couch, which sat in the middle of the room. She would pick these up later when she made a coffee.

She crept around the house as she peered all around and then viewed the burglar alarm sensors as she went. She felt stiff as her feelings gave her the creeps.

Was there a camera bug in her house?

Honey Boo went missing for the whole of the next weekend. Frances kept opening the door and calling out to him. But he never appeared, which was unusual for him.

When she woke up late Sunday night with insomnia, she went to the back-door and called out to Honey Boo again. Suddenly a flash of fur sped past her through the door faster than lightning. He was so fast Frances could not even see the white of his coat.

In the kitchen, the kitten was agitated and very hungry. He purred like an engine as she cuddled and stroked his soft fur. Then she feed him and went back to bed. As she lay there trying to get back to sleep, she puzzled over his behaviour. Had he been locked inside someone's house while they were away for the weekend?

The next day at work, Anne called a staff meeting.

"Think about some ideas for how you would like to be seated," Anne told the staff.

Everyone had different ideas but soon agreed on something everyone was pleased with.

Phillipa had worked for Data Entry Services for a few weeks and then they did not want her anymore. Frances was not surprised. She had a very sharp tongue, and you never knew which way her moods would swing.

When Frances arrived at work one morning, she noticed Tammy and Janice staring at her. She was wearing her new jeans and blue top. She had applied some makeup for a change, to see what reaction she would get at work. No one said anything.

"You don't know which way it's going to go. It could be menopausal or maybe a bad hair day," Marge said in a sarcastic manner as she chatted with Tom as Frances seated herself at her desk.

As Frances walked along the corridor towards the staff entrance at lunchtime, Heather came out of a short corridor steaming ahead and nearly bumped into her. Heather stopped and stared at her, then steamed past her.

That night, Anita came over and banged on her door.

"Can I use your telephone? Someone is using my line for the internet," she said. "Did you see the new people next door have put a satellite dish on their roof?"

The next day Anne informed the staff about Christmas parties and the luncheon their department was having.

"If anyone is not going, please put your hand up," Anne asked the gathered staff.

Frances put up her hands, along with three other people. One of the them was an Asian worker named Xin, a very sweet lady whom Frances liked a lot. She approached Frances later to tell her she had changed her mind and decided to go, and she tried to talk Frances into going with her.

"You will not like the food," Frances told her. "It will not be Chinese food" she added.

"It is not the food but the company and being with the team," Xin told her.

Xin was being sucked into the system of lies, and they began using her, too, to get at Frances.

"You and me we will go to the luncheon together," Xin told her.

There was so much happening to Frances. She got the feeling they were deliberately sending her mixed signals—sometimes they were nice to her, then something insidious would happen as she felt the vile and evil vibes around her. Their attitudes told her they were trying to get rid of her.

Melanie appeared after Frances left early for her break.

"Have you been out here long?" she asked Frances.

"No," replied Frances.

Then Marilyn, Saul, Leanne, and Glenda appeared and seated themselves at the table.

"We left early," they said in unison and then idly chatted away.

Frances joined in the chat but soon went back to her desk.

Anne wandered amongst the desks. "You need to pay for your Christmas luncheon today," she told the staff.

Xin went with Leanne on Friday to pay for their luncheon, and she did not invite Frances to join them as she had suggested previously.

That night Honey Boo went missing again, and Frances became worried for him.

On Saturday morning, as Frances packed the car for the local market, Anita approached her.

"What are you doing?" she enquired.

"I've decided to go the local market," Frances replied.

"What are you taking to sell? Can I have a look?"

Anita browsed through her boxes and picked out a few items. She said she would pay Frances later.

"I will give you an invoice," Frances replied.

"I need a new lock on my back-door. Someone has used a

key to come inside my house when I am not home," Anita told her, smirking as she looked at the box with a door lock and key Frances was taking to the market.

"I am selling that because it is one that I had changed to stop the alien from getting into my house," Frances told her.

"Who is the alien?" Anita asked her.

"My ex. Have you seen Honey Boo? He has gone missing again."

"No. Perhaps someone has locked him up or kept him."

The market was not worth the effort but she enjoyed the chance to get out.

That night Honey Boo came home again. He did not seem as frightened as the last time.

As Frances became more aware of how far spread the stalking and harassment had become, she contacted Graham at Mental Health to discuss this problem with him. She made an appointment to see him next week.

The following Monday it was Get at Frances Day. Staff made a point of discussing her feedback forms for her work performance rather than leaving them on her desk for her to read.

Gita talked loudly in front of all the staff, pointing out all the mistakes that Frances had made. Marge did the same in a very sarcastic manner.

Xin spun around in her seat to face Frances "You forgot to put the stock total in" Xin whispered to Frances.

Frances knew she probably did make some mistakes due to her lack of concentration. But she was also aware that it would be pretty easy to sabotage someone's work when verifying it.

"I wonder if I could get tickets to the Christmas luncheon now," Tammy said as Frances sat down after her lunch break.

"If anyone wants a ticket for the luncheon, there is one available," Anne said to the staff as she walked around the desks. "We will have a meeting to discuss the Christmas parties."

"Gee, that was a funny coincidence," Tammy remarked after she had rushed over to buy the luncheon ticket.

Anne called a staff meeting, including the temporary workers.

"We have to change the staff parties," she said. "We have to change the parties and only have one. We are also going to include all the temporary staff too."

"Father Christmas will be there, and he is a handsome man." She nodded toward creeping jesus with a smile. "And if each member could bring a small gift for Father Christmas to give out."

Creeping jesus for Father Christmas. Frances cringed at the thought.

"Please spend no more than ten dollars on your present," Angela added.

The staff had morning tea the next day as they gathered in the board room.

"I remember," Anne smirked.

"I remember when Elvis's car was on display in New Zealand," Marilyn said and started the conversation.

"Oh, I do not remember that" Frances said.

"They are not going to make a fool of anyone this time at the Christmas luncheon," Anne remarked as all the staff went back to work.

Marge barged around to Frances's desk with a form in her hand. "You left number fifty out again," she said with annoyance.

"Have you paid for the Christmas party, Frances?" Anne asked her as she walked up to her. Frances picked up her purse and paid the five dollars, and then she noticed that she was the only one Anne had asked for payment.

Was that to ensure that I will attend?

"Frances, telephone for you," Melanie called. It was Graham from Mental Health, calling to confirm their meeting for tomorrow.

When Frances walked back to her desk, she noticed the staff around her were tittering, no doubt because a man had rung her. She just ignored them.

That night Frances rang Phillipa. "Would you mind if I stayed at your place tomorrow night? I have to go and see Graham at Mental Health after work."

"Yes, that's fine. We can have a catch up," Phillipa said.

The next day after work, Frances drove to the Mental Health unit to see Graham. She told him all the things that were happening at work. He listened intently then told her to make sure she took her medication. He wasn't much help this time.

Then Frances drove to Phillipa's. Then carried in her overnight bag, some desert, and a bottle of wine. Phillipa had prepared pork steaks with apple sauce and some vegetables.

"I can't abide hypocrites," Phillipa said as they chatted over the meal.

"No, I can't either," Frances replied.

"Sometimes I think I am being followed," Philippa told her.

"Do you? Sometimes I think I am, too, because of all the stupid incidents that happen to me."

After dinner Frances got ready for bed and had a very peaceful sleep that night in Philippa's guest room.

A week later when Frances went to have her hair done, Pauline the hairdresser pretended not to know her and mixed her up with someone else as she talked to her.

"Here are two magazines," Pauline told her while the perm solution was being processed. One was an issue of *Woman's Monthly* and the other *Woman's Style*. "There are two interesting articles you might like to read." Pauline flipped to a page in the *Woman's Monthly* magazine with a bold black headline: *Jealousy with a Spouse and the Problems It Causes*.

After she left the hairdresser, Frances called into a bookshop. She scanned the periodicals for the copies of the magazines, but they were the December issues. The copies at the hairdresser had been November issues. That evening she wrote to the magazine requesting a copy of the November issue.

The next day at work the staff played "be nice to Frances." They complimented her on her hair and how nice she looked. Xin spun around on her chair in a strange way and complimented her in an unusual way.

When Frances went out for morning tea, she noticed Melanie, Saul, Glenda, and Marylyn as they sat at another table. Melanie stood up to have a good look at her and no doubt made a comment on her new hairdo.

They are only doing these things to blow my mind, she thought, as she realized that Gita's attitude had changed towards her in the past two weeks.

The day of the Christmas party soon came, and Frances arrived late as she went out during her lunch break. The only seat available was between Tom and Samantha.

Tom and Margaret always pretended to be on the outer with the bosses. But Frances always suspected that they used this as a diversion for her.

Tom started a conversation with Frances and talked about Kawhia.

"The ocean at Kawhia is bad. There is a big drop, and it causes an undertow," he told her. "It is too dangerous to swim in. You could drown quite easily."

As the conversation continued, the talk of drowning made Frances queasy. Suddenly, she remembered what Phillipa had said to her a year ago: There are plenty of rips at Kawhia, and you could easily drown.

Madeline attended the party, so Frances took the opportunity to make an appointment with her after work that day to discuss the abuse she was being subjected to. Madeline had come back to the company with her own business to supervise the staff.

Frances attended her appointment with Madeline at the agency, and they discussed the emotional and psychological abuse she had been subjected to.

"Who is doing these terrible things to you?" Madeline enquired.

"Most of the department."

Frances handed Madeline a document that contained information about what Harold had done to her over the years as well as the staff at work.

"I will think about this problem over the weekend," Madeline said. "Then I will talk to the boss on Monday."

That night Frances thought over the conversation and decided it would be best if Madeline spoke to Anne rather than go over her head to her boss. Frances rang Madeline at her home to tell her. Madeline agreed.

When Frances woke early on Monday morning after a restless sleep, she was ill with worry and had been all weekend. Most of the day she spent dozing after going to the dairy to buy some smokes and the morning paper. Honey Boo was missing again.

After dozing off, she woke to a loud bang on her ranch slider door. When she opened it, Anita stood there.

"I just popped over to see if you are alright."

"I have not been well," Frances said and started to cry.

"Maybe it was poison," Anita said to a startled Frances. "Is Honey Boo inside with you?"

"No, I'm worried about him. He is missing again."

"Perhaps someone has stolen him." "I got some poison for the garden this weekend. And I see that Mary has a satellite dish on her house, too."

Honey Boo came home later that morning, skitterish and hungry.

Anne steamed past Frances as she sat at her desk and startled her as she had tried to be fair.

"Good morning, Frances," Anne yelled venomously.

It soon became obvious to Frances by her work-mates' actions and remarks that they had been told she had made a complaint. Marilyn smirked at her. Samantha did a funny hoity-toity stance towards her and then stared continually at her. Marge was her usual ignorant self. Frances simply continued with her work.

I have found my tongue and I intend to defend myself from now on.

Later when Frances stood by the shelves filing some forms, Sandra, who was seated behind her, started talking about rat poison in a loud voice. Sandra was the sister of Jeanette, the supervisor in files.

No matter how hard Frances tried to give up cigarettes, she failed. She started using roll-your-owns without much effect and occasionally brought a packet of real cigarettes. She had purchased a quit pack. But because of all the abuse, she was unable to stop smoking.

At lunchtime one day, Frances drove to the bank and

smoked a tailor-made cigarette while she stood in the queue for the automatic teller. Frances was surprised to see Pauline stroll towards her.

"Caught you," she said to Frances as she stepped behind the man at the end of the queue. Frances dropped her cigarette immediately and ground it out on the dirt patch on the grass as she waited.

"The price of petrol is high, isn't it?" Pauline said to her.

She withdrew fifty dollars from the machine which whirred away and spat out a printout, and she walked into the bank to bank her foreign currency. Pauline followed her not long after. When she came back out, Frances thought she had better pick up the butt, but when she went looking for it, it was gone.

That night she puzzled over the event. She was sick of being followed, having her telephone bugged, and every little habit or word she spoke being used as abuse against her.

The next morning Frances approached Pauline as she talked to another woman.

"Here, you can put your own butts in here," Frances said angrily as she shoved an empty cigarette packet into her hand and went back to her desk.

"I would like an apology," Pauline cried to Frances when she approached her. "You can give this to whoever it belongs to." She handed the empty packet back to Frances. With a flick of her hand, Frances tossed it in the bin beside her and continued working.

Frances mulled these events. What if she had been wrong, that maybe someone else had picked up that butt?

"If you did not pick up my butt at the teller machine, I am sorry," Frances said to Pauline when she approached her.

Pauline turned and there were tears streaming down her face.

"I didn't do it," she cried. "I'm sick of this place. No one talks to me. My divorce is coming through soon. My husband used to beat me. And you are the only one who talks to me. That breakfast you are having this morning, I wasn't invited to join that either. Nor was I given a small gift from May when Melanie distributed them after May had resigned."

Pauline appeared to be genuinely upset. Appalled at herself, Frances hugged her and asked her to join her for morning tea.

Melanie arrived back with the breakfast from the takeaways and gave them to those who had ordered. Frances felt guilty about Pauline not being included and decided to offer her some of her breakfast. She found Pauline missing and went in search of her. Eventually she found her seated outside, bawling her eyes out.

"They're always horrible to me," Pauline cried.

"Well, maybe you should have a talk to Madeline," Frances advised her. "Would you like to join me and have some of my breakfast?"

"No, I will sit out here for a while," she replied.

When Frances went for her morning tea break, she stopped to collect Pauline on her way out.

"I've wasted enough time this morning, so I won't come out this morning," Pauline said.

Frances became suspicious, so she kept an eye on Pauline at her desk. Later Pauline got up and walked towards the cafeteria. After a few minutes Frances grabbed some money and walked towards the cafeteria to buy her lunch early.

As she stood at the counter, she perused the room and was not at all surprised to see Pauline seated with a large group of staff, all happily chatting away. So, she did lie to me, Frances thought.

The next morning, she arrived at work early and placed

Anne's neatly wrapped gift on her table, hoping no one would see.

"Have you got a secret admirer, Anne?" Melanie piped up as Frances became aware of the conversation around her.

"Who are the chocolates from?" Tammy enquired as Anne showed them her gift.

Twice during the morning, as Frances went to collect more work from the trolley, Anne approached her. But she was interrupted and continued walking past Frances with a smirk on her face. Finally, Anne had a chance to thank Frances for the gift.

The next day was Saturday, the last day at work before the Christmas break. Frances had dressed neatly but arrived late at work.

"You're late," Tammy remarked.

"Good morning, Pauline. How are you today?" Frances said.

"Good morning, Frances," Pauline replied as Frances walked past her.

At morning tea break, a Chinese man started a discussion with Frances.

"What are you doing for Christmas?" he enquired.

"I am having Christmas with my daughter and granddaughters," she replied. "All I want to do is go home and sleep."

"Even now at this time of day?" he said.

"Yes, I have been tired because of all the long work hours."

Creeping jesus, who was on duty, appeared at the door.

"What time are you leaving today, Frances?" he called, leaning against the open door.

"One at the latest," she replied as she stubbed out her cigarette and went back to work.

A few hours later, Marge stepped away from her desk and

wished everyone a merry Christmas. Then as an afterthought, she turned and wished Frances one, too.

"Merry Christmas," Frances called out to those who were still working as she left the building. Theresa was the only one who returned her wishes.

After work Frances drove to the fruit and veggie outlet to purchase some strawberries and raspberries for Christmas day. Then she stopped by the home of a man who had contacted her about looking at several boxes of books he wanted to sell. John was a stall holder at the Hamilton market and part owner of an antique shop in Hamilton. His trade was a master painter. He collected books that Frances was interested in. He was a nice man who always treated her with respect. John wasn't home, but she decided to wait a few minutes in case he was running late. Finally, she left.

Later that day she felt guilty about not waiting longer and rang John.

"I left at one forty," she told him.

"You must have missed me by seconds," he said. "I'm sorry."

"I will come over tomorrow if that's suitable," she said.

"If I'm not home, just go into the garage and sort through the books," he told her. "Jan should be home anyway."

The next day Frances decided not to travel all the way to John's. She had other things to occupy her, and she rang to tell him.

"Jan speaking," said the voice who answered the phone.

"I'm Frances," she told the woman. "I was coming to your place today to take a look at some books I've been talking to John about. But have decided not to. Please tell John I will arrange another time. This is the day before Christmas and I have a lot to do"

"Oh yes, I know all about you, John told me" Jan said sarcastically as Frances stood there stunned by the remark. Then she hung up and dialled Jacinta.

"Frances here. Merry Christmas," she chirped on the phone.

"Are you doing the market at new year?" Jacinta enquired.

"Yes, I am," Frances lied, and they arranged to meet. Frances was not feeling up to going to the market.

Frances had already made the decision not to go, as she was exhausted because of all the abuse. Fear was controlling her life, and she could always email Jacinta later.

Cindy and the girls arrived later the next morning for a nice Christmas meal. Sheryn was tall, with long blonde hair. Kirsty had short dark hair, and Robin was also blonde, with a light curl. They were beautiful teens.

"Hi, Mum," Cindy said as she gave her a big hug. Her three granddaughters gave her big hugs, too. They put their gayly wrapped presents under the Christmas tree.

"What's for lunch?" Cindy asked her. "It smells delicious"

"Roast lamb, pumpkin, potatoes, and kumara with minted peas. For dessert there is Christmas plum pudding with cream and pavlova with raspberries and whipped cream. I also have a bottle of sparkling grape juice."

They all made noises of delight and anticipation.

"While we are waiting for the lunch to cook, why don't we open the Christmas presents," Frances said.

"Where's Honey Boo?" Sheryn asked.

"He's outside somewhere," Frances replied. "I am so glad I got him. He is gorgeous."

"Okay," Cindy said as she bent down to pick up the presents. She passed them to everyone.

Cindy and the girls got a box of Tresor Dore chocolate seashells and a voucher for perfume at the local chemist. They gave Frances a box of Ferrero Rocher chocolates and a voucher for Miller's women's wear shop. They were all delighted with their presents.

Frances then dished up the lunch. She also opened the bottle of sparkling grape juice and poured it out in the wine glasses set for them.

They chatted for a while, then Cindy spoke up.

"Mum, we are going to the Gold Coast for the May school holidays," she said.

"Yes, that is going to be great," Sheryn piped up. "We will be able to go to the theme parks and have fun."

"That's great, have fun!" Frances said.

"Yeah, we will," Robin said.

"Is there a market on these holidays?" Cindy asked her mum.

"Yes, but I am not going because of the stalking," Frances told her.

Frances cleared the table and put the dishes in the dish washer.

After finishing the sparkling grape juice, it was time for them to go home.

On Tuesday morning Frances emailed Jacinta and told her she was not attending the market. She soon received a reply from Jacinta who tried to talk her into going where her friends were. Then the phone rang.

"You left two messages, so I thought I would ring you," Phillipa said. "What's wrong?"

"It's just all this stalking, it's getting me down," Frances said with distress.

Frances then told Phillipa about some of the incidents that had happened lately.

"Did I tell you what I did to my friend Rita?" Frances asked her.

"No."

"I carefully wrapped three dollars in a parcel and sent it to Rita for a Christmas gift," she laughed gleefully. "I wrote on the note, 'Here is three dollars so you can put your food on a plate next time you eat out.'"

Frances could hear a strange noise on the line, like a tape recorder whirring. "What is that noise" she said to Philippa.

"I can't hear it," Phillipa replied and then ended the conversation.

On Thursday Frances drove to Hamilton to do some banking and browse the shops. She wanted a long petticoat to wear under her new skirt she had brought in Melbourne.

Then she called in for a coffee at Phillipa's before she drove home. Phillipa's house was a mess as usual. It was late when she left for home and then discovered along the long lonely road, she had a puncture. The car was pulling to the left so she stopped to look at the tyres. She attempted to change the wheel.

The wheel was stuck on tight, and she could not remove it. But a kind man came along and persisted with the wheel until it broke free. Frances was extremely grateful. She made a note of his number plate to send him a gift.

When she arrived home in the dark, she was hot, flustered, and sticky. She stripped down to her underwear while Honey Boo sat and watched.

She heard meowing coming from her back-door, so she went outside to feed the neighbour's kitten. As she did, the door slammed shut behind her. When she turned to open it, she found that somehow the lock had jammed on the door. After trying numerous ways to get inside, she broke a window and climbed through the hole. She'd have to have it repaired the next day.

Before heading to bed, she sat down to check emails. In the first one she looked at, a customer complained about the condition the stock had arrived in, so she closed down the computer and went to her bed.

The next morning, after she had typed up her diary, she searched the internet looking for a writers' site and emailed a man named Gary who invited people to chat on the topic. When he replied, he said he wrote for the BBC.

A day later Frances received a strange email from Gary. "I just had a big puncture and had to buy a new tyre," he wrote. "Then the car would not start and it took two big diesel engines to tow it, because the battery was flat."

Reading Gary's comments made Frances remember how the guy had been eyeing her battery while she was fuelling up a couple of days ago. She got up and dashed out to her car. She opened the bonnet to find the battery was corroded all over. Then she looked at the date and saw that the battery was older than her car.

When she tried to start the car, it would not start. She found that someone had put the alarm in safety mode, which she never used.

The next day when Frances went down to the mailbox late, the postie woman roared over to her on her bike from over the road.

"I am late today," the woman told her. "I had a puncture, and then my bike would not start. I had to get a mechanic out from the garage to attend to it." Frances collected her mail and while walking down the drive to her place, she pondered the happenings of the last two days. Was there a connection, especially with her car in safe mode?

CHAPTER
TWENTY-FOUR

New Year's Day of 2001 dawned as a drizzly day. The weather that summer was atrocious, and all campers in the Wa Kawai caravan and camping grounds were packing up their belongings to go home. It was not much fun camping in this weather. Frances was glad that she was at home.

After a leisurely breakfast, Frances peered outside through the ranch slider windows as the fine rain drizzled down onto the lush green grass in front of her deck. She noticed that Anita was home, so she walked into the lounge. There was a bookcase on one wall filled with books, the dining table and chairs set in the alcove off the back wall of the lounge. The lounge corner suite sat in the middle of the room facing a wall, which was lined with two China cabinets and a TV set on a small table. She picked a gaily wrapped parcel off the bookcase. Leaving by the ranch slider in the lounge, she walked over to Anita's.

She gazed around the garden as she tapped lightly on the ranch slider door.

"Happy New Year, Anita" Frances said as she handed her the gift.

"Why, Frances, that is very sweet of you," Anita said. "The weather isn't the best, is it?"

"No, it keeps you inside," Frances replied.

"I go into hospital next week," Anita said, "I have to pack the items I want to take; I have a lot of editing to do for the BBC"

"Oh, you do editing," Frances enquired. "I have been busy on these wet days, too, writing my book."

Then her mind wandered back to the email from Gary the other day. "I do editing and writing for the BBC," he had written.

After a short conversation, Frances wandered back to the safety of her own home.

The telephone rang the next morning, breaking Frances' chain of thought as she sat at the computer.

"Hi, happy new year," Phillipa's voice boomed into the receiver.

"Happy new year to you, too. How are things going with you?" Frances said.

"Are you doing much with this shit weather?" Phillipa asked.

"Yes, I have been pretty busy with my book the last few days," she replied. "What's that funny crackling noise?"

"What noise? I can't hear any," Phillipa replied.

It was a hollow, echoing sound, like a tape recorder being used again.

"It has gone now. I don't know what it was," Frances lied.

"You better watch out. Harold might write a book in retaliation about you," Phillipa said. "When are you coming over again?"

"Soon, will give you a buzz when I am," Frances said. "Must away. I have to take my car for new tyres, a battery, and a warrant of fitness," Frances said.

Bill, one of the mechanics at the garage where Frances got her car serviced, walked in while Frances stood in the office, waiting for a ride home. He was five foot nine, with straight blonde hair.

"We got the tyres in for you, Frances," Bill said as the office assistant stood beside him and listened to the conversation.

"I will take you home now," Gary the mechanic said when he entered the office.

"I've got a house with a good view of the harbour," Gary told her as they drove towards her home. "It's a large old house, but the wardrobe is tiny. Too small for all the wife's clothes." He continued.

"The house that jack built," Frances laughed.

"What do you mean?" Gary enquired.

"Nothing much," she laughed again as her mind flew back to over a decade ago when she and Harold had built their own home.

Years ago Harold had left all the floor plans for Frances to work out, and he agreed with them. To make sure that the plans would all fit together, Frances asked Harold to check them all, as he was a wiz with that type of thing.

Gil was not a friend nor visitor to their home before, except once for a New Year's party, so why did he come that time? He had just stood there just inside the ranch slider door near the table, his eyes glancing slowly around the room. At that time the dining table was in the wrong spot and where it was positioned made the dining room look too small.

Then suddenly Frances remembered Horrible Harry's question that time at work. "Did you do all the plans for your house?" he had asked.

How did he know about that? In addition to this, she remembered that prick from Tauranga, too, Lester Wrightson, and his comment when he came to see her about some item she was going to sell for him on the internet. "Oh, the house is bigger than he said it was," he said.

Then there was Julie that time, too, when she came to collect Frances for an Elvis function. Julie had made sure she had to walk right through their house to get out of the garage. Frances had wondered why Julie just stood at the garage door and looked back into the house with bewilderment on her face. Frances had brushed it aside, but the incident stuck in her mind.

That afternoon the telephone rang as Frances sat tapping on the keyboard as she worked on her manuscript.

"It's Gary," the man's voice said. "Your car is ready. I will pick you up soon."

Frances stood in the bedroom and watched as her familiar station wagon drove up her driveway. Gary tooted the horn, then he drove her to the office to pay her account.

"Did you supply the tyres?" the office assistant enquired.

"No, you did," Frances replied.

Gary entered the office, walked over to the computer, and fiddled with some papers beside the computer as he peered over the receptionist's shoulder to check her invoice on the screen as the assistant processed it.

After Frances arrived home, she phoned Phillipa.

"Hi, I'm coming over this afternoon. My cars fixed. I have new tyres, a battery, and a new warrant."

"That's fine. What time will you arrive?" Phillipa asked.

"Say around three o'clock," Frances replied.

"Yes, that's fine. Will see you then."

When Frances parked her car outside Phillipa's, she was dumbfounded when Phillipa drove out of her driveway and onto the road. Frances stepped on the roadway then Phillipa slammed on her breaks and stopped.

"Here's the paper about the Alegria show," Frances said as she handed her the advertisement.

"I'll look at it later," Phillipa said as she put her car into gear and took off. Phillipa didn't give Frances time to ask her why she was taking off.

As Phillipa drove off, Frances heard a rustle behind her. She was startled to find that Phillipa had flung the newspaper out of her window and onto the road.

Later that night Phillipa rang her, but Frances hardly listened as she rambled on. She was annoyed with her for taking off like that when she knew that she was arriving for a visit.

Then Frances pricked up her ears when she heard Philippa mention a warrant. "It's two weeks overdue," she was saying.

When Frances hung up the telephone, she was deep in thought as she walked through the house to the garage, opened her car door, and peered at the sticker on the windscreen. She saw that her warrant of fitness sticker was dated the 14th of January 2002, when in fact it should have read the 3rd of January. Another piece of information from that bitch, she thought as she went back inside.

Saturday morning Frances drove to the local dairy to buy the morning paper and a treat of a packet of cigarettes. She noticed the local market was on. The smell of onions and sausages cooking on a barbeque wafted through the air as Frances approached the market with its usual junk stalls and local artists. Then she paused and noticed some View-master reels and picked them up to examine them.

"I had some royal family ones," the woman said to her as she sat on the ground watching Frances.

"Oh, did you?" Frances replied.

"Yes. Someone came along and brought them not long ago."

Then Frances noticed an old post office money box and enquired how much.

"Fifteen dollars," the woman replied.

"Would you hold it for me? I need to go to the EFTPOS machine to get some cash."

"Yes, sure," she replied.

After she collected the money from the teller machine across the road, she noticed the woman was nowhere to be seen. A young child sat in the woman's place.

"Your mother put this away for me," she said, pointing to the money box. "She said it was fifteen dollars." She picked up the money box and gave the boy twenty dollars.

Suddenly Frances became aware of someone standing very close behind, listening to her. She whirled around and saw that woman there listening to the conversation. After Frances collected her change and drove home, she was sure that woman was checking to see if she was honest.

The staff chattered idly at the workstation while they worked the following Monday. Tammy talked about various spots and moles she had on her body.

"I have a funny spot on my leg," Frances said as she lifted her trouser leg to show the spot to Tammy and Melanie.

"Do you use a finger stool when working, Frances?" Tammy enquired. Frances ignored her and continued working. Later that afternoon, Frances caught a fleeting glimpse of a person who approached Dulcie's desk opposite her, and she glanced up. Creeping jesus was standing there staring at her. Frances lowered her head and continued working as she licked her finger and flicked through the pages.

The next day Frances arrived early, after rushing through her morning routine and drive, because she wanted to leave work early to see the movie *Young Nickie*. She hadn't had time to comb her hair or spray some perfume on in the car before she walked into work.

After she sat at her desk, she unzipped her handbag, grabbed her comb, combed her hair, and then sprayed on some perfume. Then she slung her handbag under her desk and walked over to the trolley to pick up some work.

As she idly walked back to her desk, she became aware of Marge angrily scooping something into some tissue paper off the empty desk beside Frances and threw it into the bin.

Frances glanced at the desk at the end of the bay of workstations and saw there were some sweets in a tray set out.

"You shouldn't have done that, combed your hair," Marge said sarcastically as she scooped up the rest of the sweets and put them in the bin.

"I didn't know they were there," Frances replied innocently.

"The wrapped ones will be alright," Marge replied as she walked off in a huff.

"My hair is always clean. I wash it every morning," said Frances as she turned around to Tammy and Melanie. "It does not matter what I do, I'm always in the shit." She settled down to work, idly flicking through her papers. Then she caught a fleeting glimpse of someone walking around to Dulcie's desk and was startled to see creeping jesus standing watching her again.

No one else ever put birthday shouts on a table they always walk around handing them out so Frances knew Marge had set her up on Marge's birthday. Frances sat working hard and ignored her surroundings. No one offered her a sweet and she would not touch them, as she fumed about Marge and the way she had been set up.

"I would like to have a chat with you," Madeline said when she approached Frances the next morning. "Nothing serious."

She led Frances over to the other side of the room and into an empty office, where she offered Frances a seat and shut the door.

If it's nothing much why go to this extreme? Frances wondered as she sat down.

"Don has been looking at the forms that come in," Madeline started. Don was creeping jesus. "Some are really dirty. One even had a nail in it. You do not use a finger stool, and you lick your fingers to turn the documents over. This is not good for your health. You also comb your hair a lot."

Frances sat there listening and did not say a word as she wondered where this conversation was leading to. Then Madeline mentioned briefly the code of ethics and the oath that all employees had to sign.

"*Don (creeping jesus) cares about you!*" Madeline yelled.

Frances was struck dumb. She had no answer for that as the conversation abruptly ended. What a stupid thing to say to a worker. Who did she mean? she wondered as she walked back to her desk.

Back at her desk, Frances glanced over to where she had just come from, and she saw Madeline standing there talking to Don.

Therefore, I am dirty and I pass on germs because I lick my fingers when turning the documents over.

Heather approached Frances as she sat outside during her break that afternoon and sat down beside her without saying a word. Frances was surprised to see her, as there had been a memo that she would be away for her holidays. As Frances left her seat to go back inside, she glanced at the wall and Teina sat there staring at her with a puzzled look on her face. Until now Teina had played no part in her abuse.

As Frances puzzled over Madeline's words, she suddenly remembered the familiarity with the way that she said it and not really what she had said. It clicked as she drove home. "Your husband must be a powerful man," Anne the supervisor had shouted to her all those months ago.

After analysing her predicament over the weekend, especially the accusation that she had broken the code of ethics and the oath, Frances decided to speak to Madeline again. On Monday morning, she rang Madeline before she left for work and left a message on her voicemail.

She was surprised to see Madeline at work so early when she arrived. Frances had already taken her glasses off because she did not need them for work. She had been crying, and her eyes were extremely red and all puffy.

"Would you like to see me now or later?" Madeline asked as she approached her.

"At your office please, Madeline," she replied. She felt that she would burst out crying again while at work.

"Will four o'clock suit you?" Madeline asked.

"Yes, that's fine."

Later that day Anne came around and enquired as to whom would be working on the 5th of February as the 6th was Waitangi Day, a statutory holiday. Anne hesitated at Frances' desk, and Frances got the impression that Anne was probing to see if she would resign before then. She felt uneasy, as she had written her resignation letter, which was in her handbag, but she decided against it as the day dragged on.

Frances had had enough of the abuse. "Dear Madeline, I wish to resign from my job, it is all too much for me," she had written.

"Hello, Frances," Madeline said pleasantly as Frances walked into her office at four.

"I have read the code of ethics, Madeline, and I think I have broken the code," she said. "That is why I wanted to see you. I run a small business from home on the internet. I never mentioned it when I started, as I assumed the first thing they would check on was your records. I may not be at work much longer due to health problems. I find it difficult to sit for long periods of time due to the pain in the top of my legs."

She was extremely surprised that she did not cry in front of Madeline.

"You have not broken the code. There are quite a few people on the staff who run small businesses," Madeline said.

Frances had a large collection of articles on abusive situations, especially psychological abuse, and as she was tidying up at home that night, she found an article on verbal abuse she had not filed away. "You lose the ability to feel compassion," the author wrote. "If you can't feel compassion for yourself, you cannot offer it to others either."

Creeping jesus walked past Frances's desk early the next two mornings. "Good morning," he said, reminding her that he was watching her.

Xin chatted non-stop, asking Frances questions. She was curious about her financial status, which lead Frances to believe that someone had put her up to those questions.

"Will you go on a benefit when you leave work, or do you have some money aside?" she asked.

"I have no money, but I do have a superfund I can use and hopefully my part-time business," Frances replied. "I am too proud to go on a benefit."

Later that day Madeline approached her desk. "Would you like to move from this area and shift over there?" she asked, pointing to the empty workstation at the back of the room. "We are arranging the area. It would be good for you away from the others, since you comb your hair a lot. It would be good for your skin condition, too. You can start moving on Tuesday."

As time went by, Frances became upset about the discussion, recalling the small spot she had pointed out a few weeks ago to some of the staff. She had been crying for most of the day when she attended her doctor's appointment.

"I want you to see what they are doing to me and to look at this dry spot on my leg," Frances told her doctor.

"That is no problem at all. It is just a dry spot," he replied as he looked at her leg.

"I can't do anything about this abuse," she said. "The cops are corrupt. I have already tried three times with them."

"Here is a medical certificate for the day off work tomorrow and some sleeping pills," he said as he handed her over a prescription.

Too upset to work, she did stay home the next day.

———

Two days later, Frances broke a tooth and had to find an emergency dentist to pull it. After asking around at work, one woman recommended her dentist, and Frances made an appointment for the next day. Frances attended the appointment to have her tooth pulled out. The dentist gave her some pain killers and antibiotics to ease the pain. By now she was supersensitive to all this abuse. She did not trust anyone at all. She had her prescription filled on the way home.

She climbed into bed exhausted and fell asleep. When she woke, she felt very ill with nausea, diarrhoea. and stomach ache, in addition to the pain in her mouth.

That night she received an email from Anne, an overseas e-pal. In her reply, Frances told her about her tooth and how ill she felt.

The next day she received a reply from Anne, asking what the dentist had prescribed. The wording of the email made her suspicious. Frances replied telling her that he'd prescribed penicillin, metronidazole, and Synflex. After sending the email, she grabbed her prescriptions and looked up the medication on the internet.

Metronidazole, she found is used to treat infections caused by bugs that do not require oxygen to grow and multiply. There was no mention of using the drug for oral surgery. Frances was mortified at what she read.

A few days later, Frances was washing her linoleum floors around nine p.m. As she knelt down on the toilet floor, she felt a sharp pain in her knee. She raised her knee to look at it and was puzzled at the blood streaming from her knee. She realized she must have left a small sliver of glass on the floor after she broke the window not long ago. She grabbed some cotton wool, sticking plaster, and gauze and dabbed at the cut. It was very tiny for so much blood, she thought as she applied the gauze and plaster.

When she climbed out of bed the next morning, Frances was stunned. Her knee was extremely stiff and sore. She could hardly walk. She thought this strange for such a minor cut.

There was an auction on the next day in the Coromandel, and she wanted to attend it. She intended to go away for the night. That way she could view the auction lots the next morning. She phoned the doctor's surgery to find they were on duty that weekend and made an appointment.

As Frances lay on the couch, the doctor prodded the small cut.

"I can't find anything. Would you like me to have another look or do some mini surgery?" he asked her.

"Have another look please," she said, horrified at the thought of mini surgery.

"I got something out," the doctor told her as he prodded further with his instrument. Then he bandaged up her knee.

"I will fill in an ACC form for you and get you to sign it," the doctor said as he departed the room. When he returned, he handed her the form? "Could you sign here? I have put the accident happened at nine o'clock last night."

How did he know what time the accident happened? I never told him.

Frances signed the form, and he handed her a copy for her records and a prescription for antibiotics.

Tuesday morning at work, Frances moved her belongings over to her new desk. There was no one else allocated there, and she sat in Coventry. There was no one else seated there and Frances sat all alone. There were two women seated further down from her but not within talking distance. *That's fine, I have the radio to listen to back here*, she thought to herself.

Creeping jesus and Anne were talking together and walked towards her. He broke away and walked directly towards her. "Good morning, Frances," he said as he walked past her.

When Frances left the office for morning tea, she stopped for a chat with Pieta, who enquired about her limp. Frances related the story of the broken window at Christmas and how she cut her knee.

"It's so tiny, I am amazed at the problem it has caused me," she said.

"Did you feel like me you were too big to get in the window?" Brenda piped up.

"No," Frances replied curtly.

"Was that the day you only had half a brain?" Brenda asked.

Pieta was stunned at Brenda's remarks and gave Frances a sympathetic look as she walked off humiliated.

Pieta came over to speak to Frances when most people had gone for lunch. She was horrified where they had seated her.

"Why did they do that to you?" she asked Frances.

"Just the games they like to play."

Frances constantly eyed the group area she had been moved from as she tapped away on her keyboard. Annette, who had been sitting on her own, had moved next to Xin, and Mary was sitting at her old desk.

That night Frances decided to test Anita out about Lennie the builder. Frances had Lennie come out to give a quote for a roof over her patio. He denied knowing Antia. When she arrived home, she ambled along the drive and up the steps onto Anita's deck and knocked on the door. A face peered out from behind the drapes.

"Is it alright if I use your hose to water the flowers along the driveway? My hose won't reach that far," Frances asked as Anita opened the door and stepped onto the deck.

"Yes, that's fine. I was going to do it myself today anyway," Anita said.

"Do you know Lennie the builder?" Frances enquired.

"Yes, I know him well," she replied. "I chatted to him on Friday when he came to your place. His family lives in Australia," she added.

He denied knowing her when he spoke to me, she thought.

Frances grabbed the hose and started to water the flowers along the driveway. She was fuming.

They think I am thick. They should get their stories right, she thought as the jet of water sprayed over the plants in the garden.

I cannot go out. If I do, I am stalked and abused. I cannot run a business to be self-supporting. In fact, as far as they are concerned, I cannot do anything. I am not even allowed an income.

Frances had the next day off work because she was so sick. She had to rinse her mouth out with a salt solution.

Arriving at work after her day off, Frances walked past Brenda's desk and said loudly, "All good things come to those who wait." As she glanced at Brenda, she noticed Samantha was there too.

She sat at her desk all alone, and all the staff commented on her being alone. She bravely put a smile on her face and told them that was what she wanted as she cried to herself deep down inside. Even creeping jesus walked down and passed her desk way over in the corner and said good morning to intimidate her.

Later that morning, Anne walked past Frances with a huge smile on her face.

Pauline approached Frances while she was picking up work from the trolley.

"How are you today?" she enquired.

"Not bad. Loopy's birthday today," Frances said.

"Who is loopy" Pauline asked her.

"Loopy is my ex-husband" Frances replied.

"What makes men do something like that? Your husband sounds just like mine, Just like my husband, only he beat me up," Pauline said. "He went to live with his grandmother when he was five because he suffered from asthma. His parents were told by their doctor to get rid of their animals, as he was allergic to their hair and fur. They got rid of him instead. They much preferred their animals."

That night Frances found there was a cheque from Canada in the letterbox, payment for stock she had sold.

Please fill in your name, as I don't know your surname, the enclosed note glared at her as she stared at the blank cheque.

Strange, Frances thought. *That is the second cheque I have received like that.* These people know my business name. I always send full details when an item is sold.

The next morning Gita came over to Frances. "Want some plums?" she said, offering her an open bag. Frances picked two plums out and thanked Gita, then started nibbling away at a plum.

Later in the morning she started to eat the second plum when suddenly she felt violent pains in her chest. She turfed the plum in the bin.

The pain would not go away, so she got up and slowly walked around to ease the pain. She came across Angela and Anne as they walked along the corridor. Frances tried to walk normally as she tried to cope with the pain.

She turned to face them after they walked past her, and she thought they had disappeared, but Angela had turned around and was approaching her.

"Are you alright?" Angela enquired.

"No, I have a severe pain," she replied. "I'll be okay soon."

The pain continued for two hours. She was mystified. What had caused it? The plum?

She left work at eleven-thirty for an early lunch. She drove to the city and parked outside DeKa. As she browsed the clothing racks inside, Frances caught a fleeting glimpse now and then of a woman who appeared to be watching her.

Frances found a nice blue short-sleeved blouse, paid for it, and then departed the shop. Outside, she headed down the road with her bag in her hand to the bank. The market was on again tomorrow, and she needed a float. Fortunately, the queue at the bank was short, and her transactions proceeded quickly. As the teller flicked through the notes, Frances noticed a bright blue ten-dollar note and remarked on its colour.

"There's not many in circulation," the woman replied. "It is a new millennium note. You should keep one for an investment. Would you like this money in a plastic bag?"

"Yes, please."

On the way back to work, Frances stopped at a dairy around the corner from work to purchase some cigarettes. She handed over a twenty-dollar note.

The woman assistant handed Frances her change all in coins.

Just a damn nuisance or coincidence! How did that teller know I needed change for the market?

At afternoon tea, Dulcie called out to Frances. "Doing anything this weekend? Perhaps you would like to come out with us."

"No," Frances replied.

Strange, Dulcie being out there. She had never seen her at her break before.

Later that afternoon Dulcie came over to Frances, seated at her desk. She carried a keyboard and other items.

"I'm cleaning my desk and keyboard," she said to Frances.

Strange. She has plenty of room on her desk to do that.

"We are not meant to clean our own keyboards," Dulcie chatted gaily as she took the keys off the keyboard and wiped them as she went. "I would like to buy my own home. Maybe even two units for an income."

"We had two rental units. Lived in one and rented the other out to pay the mortgage," Frances said. "My ex was a control freak. He destroyed everything I ever worked for. I should be retired now. I worked and saved so hard. But what the hell, it's only money."

"Do you own your own home?" Dulcie enquired.

"Yes, at least I was able to be mortgage-free," Frances replied. "It's too expensive living in Wa Kawai and working in Hamilton. I need all the income I earn just to live."

"Do you have a computer at home?" Dulcie asked. "Are you on the internet?"

"Yes," Frances replied, not wanting the discussion to continue.

At home that night, Frances made a quick tea and sorted some of the boxes in the garage for the market the next day. She chose her stock with care and packed enough boxes for the next day.

Early the next morning, Frances drove into the township to enquire if there were any stalls available at the market. There were, so she drove home to ready herself for the market.

Anita appeared around the side of her car as she was loading her boxes into the car.

"I'm having a stall at the market this morning. I had a clean out last night," she said to Anita.

"Can I have a look first, then give me a lift to the village?" Anita asked.

"Yes, sure. Don't hold me up, though. The market starts soon," Frances replied.

An avid reader, Anita chose three books.

"That will be fifteen dollars. You can pay me later. I will bill you," Frances told her.

"There's a parcel in your letterbox," Anita said. When Frances drove down the driveway, she stopped and retrieved the parcel from her letterbox before heading to the market.

Arriving back at the market, Frances found that her stall was located next to Josie's. It was beside a fence that ran along the roadway. Josie was five foot two inches with blonde, curly hair. She was neatly dressed. Josie had had a stall next to Frances before.

"Did you hire a table?" Josie enquired as she helped Frances unload her car.

"No, I had it at home. It is very handy to have."

"I come to the market quite often," Josie said. "It's fun. I enjoy it."

As Frances seated herself comfortably on the wall, she spotted Anita's landlady Jean amongst the gathered crowd not far from her.

"Jean," she called. Jean spun around, saw her, and came over to chat.

"I've just brought some veggies," she said as she proffered her open bag for Frances to have a look.

As she sat on the top of the concrete block fence, Frances glanced idly around the area. She unwrapped the parcel she had received in the mail. Inside the parcel was the miniature China she had ordered. It was always popular. She popped a few pieces on her stall, pricing them as she went. Three pieces sold almost immediately.

As they were sitting there passing the time, Josie asked her with a smile, "What do you call a queue of men waiting for a haircut?"

"I don't know," Frances replied.

"A barbeque!" With barely a pause, Josie went on, "What has four legs but cannot walk?"

"I don't know."

"A chair. What do elves learn in primary school?"

"I don't know."

"The elfa-bet!"

Frances burst out laughing. It was a good morning, and Frances enjoyed herself, the first in a long time.

As the afternoon began to turn into evening, Frances began to pack up her stock. Anita strolled along the road with a young woman and stopped on the path near Frances.

"Did you have a good day?" she asked Frances.

"Yes, I think so. It was fun anyway," she replied.

Frances walked over to her car parked in a side street and found the passenger front window open. It was clear that items in the back of her car had been moved around and her car had been searched. She had made her abuse evidence into parcels addressed to someone in the USA so if her car was searched, they wouldn't open the parcels.

She was exhausted when she arrived home. She sat down for a moment to make a list of the books Anita had taken earlier that morning, then lay down on her bed and fell fast asleep.

Frances woke to a hard tapping on the door and glanced at her watch. It was 6.45 p.m. She rubbed her eyes and made her way to the door, surprised to see Anita standing outside on her deck.

"Will you check this list to make sure I have all the book titles?" Frances asked her as she handed the list to Anita.

"Yes, sure. I would like to look at all your books," Anita said.

As Frances led Anita through the lounge into the hallway and then her office, she noticed Anita's eyes were everywhere, taking in the details as she followed her.

Bookshelves filled with books neatly displayed lined the walls of her office. Anita surveyed the room before she browsed the shelves of books and chose some to purchase.

"You don't have to buy them all, you can borrow some," Frances offered.

"Thank you, I will let you know which ones I want to keep," Anita said.

The phone rang the next morning, it was John. He supplied Frances with books occasionally.

"Would you like to come over and look over my books today? I thought today might be a good day, being a holiday," he said. Frances remembered that it was Waitangi Day.

"Yes, I have nothing to do. I would like that" Frances replied.

After she arrived home from John's that afternoon, she unpacked the boxes of books in her driveway. Anita appeared beside her and peered into the boot of the car.

"Oh, I see you have more books," Anita said. "I am looking for some Jewish books with Jewish topics."

While Frances unpacked and shelved the books, she noticed there were two Jewish books amongst her purchases.

Was that a coincidence.

The next day at work Frances noticed that Lynn had called a meeting of all the staff. She was not informed, so she sat at her desk and tapped away on the keyboard.

Later Robyn came over after the meeting and started a conversation with Frances. She did not mention what the meeting was about.

Frances related some of her life story to Robyn. Then she noticed that Pauline was standing beside Robyn listening as Frances said, "I have a big box of abuse evidence at home."

"I hope you lock it," Pauline said.

"No, it is in a cardboard box and my house is alarmed," she replied as she walked off.

Seated back at her desk, Frances noticed that Robyn, Pauline, and Brenda were having a conversation together. Robyn came over to talk to Frances.

"I was out shopping with my father one day," she said. "He disappeared, and when I found him, he was fishing in a rubbish bin on the street. My father keeps wanting to steal a kitten."

"The alien used 'TCB' the clever boy'—when he was setting me up at home, to make me look bad. It is Elvis Presley's motto," Frances told Robyn the next day.

"Who's the alien?" Robyn asked.

"My ex," she replied. "You know, my ex was so bizarre, one day he scattered bird shit and feathers from the birdcage in his library and hung up a sign 'beware mice.'"

"Why did he do that?"

"To make people think I am a dirty housewife. I told my solicitor about it, and she was astonished. She said it was so bizarre. You want to know what I did back to him?"

"Yeah, what did you do?"

"Well, he had tried suicide twice, so I decided to pay him back. I sat half a day making an effigy of myself. I used a pillow for a body, panty hose for the legs and feet, and stuffed them with sheets. We had a polystyrene head in the loft with a dark wig on, so I used that for the head,

"I attached myself to a rope and hung myself up in the garage by the door to the library. I used nails to keep me in the right position. I put on a pair of my slippers on my feet. I knew he would be home late; it would be dark. I left a stepladder under my 'body.' My effigy looked good, realistic.

"When I heard his van come down the drive, I hid myself in the rumpus room. The automatic door opened, and he backed in. He screamed 'Oh no' very loudly.

"I jumped from behind the door, and he realized what I had done.

"'Bloody bitch!' he yelled and walked off in a huff.

"'Now you know what it feels like when I found you like that twice!' I screamed at him. I took a photo of myself.

"I was sorting through junk I brought with me when I moved house. I cut all the photos of us together in half and sent his half to him, including me hanging. I enclosed a note that said, 'your half.'

"Did you really do that" Robyn asked her.

"Yes of course I did" Frances replied. "I had no need for them anymore"

Frances began to notice that whenever anything happened, it usually came in pairs. In the data department or cafeteria, someone was informing Heather Morris that she was out on a break. Heather then would appear to reiterate that the abuse or intimidation was taking place.

Sheryl, the woman who worked in the cafeteria, was the 'look out' person who advised Heather and other people when Frances was having a break, and then they would come out and intimidate her.

Frances had sussed that out by changing her break times to unusual times and yet still the intimidation continued.

Frances finally reached the point that there was no use continuing her life as she felt that this is what the remainder of her life would be. Full of stalking and abuse. She had tried hard to stop the abuse, but no one would help her. They took absolutely no notice of her. They would rather believe her lying ex.

Harold sat nervously in the kitchen, sipping a cup of coffee. He couldn't wait for Mary to go shopping. He had an important phone call to make.

At last Mary left, and he picked up the phone and dialled Data Entry Services.

"Good morning, Data Entry Service, Helen speaking," the receptionist said.

"Hello, Helen. I am Harold Jones," he said. "I wish to know if your company is still abusing my wife Frances Jones," he continued.

"Yes," Helen said. "They abuse her every day, and she gets very agitated and upset."

"That's good. Keep up the good work," Harold said and hung up. He was pleased with the conversation.

CHAPTER
TWENTY-SIX

The humming increased inside the house, sounding like an electrical disturbance. It was disconcerting. It had started since those new neighbours moved in. There were two adults and a child of around five years old.

After Frances carefully wrapped the parcels, she left home for the post office. Derek, the manager, served her. He repeatedly abused her whenever she mailed there.

"Thirty-five dollars ninety-five cents," he said.

"Could I have a receipt, please?" she said as she handed him a cheque.

"Yes, certainly," he said as he pressed the button.

The till whirred as it spat out the receipt. Derek tore off the receipt and handed it to Frances.

"Thank you," she said as she grabbed the receipt.

She perused the receipt on the footpath and was dismayed to note the ID as manager and not the manager's name. Even more surprising was that it was issued as cash with five cents change.

Smart bastard, she thought. She dashed into the dairy and purchased a packet of cigarettes.

As she walked back to her car, she heard a tinkling noise on the pavement behind her.

"Excuse me, you dropped this," the stranger said as he handed her a five-cent coin.

When she arrived home, Frances pulled out her accounts payable file and quickly flipped through the receipts, reading the Wai Kawai post office ones only. There were many issued for cash, yet she always paid by cheque.

Frances left work early that Thursday for her appointment with the specialist about the pain in her back legs and hips. Locating the address, she did a U-turn and parked outside against the curb.

After she walked up the ramp and pushed the door open, Frances found that reception was directly in front of her.

"Hello, you must be Frances. Could you please fill in this form?" the receptionist said as she handed Frances a form.

Frances gave the form back after hastily entering the details.

"Could I have your x-rays, please?" the woman asked. "Take a seat over there." The woman pointed as Frances handed her the 14 x-rays.

Frances turned to her right and walked towards a large, oblong room. There were two doors leading off each end of the wall opposite her. A large blue lamp sat on a wooden table next to the left-hand door. As Frances turned her head, she saw there were large comfortable chairs against the back wall. She walked over and sat down.

The door on the right opened and a tallish man with a long, thin face and grey hair stepped out. He wore round spectacles set in a light frame.

"Frances, will you come this way," he said. He led her into the room and offered her a chair. "Doctor Michaels referred you to me. Are you still working?"

"Yes, but not for long," she replied.

"So, you have resigned," he said.

"No, not yet," she replied

"So, you've come to me for an operation. Please lie on the couch face downward," he asked her.

Frances stood up, climbed onto the couch, and lay down. He examined her spine from top to bottom.

"Sit with your legs over the side," he asked.

She sat up and swung around with her legs dangling over the side of the couch. He used a small hammer instrument and tapped at her kneecaps.

"Walk up and down these steps." he said as he pulled a small bank of steps from under the couch. She did so while he watched, nodding, and then sat down.

"I have viewed your x-rays. I can find nothing wrong." He said pointing to her x-rays in the illuminated box on the right-hand wall. "I can see nothing wrong," he said as he raised his eyebrows and sneered at her. He was brazenly open about his attitude towards her and had a contemptuous disregard for her rights,

Frances became anxious at his manner. She was certainly living in a thick fog these days and could not find her way out. This man's manner alarmed her immensely.

He grabbed a pointer and continuously pointed around the hip joints. "I can see nothing," he reiterated as he continued pointing in a circular motion around her left hip.

She became agitated. Anxiety set in. Her heart began to race as she left carrying her x-rays and was unaware that one was missing. The continual pointing mesmerized her. This was ingrained in her mind.

When she left the surgery, Frances drove along the short street and came to an intersection at the main road. She glanced into her rear vision mirror and had a fleeting glimpse of the car behind her. This car had an L plate made of cardboard on the right of the front window this was for a learner driver. This driver peered intently at her as she waited to turn left.

Startled, she turned left and drove along the road, turning left and right, then left again back on to the main road. She looked quickly in her rear vision mirror to find that she had managed to lose him in the heavy traffic.

She felt more comfortable and drove straight ahead towards her solicitor's office. A quick peep in the mirror frightened her. The vehicle with the L plate was back. This time the L plate was on the left-hand side of the window. Befuddled, she did not note the colour of either car. Was it the same one?

She managed to lose him again as she swung into Harrison's car park. Then suddenly she heard the sound of tyres on gravel as a car pulled into the grounds of the building next door, only a small curb separating the two buildings. The driver braked, and the car screamed to a halt.

Frances looked at it carefully through her window. There was an L plate on the front window of the car, a man seated inside looking at her.

She opened the door and got out. The February sun warmed her face. Distressed, she forgot to note neither the car number plate nor the colour of the car.

Dust and leaves swirled around inside the doorway as she entered the building with her solicitor's office. She hurriedly climbed the stairs in front of her.

When Frances reached the first floor, she pushed the glass door open and stepped inside. There was an office to the left of the reception desk, where a woman with arms folded stood quietly inside against the back wall, watching. She appeared to be waiting for her.

"Can I help you?" the pleasant, black-haired receptionist asked.

"I would like to make an appointment with Karl Harrison," Frances replied.

"Could I have your name?"

"Frances Jones."

"I heard that," the woman said as she stepped from the side office. "I am Mary Saunders. I took over when Jane left."

The woman led Frances into the office. "I have not much time. Could you give me a brief outline?"

Frances slowly started talking. Tears rolled down her cheeks as the fear rose within her and her shoulders tensed with stress.

"I want action this time," Frances demanded. "Not like last time, Jane said she never got a reply from Wa Kawai Police Station, despite repeated calls." Her voice had become loud and ragged.

"Are you threatening me?" Saunders asked.

"No, I am not. You can see the state that I am in. I just want some action this time. Please!"

"Will two p.m. Tuesday suit?" Mary said as she eyed Karl's diary.

"Yes, fine," Frances replied. "Could you write it down on a card?"

As Frances left the office, she was perplexed and drove home quickly. When she arrived there, she parked her car and walked inside. Exhausted, she lay on the bed and fell asleep.

When Frances woke the next morning, she felt no better. Her mouth throbbed, and her knee was sore. She phoned Madeline to ask for the week off work on sick leave.

The following Tuesday she attended her appointment with her solicitor. Karl was not available. She was annoyed at that and she told Mary that she had made an appointment with Karl not her

"I will help you," Mary Saunders said as she ushered Frances into the office.

Frances gave her the evidence. She perused the first few pages and asked some questions to some of the documents.

"Did you follow this one up?" she asked, holding up a letter from August 1997, written for a refund of services not used from the travel agent.

"No, I couldn't see the point," Frances replied.

"Is this safe?" Mary asked as she gingerly picked up the sample of poisoned cereal.

"Yes, it's well wrapped," Frances answered.

"I will have to read this and get back to you," Mary said.

After Frances arrived home, she decided it was time for a

break for a couple of days, away from this unpleasant atmosphere. She packed her overnight bag and drove away. Anywhere, it did not matter, as long as she escaped the terrible nightmare that she was living in. She headed toward New Plymouth.

There are plenty of stops for me, I may pick up some stock, she thought as she drove along. When she arrived in New Plymouth, she went to Past Times Antiques. After that Frances discovered a new shop around the road, Past Centuries Antiques.

"Are you Andrea, the woman buyer in the area?" the male shop assistant asked her as she stepped inside the door to his shop. "I have heard she is coming around New Plymouth. She sells on the internet."

Frances ignored the man and browsed his stock then settled on two nice vintage glass items for her own collection. After she completed her purchases, Frances went to the camping ground and obtained accommodation for the night.

She needed the break so much she collapsed on the bed and wept herself to sleep. She was exhausted after all the turmoil in her life in the past few weeks.

The next day she drove off towards Wairata. She stopped and browsed the shops on the way. But there was no stock for her this time, although the rest of the trip was a pleasant one.

After she arrived home, Frances unpacked her parcels, and a five-cent piece fell out from the Past Centuries Antique shop parcel. Terrified, she remembered all those other times.

That night her mind flew back over the past few months, she was totally fatigued, no one would help her regardless of where she tried. She recalled the specialist. *I should check my x-rays*, she thought, remembering his continual pointing around her left hip joint area.

The next morning, she pulled the packet of x-rays out and

counted them. There were thirteen. One x-ray was missing. She tried to eye each x-ray through the light of the window. It was hard to see, but there appeared to be nothing major missing.

She immediately turned on her computer, typed a note to the specialist, and faxed it to him. She asked for the return of the missing x-ray. However, she received no reply.

In the mail that day was a reminder to have another blood test at Test Laboratories, Ltd. *Strange, they have never done this before,* she thought.

She drove to the post office that morning and parked her car right outside. After mailing her parcels, she went back to her car.

There was a red van double parked, blocking her car. She vaguely saw writing on the van, so she moved around to read it. *Test Laboratories* glared back at her, the man sitting in the driver's seat sat staring out at her.

Back at home she tidied up and dusted her China as she went. When she picked up her lovely pink art glass bowl, she was alarmed to see a five-cent coin in it. Placing coins in obscure places was not a habit of hers.

Who has a key to my house?

Who were these people? Complete strangers who dreamed up a theme to follow her. It was designed to twist and distort her mind.

Later that afternoon Frances decided she should get her accounting books in order. She printed out a Debtors Overdue list to work on. Eyeing the three-month-and-over column, she saw there was an amount for $21.47. Intrigued, she went back over her invoice file and finally found the outstanding invoice. She was aghast as she comprehended what that invoice was for.

The horrific memories came flooding back like yesterday,

and all her problems fell into place. The staff were commenting on receiving overseas cash in the mail, then the penny dropped.

She had received nine American dollars cash in the mail. Frances had needed American cash to send overseas. Rather than pay ten dollars bank fee she had kept that cash. However, she had invoiced the amount in her Debtors Ledger, meaning to bank the money in New Zealand dollars.

The humiliation and abuse had started again, and she had forgotten to bank the money. But then she had forgotten many things during those months, so severe was the abuse. The abuse was about receiving US cash in the mail. It was a registered letter, so it had to be delivered to Frances at work. They have a machine that they use looking for cash in the envelopes.

She lost the ability to think, to focus, or even remember her daughter's phone number. She had to email her daughter to ask for it. The abuse was vicious and occurred simultaneously from all directions. Frances lifted the receiver; she rang Madeline to explain what had happened. She was not there, so she left a message. Madeline did not reply to the message. She rang repeatedly but received no response from her at all.

No wonder I didn't know what Madeline was talking about. She said the code of ethics, the oath, he cares about you. Frances was appalled at their despicable behaviour.

She typed a fax to her solicitor and outlined the details of the US cash she had received in the mail. "This round of abuse has been based on assumptions," she typed. "You will note 'assume nothing' in my documents, something I hung on my office in the late 1980s."

That night as she sat on the lounge suite. She had a clean out, ripping up notes and putting them down the toilet. Nothing sinister in that; just she did not want them to use every little thing they obtained about her as emotional abuse. Who knows, they may even have been searching her garbage bags.

When she took some of her screwed up paper out to the garage to put in the rubbish bag, she noticed Jean was peering through the window. It was early evening and Frances could not understand why she would do that. What did she expect to see?

The next morning there was a knock on the door, and Frances ran to open it. Anita was standing there. She immediately walked inside.

"I would like to look at your books," Anita said as she glanced at the pile of paper on the lounge suite.

That is the second time she has come over recently when I have my personal papers out, she mused.

Anita walked through the lounge to the hallway and looked into her bedroom at the unmade bed.

"I slept in," Frances said. "I am not well." Tears now flowed freely. "The abuse is getting me down."

"Oh, I'm sorry to hear that," Anita said. She put her arms around Frances and gave her a big hug.

After choosing some books, Frances walked Anita to the gate to see her off. Frances glanced up to her TV aerial and noticed a light shining from it. What was that?

The next night when Frances came home, she found her art glass bowl had been shifted from the table, the book she was reading sitting there in its place.

Who has a key to my house?

That night she pondered over an advertisement for volunteers for Victim Support. Frances decided to improve the quality of her life, to fight the abuse, and to achieve something rewarding. She wrote away for details and two days later was advised that there would be a meeting on the following Monday.

Frances arrived at the hall on time. Six women attended the meeting in the community hall. The team leader, who introduced herself as Caroline, explained what was required of a support person and the type of crimes involved. She was short, with shoulder-length black, curly hair. The other five women were in their thirties and were friendly towards Frances.

One woman said, "Yes, I have people come into my house all of the time when I am not at home. The door is locked and alarmed, but they still get in and move things around my house."

The woman next to Frances handed her a slip of paper. It was a calendar with the perpetual dates of Easter on it, starting with the coming of Easter. This woman also handed a copy to Caroline.

Frances remembered the discussion with Marylyn at work about the equinox and Easter dates. Frances had even looked the future Easter dates up on the internet for her.

When it was Frances' turn to tell her experiences, she sobbed profusely.

"I am afraid Frances you are not a suitable candidate for Victim Support. You are too emotional and need time to heal. Come back in a year's time and we will reconsider," Caroline said. Frances was upset, she wanted to help victims and Victim Support wouldn't have her just yet,

Opening her emails after the meeting, Frances had a welcome one from Shirl. She read it eagerly, taking in this year's Easter date and a function that Shirl mentioned.

Then suddenly she remembered that sign for a function on the same date in the village. Anita had pointed out the sign as she drove her to the township the other day.

The next morning there was a tap on the door. It was Anita, returning some of the books.

"Finished with these," she said as she handed Frances the books.

Frances noticed a slip of paper peeping out of the top of one of the books. She opened the book where the slip was, and a souvenir page of the royal family fell out onto the floor. This was obviously to let Frances know that she sold royal commemorative items on the internet.

That night Frances knelt on the carpet and just about shot through the roof. Inspecting her knee, she saw that it was inflamed, red, and raw, and pus was oozing out around the spot where she had cut it. She knew then that Doctor Michaels had failed to get the glass out a month ago.

Damn, she would have to see a doctor again.

CHAPTER
TWENTY-EIGHT

"Change your password," the wording of the email from an unknown person glared back at Frances as she cleared her emails. *Strange message,* she thought as she promptly deleted it.

Frances had decided that she should see a doctor at the Family Medical Centre in Hamilton. She did not feel up to facing Doctor Michaels this time. She felt he had abused her and pretended to get the glass out of her knee when she visited him a month ago. She also felt that the letter regarding her blood test was part of the plot; they knew she would have an infection by now.

Frances drove over to Hamilton. The Family Medical Clinic was in a new building, with a fresh, clean feel about it. While she waited for her turn with a doctor, she grabbed a women's magazine and started to read.

"Frances Jones," a man's voice boomed out into the waiting room.

"Yes," Frances replied. She stood up and followed him to his office.

"I am Doctor Smith. What can I do for you today, Frances?" he asked.

Doctor Smith was a large man with a spotty, unshaven face. He had short, dark hair and a long nose.

"I think I have some glass in my knee," she replied. "I cut my knee a month ago, and thought it had been taken out by Doctor Michaels. But apparently it was not."

Doctor Smith looked closely at her knee and prodded around.

"Ouch, that hurt," Frances said as he pushed hard around the small cut.

"I will need to get a soft tissue scan to find out where the glass is," Doctor Smith said. "I will get the receptionist to make an appointment for you at Radiology, Limited. Have you any other symptoms?"

"Yes, I have a temperature and I have had a tooth out."

Doctor Smith proceeded to examine her throat, looked into her mouth, and used the stethoscope on her chest.

"Report to reception for the appointment," he said as he dismissed her.

At the reception, Frances picked up her appointment for the scan and paid the excess ACC fee, the remainder to be paid by Accident Compensation Corporation.

The next morning Frances attended Radiology Limited, for her soft tissue scan.

A radiologist named Barbara used a blue whiteboard marker on Frances's knee to mark the spot as she scanned it. Then she wrote a note and gave the note and scanning sheet to Frances to take back to the Family Medical Clinic.

"Ectogenic foreign body five millimetres by three millimetres, the cross marks the spot," it said.

Back at the clinic, Frances waited again to see the doctor. Finally, a new one approached and ushered her into a treatment room. He was tall, with dark wavy hair and had a long narrow face. This man did not wear a name tag on his white coat.

"I have a devious plan," he said, "to get this out." He was abrupt and his manner horrified her as he prodded and poked around her knee. He cut into her knee with a small scalpel but could not find the glass.

"I will need an x-ray of your knee," he said as he attached some cotton wool and plaster over the wound, then sent her to have an x-ray.

As Frances walked around to the x-ray department with her trouser leg pulled up above the knee, blood streamed down her leg from the wound

The woman attendant attached some tape that held two small metal pins, then she proceeded to x-ray her knee. Then she moved the tape and pins on her knee and took another x-ray.

"Take these back to reception where the doctor will see you again," the woman said as she handed Frances the x-rays

Frances perused the list of doctors in attendance that day. "I'm not sure of the doctor's name," Frances told the woman behind the desk. Then, noticing him standing near the other side of the desk, she said, "It is that doctor over there."

"He is Doctor Simonsen," the woman said.

She noticed that Doctor Simonsen's name was the last name on the list. It appeared more as an afterthought and was written in a different colour pen.

Strange, the last doctor on the list. Also, a line between the last name and all the rest.

"Did you bus in?" he asked her in a peculiar manner as he worked on her knee.

His manner alarmed her, and she became frightened as he finished getting the glass out.

"Here is a prescription to combat any infection," Doctor

Simonsen said as he handed her a slip of paper. "You should get the prescription filled soon at the pharmacy next door."

Frances's mind went into overdrive. Something—she did not know what—told her she needed a photocopy of that prescription before she had it filled.

"Is there anything to pay today?" Frances enquired at the reception desk.

"Yes, here is your account," the woman said as she handed the slip of paper to her.

Frances was alarmed. The fifteen dollars she had paid for ACC excess yesterday had been changed to a full consultation fee for forty-nine dollars. The remaining thirty-four dollars was the outstanding amount.

"This is not correct," Frances told the receptionist. "I am covered by ACC. I did not have a full consultation. I came for glass in my knee."

"Oh yes, I'm very sorry. We have made a mistake," the woman answered as she crossed off the outstanding amount. "There is nothing to pay today."

Later at home Frances photocopied the prescription and then drove to the pharmacy to have it filled. Back at home, she tucked the papers away and took the medication.

Frances became doubtful about her treatment and decide she would attend the hospital and have them check her knee out that night. She was doubtful of the treatment she had received.

By now it was dark. The streetlights dimly lit the road as she made her way to the main road to Hamilton. She noticed the Main Road Street sign leaning against a lamppost, though it was certainly not on the main road. She drove miles to the hospital and waited for hours for a doctor to see her. The doctor who saw her said her knee was fine.

"It is painful," she said. He gave her a prescription and some pills to take at once.

It was nearly midnight when she finally made her way home. She scanned the x-ray of the glass in her knee. As she looked at it, she could only see the pin that the woman had put there. The two small heads on the pin showed up brightly against the black x-ray.

They can't scan for glass. It would not show up, only the bones.

There was that electrical humming noise again. What was it? Was it a transmitter sucking information out of a camera bug inside her home?

A week later, before Frances went to Doctor Michaels to have her stitches removed, she was alarmed at her predicament and decided to use her scanner to copy the x-rays of her knee. She was afraid of keeping her x-rays at home, sure that someone would come inside and destroy them.

Frances's burglar alarm started to beep incessantly. It was still under guarantee, so she phoned the security company and asked them to inspect and fix the keyboard on the wall.

A man named Malcolm came out the same day. He fiddled with the keyboard and could not get the pin number to change. Standing in her hallway, he phoned the supplier and described what was going on with it. Whoever he spoke to told him the faceplate and keyboard were faulty and to send it back to them for replacement.

He showed Frances how to disconnect the wall box and asked her to bring the wall box in on Thursday when the new keyboard and faceplate would arrive at his company in Hamilton.

"Repco," Malcolm said. "You brought the alarm from them, did you?"

"Yes, I think I did," Frances replied, though it had been so long she wasn't sure at all.

"All you have to do is reconnect the wires when you pick up the wall box," Malcolm told her.

On Thursday, after Frances picked up the new wall box, she

was baffled as she tried to wire the alarm back together. The wall box sat too high on the wall for her to hold the panel and screwdriver and keep the wires attached. In the end she gave up and contacted Malcolm.

Malcolm refused to come out again. He told her to contact the suppliers, who should be able to help her by phone.

Frances emailed the supplier who gave her instructions by email. But they baffled her, too. Due to her state of mind, she was not capable of following them.

When she finally wired the alarm, the lights that were labelled "PANIC" "FULLY ARMED" stayed on. She could not disarm the alarm, and when she tried again, she had difficulty attaching the wires.

In desperation Frances rang the local electrician. He arrived an hour later, but he could not get the alarm working either. He used the ladder and climbed up to the siren box under the eaves of the house. He fiddled with both the box and the external siren. He could not find any problem. He then contacted the supply company, and they advised him what to do. He checked everything, and still the alarm would not work. Then he decided that perhaps Frances should try some new batteries in the sensors. Maybe that was the problem. She was to ring him when she had purchased the batteries.

In the meantime, Frances had emailed the supply company and her emails were returned to her with a UCE/Spam filter stating that the service was unavailable.

She was determined to have her alarm working. She had too many reasons to be concerned for her safety. She typed a letter and faxed it to the supply company. "You have not responded to my emails, and now you have put a block on them," she stated in the letter. She threatened to go to Consumer Affairs with a complaint if her alarm was not fixed in the next few days. "Everywhere I try to get help for anything I am blocked and therefore will lodge a serious complaint."

The reply was almost immediate. They gave her instructions on how to check the alarm. Frances immediately faxed them back, told them her alarm booklet had been stolen and she was not capable of following the instructions.

The next day, after she purchased the batteries, Frances rang the electrician again. He arrived later that afternoon.

With the help of the supply company by phone, the electrician got the alarm working. But the external siren still would not work. He climbed up the ladder again and when he came down, he showed Frances a small metal pin.

"That's a tamper pin," he said, nodding at it sitting in his beefy hand.

"A what?" she asked/

"It's a battery-isolating pin. It would stop the external alarm from working. I guess your guy from the security company—Malcolm must have inserted it. But I can't imagine why."

That night after the alarm was working properly, Frances emailed Malcolm and asked why he put the tamper pin into the external siren.

His response by email was almost immediate.

"If you remember," he said, "I did not touch the external siren at all. I only worked on the keyboard. Someone else has done that, or else they are having you on."

Frances replied and thanked him for the information. Then she popped the pin into a small plastic bag and stored it with the mountain of evidence she had hidden inside her home.

Suddenly she remembered that strange email telling her

to "change the pin number" and wondered if that had something to do with the alarm. When she lodged the documents with her solicitor Karl Harrison, she had taken photocopies of most of the evidence and hidden them inside her wardrobe.

Frances was astonished when she searched the wardrobe. The bag of evidence was nowhere to be found. Someone had been inside her home again and this time removed vital evidence. She had some copies elsewhere, but some of the stolen items were the originals of which she did not have copies.

Somewhere, someone out there, she mused, is getting afraid of the evidence she has managed to obtain against Harold.

Immediately Frances typed a letter to the Wa Kawai Police Station and advised them of the break in.

"I do not expect you to do anything about this harassment, as you never believed me the last time I lodged a complaint. This abuse has been vicious and detrimental to my mental health," she wrote.

Frances then thought more of the alarm. *Why did the panels and keyboard need replacing? Was the alarm bugged when it was installed eighteen months ago? Was that where the camera bug was installed?*

That night Frances searched the internet for camera bugs. She was amazed at what she found. A miniature camera bug could be installed in a burglar alarm keyboard panel or even in a smoke detector. Frances had smoke detectors in every room of the house.

As she read on, she was even more appalled. Night vision camera bugs could watch you deep into the night, even without the lights on. There were also bugs that could be installed into your telephone and car bugs that could be attached outside the car to monitor your every move. The more she read the more astonished she became.

In the end Frances thought about it and decided to email support at how2spy.com for further information. She wrote,

I am writing to see if you can help. I have every good reason to believe my home has been bugged with a surveillance camera due to various incidents over a long period. The keyboard of my burglar alarm has since been replaced.

Can monitoring of all inside movements be actioned through a camera bug? How is this information transmitted to those who have installed these bugs? Is it possible that this could be transmitted by satellite dish and how far would the maximum distance be for transmission? What do these bugs look like?

How do they receive the information? Would they make a noise while transmitting? EG. An electrical generator or humming electrical sound? I look forward to receiving a reply from you.

However, she received no response from them. All this wealth of information intrigued her. The unexplained suddenly became much clearer. Frances had already noticed that there were satellite dishes on the houses on each side of her.

Stunned, she remembered that night in the dark. She had slowly crept out of bed pulling the small suitcase from under the bed, unlocking and removing the evidence that she had collected of her abuse, and hid them elsewhere. When she had finished, she put the lock and key under her pillow.

The next morning, she went to the village and forgot to put

the lock and key away. After lunch she remembered to put them away, but they were not under the pillow. The lock was missing, and the key was on the floor. Weeks later when she tidied up her office, she found the lock hidden under some documents.

How could anyone have known I did that in the middle of the night in the dark?

Someone had been inside her home again. It was like they had free range to do whatever they could to block her in her quest for justice.

Therefore, they removed the evidence. Not only that, the electrical humming noise had also ceased.

The campaign of terror continued for Frances. She became worn out, did not trust anyone, and became afraid to go out. She was not up to working, as she could not think straight nor concentrate on anything for even a short period.

She faxed her resignation to Madeline at the agency and never received a reply. They just paid her holiday pay into her bank account.

As she was reading the local paper, she noticed there was an advertisement for the next local market. "*The big one* for the year," it was called.

Later that day at the Hamilton Post Office, she was served by Marion, a woman who had abused her before.

"Would you like a big one?" Marion asked a confused Frances.

Marion then held up a large customs declaration form for Frances to read.

"No, I do not need one of those," Frances replied hastily.

"What are you going to do now?" Marion asked her. "Sell your house and move right away from the area?"

Frances was appalled. What did she mean by that?

As Frances sat in the car, suddenly the words that Marilyn had said to her months ago at work came to mind.

Did they kick you out of Wa Kawai?

Two days later Frances decided to mail her parcels at Centre Place Mall. The assistant asked her the same question "Do you want a big one?"

On her way to the stationers in the same mall, Frances became aware that there was a man following her through the mall. He stopped before she went into the stationers as she pulled out the staple box she wanted to replace.

Outside the stationers, there was a stall of discontinued lines and an antique catalogue sat glaring back at Frances. When Frances picked up the first box of staples to check the size, it had a sale price sticker on it. An old-fashioned cheap sticker, the same kind Harold used.

She picked up more boxes, but these had the normal stickers on them. On her way to the counter Frances picked up a ream of Pacesetter Premium all-purpose A4 paper as well.

"Would you like a printer cartridge as well?" the young woman assistant enquired.

"No, just these staples and paper," she replied warily.

On the way home, Frances called into her local garage to pick up the new wheel brace she had ordered. Lizzie, the assistant, ran around the shop like a scared rabbit when Frances enquired about the brace. Finally, she went into the back room and emerged carrying the wheel brace.

"I was looking for a big one" Lizzie told her. "It came in a big box. Someone must have taken it out of the box."

Frances stood there dumbfounded. These people had dreamed up another theme and made sure it followed her around. She was horrified as this treatment screwed her brain up and made her even more confused and perplexed. How much more could she stand.

Back at home Frances lay on her bed and tried to comprehend what they were doing to her and how the psychological abuse had affected her.

I will teach them a lesson she told herself. I cannot take anymore; I will commit suicide and I will take some of them with me.

She sat down, pulled out a sheet of printer paper, and began to write.

> *Dear everyone,*
> *I am sorry to have to do this, but it is the only way out.*
> *I cannot go on with all this stalking and abuse.*
> *Please look after Honey Boo.*
> *I love you all.*
> *Love, Mum*

Each night for the rest of the week Frances practised driving from Wa Kawai to Hamilton during the peak hour traffic. The drive was a long, winding road, and she cautiously noted how the cars drove so close to each other.

That would be easy, she thought. *Take off my seat belt and drive full bore into the leader of the row of cars. That way I could take more than one person with me. It will teach the narrow-minded community a lesson, give them something to think about and what their nastiness has caused. Complete disruption in the community and only themselves to blame.*

When the local newspaper arrived on Friday, Frances was appalled there was an article about certain death if you drove without a seat belt.

Did they watch this while I wrote my suicide note? Do they know I was going to kill myself?

She was afraid to do it and she took off her seat belt and was ready to ram into the cars coming the other way. But she could not do it, no matter how hard she tried.

She drove home in despair that the one thing she wanted most she could not do.

The next day Frances gathered some shells at Ocean Beach. She already had others, imported shells she'd purchased to make jewellery for the markets. She did not tell anyone what she was doing. She sat at the dining room table making earrings for the next market.

Later that day Frances called in to see Josie for a chat. Josie did the markets also. Josie had a pile of boxes sitting on the floor of her lounge.

"I'm having a garage sale on Saturday," Josie told her. "Would you like to look at my stock?"

"Yes, thanks," Frances said as she knelt on the floor among the stock. She picked up some purple shells. "These are beautiful."

"Oh, those aren't for the market," Josie said. "They should be in that pile. You can have a few if you like. They come from Ocean Beach. They are only found in August when the sea sweeps them into the shore."

When Frances arrived home and parked her car, she walked down the driveway to the letter box to check her mail. She was astonished to find shells scattered along the driveway, so she picked them up and took them inside. Suddenly Anita appeared beside her.

"Here is an orange for you," Anita said as she handed Frances an orange. "It's a big one."

Later that day, Frances attended her appointment with Doctor Michaels. She needed a new prescription of Stelazine.

"You seem down today," he said to Frances.

"Yes, I am having more trouble with the stalking and harassment," Frances told him.

"I think I should notify mental health again, have them send a support worker out to see you," Doctor Michaels told her. "I will contact them today."

Frances despaired over this, but she knew it was for the best. Her ritual checking of everything she did had come back to an unusual extent. She knew now that this was caused by the abuse over the years.

The following Wednesday, Graham from Mental Health arrived at her home to see her. He had a young woman undergraduate with him. They sat and talked for a while, and Frances told him about the ritual checking.

"Harold used to point it out to people," she cried. "They used to laugh at me because of it."

With that Graham jumped up and said, "I can help you with that. Would you like me to make an appointment with a psychiatrist?"

"Yes," Frances replied uneasily.

"I will make another appointment for me to come out, too," Graham said. "Wednesday the fifth of April at four p.m." He handed Frances a card.

"Data Entry Services have been continuing their abuse, too," Frances told him.

"They only do that to their clients," Graham replied.

"No, they do not they do it to staff as well."

Frances saw an ad in the local paper for continuing

education courses available for the following term. She decided to do a picture framing course. She filled in the application form with her credit card details and faxed it off to the facilitator.

On the first of April, another bombshell was in store for Frances. When she powered up her computer, it when straight to the time clock. Time to update to daylight savings time, the computer prompted her. That was strange. It never asked that when daylight savings started in October.

She searched her computer and found some old data. The support company had told her all data had been removed, but it was still on the hard drive.

There was also an email from a woman in Britain named Alma, who had purchased quite a lot of royal family items from her.

"You will not hear from me for some time," Alma wrote. "I am going on a cruise and visiting Vancouver Island."

Frances was astounded, as next to her on her desk was a postcard from a customer who lived in Vancouver.

Who was watching her every move and used items in her house to baffle her? Someone was still watching her every move. Frances never heard from Alma again.

It was the first of May and Frances went to the hairdressers for a cut and blow wave. She left her car at the local garage for a lube. She found it was nice and relaxing for her as she sat in the swivel chair while her hair was being attended to. When Frances paid the hairdresser, the woman said to her "Are you going straight back to your car?"

"Yes," Frances replied as she left the shop.

The garage had completed the work on her car, and she found it parked on the Main Road opposite the garage.

When she entered the car, she was astonished and upset. They had not locked the car, and it was very apparent to her that her car had been searched. The book and back seat items were all jumbled up. She was thankful that she had been thoughtful enough to wrap the evidence she held about Harold into a parcel and addressed it to Barry Smith overseas. She had made it look like some stock to be mailed.

From there Frances drove over to Hamilton to do some banking. Judy served her.

"I know someone who bought some earrings off the internet," Judy told her.

"Do you?" Frances said as she clammed up inside as she thought of the earrings she was making at home.

Some months previously, Judy had told Frances that she knew someone who worked at Data Entry Services. She knew that she was involved with someone at Data Entry Services who was ordering this subtle abuse.

Frances decided it was time to escape from this abuse. She was terrified and afraid for the state of her mental health. She rang Shirley at the land agents and asked to come around to inspect her home and give her an idea of price.

Shirley was a short woman with long straight hair and wore trendy spectacles. She advised Frances about the house, and they agreed on the price with her, so she listed that day.

Two days later Shirley rang.

"I have an offer on your house," she told Frances. "Can I bring it around now?"

"Yes," Frances replied.

Ten minutes later Shirley arrived.

"You will not like the offer. But it's my job to present all offers," Shirley told her.

Frances was dismayed at the offer and put in a counter-offer twenty-five thousand dollars higher.

"They are not going to force me out with a ridiculous offer," Frances told Shirley as she left with the document.

The time soon came around for her picture framing course, and Frances attended, delighted she had something different to do. She took with her some photos she wanted framed.

It had been months since she took her documentation to her solicitor Karl Harrison, so she wrote a letter and faxed it to him. Frances was appalled at the response to this. The letter stated that there was no evidence to suggest any psychological abuse, despite the fact that he had stated this one year ago. Frances wrote a letter back.

I am rather surprised and troubled that your decision is with a negative result. Your company took rather a long time to reach this conclusion. You also witnessed the state I was in when I attended your office. No one gets to that physical state without something happening. You were conveniently waiting for me that day.

I refer you to the letter the previous year regarding obtaining evidence about the abuse I was subjected to. You stated that I may be able to bring a prosecution of psychological abuse by getting a report from a psychologist. I went to a psychologist, but it was futile. He was only interested in my business activities. Had something been done, this problem would not have escalated beyond control. Furthermore, people who indulge in this despicable behaviour do not realize the consequences of their actions, and it can only continue to escalate and spiral out of control to the detriment of the victim. I request that you send my documents back to me immediately.

A week later, the documents arrived in the mail. She

perused them and was dismayed to find that some were missing. There was the letter to Dave Clarkson regarding her refund of travel unused in August 1997, the power of attorney document, and also a letter to Aotea Airlines.

Frances then recalled Andrew, the consultant from her last job, repeatedly saying to her, "You need a lawyer."

Tried convicted and punished for something I never did, she thought to herself.

On the seventeenth of May, at her picture framing course, Frances became uneasy. The assistant had cut the mat board the wrong size, despite double-checking the measurements. Her materials were wasted, and she had to start again.

The following week she was dismayed that the framing she had ordered had not been delivered.

"It's just your bad luck," the instructor told her.

The next week still her materials were not delivered, so Frances pondered over this as she watched the other students happy in their work.

"Mr. Walker, have you any other framing I could use?" she enquired of the teacher.

"I will have a look," he replied.

Mr. Walker slowly and deliberately looked through the pile of framing sitting on the bench at the far end of the room. Suddenly at the very back, he pulled out some framing.

"This is what you ordered, isn't it?" he asked her.

"Yes," Frances replied and grabbed the framing from him so she could start work.

Mr. Walker was embarrassed about being caught out like that. Frances did not attend any more classes, as she knew she would never finish all her frames in the next class, the last one of the course. She was way behind on her work, and it would be futile to try to catch up.

Two weeks later she received an account rendered from Mr. Walker for one hundred seventy-nine dollars.

Frances responded to the account with a payment of one hundred dollars and told him she would not be paying the remainder of the account due to the abuse he had subjected her to. She never finished her classes nor used the materials he had charged her for. Frances never received another account rendered for the remainder of the account.

CHAPTER
THIRTY-ONE

Frances felt her life was like a James Bond movie, and she became scared of the unknown. There certainly was no stability in her life. She was living dangerously in their power, feeling constantly under their control. Who were these people who were controlling her every move?

She rang the Craft Shop in Taupo. She explained to the owner that she needed earring findings. As she spoke into the phone, she was holding a finding from the Gem Company. Frances had rung them last week, but they could not help her.

Frances was astonished when the sample arrived. They were the same ones she had held in her hand when she had rung them.

She walked warily to her office and looked around. They—whoever they were—were still watching her. But how could they?

The psychological abuse was getting to Frances, and she decided to lay a complaint against Madeline with Human Rights.

When she contacted Human Rights, they said they would send her an information pack. Frances was amazed when she read the rules applicable for harassment. Her problems were clearly defined.

After filling in the form and attaching her evidence, she mailed the application form to Human Rights.

She typed a letter to Data Entry Services main office in Auckland to advise them of her action. She wanted to be fair. It was not their fault, and they had a right to know how the workers in Hamilton were being treated.

Frances wrote the details of the abuse.

I did not know what I had done wrong. When I spoke to Madeline she joined in the abuse. She tricked me into moving from my desk, and I was sent to Coventry. Because of the abuse I was not thinking properly nor able to logically think for a long time. I am still not fit for work four months later. I have had to surrender my superannuation policy to live on.

The abuse started when I received a US cash payment in the mail. I never banked that money, because I needed US dollars. I intended to bank a cheque to cover the amount. I invoiced that payment through my debtor's ledger. I never banked the cheque because the abuse started again.

When I found out that was why the abuse started again, I was shocked that anyone would treat a person like this for such a small sum. Why did Data Entry Services not have Madeline approach me? They would have found out the truth. Instead they started the abuse in full force.

When I phoned Madeline after I discovered the reason for the abuse, she never responded to my repeated phone calls.

*I was told at Christmas how and where to commit suicide by
a staff member. I almost did that on the eighth March. It is
unfortunate for your company that a minor branch would
be involved in such a complaint. I have nothing to fear from
Data Entry Services and therefore have taken this action
regardless of whom they are.*

*I know now that my ex-husband is behind this abuse and
that he has contacted every company I have worked for since
1976 and have them abuse me.*

When she finished, she went and posted the letter at the local post office.

Queen's Birthday weekend came, and Frances was attending the market down south with Phillipa. When they arrived, Julie, the organizer, was very nice to them and helped them settle into their stalls. Julie browsed Frances books and asked if she could take two away, she would pay for them later. Frances agreed.

Frances and Phillipa's stalls were changed for Sunday, and they were separated for the day. Phillipa looked after some of Frances's items on her stall.

"Here is some money, I sold some items earlier," Phillipa said to Frances as she pulled a five and ten dollar note out of her pocket. Phillipa stared at the money and started to give Frances five dollars, then changed her mind and gave her ten dollars.

Later that day Julie came around to Frances and paid for her two books.

"Two five-dollar notes," Julie emphasized as she handed Frances the money.

It was not a very successful market, but at least Frances had a break away from some of the stalking.

The following week Frances was sharing a stall with Jacinta in Wellington. She was looking forward to this fair. She had never attended a fair so far from home.

She idly looked through the yellow pages for a cattery. She needed one that was on the route to Wellington rather than travel to her usual cattery. She found one and rang them.

"The fee is five dollars," the woman said. "Everyone has five dollars in their pocket." "How much do you usually pay?"

"Six dollars," Frances replied.

"Oh, gee, I must have been busy," the woman said. "I have to turn my calendar over. I am still in May."

Frances was astounded when she hung up the phone. She grabbed her desk calendar and found that it was still on the month of May. She cringed.

Human Rights rang Frances just as she was about to leave on the long, winding drive to Wellington. They had a query on her application.

At the cattery, the woman was very talkative

"Your Honey Boo will love it here," the woman told her. "Look at this little fellow." She pointed out a cat with three legs. "The poor thing is disabled, but he manages."

On the way to Wellington, Frances stopped at antiques and collectors' shops in her bid to find new stock. At one shop, she purchased some books.

"I am sorry," the owner told her. "This is all the notes I have." He handed her thirty-five dollars in five-dollar notes. She cringed.

On arrival in Wellington, Frances found the hall where the market was to be held. Jacinta was already there unpacking.

"This area is yours," Jacinta told Frances as she lugged boxes of stock into the hall.

After setting up their stalls, Jacinta took Frances to a local collectors' shop, where Frances purchased six sets of salt and peppers. Then they drove to the camping ground where they were to stay for two nights. They both approached the manager as they offered their money separately. The man wrote out a receipt, then bang went the company's stamp onto the document. Frances was frightened—she had heard that bang before at Wa Kawai second-hand shop. Frances was annoyed. They paid separately, but the man gave her a receipt for both of them.

Frances was aware that the abuse was starting up again. Funny that, she mused. As soon as Human Rights contacted her. Jacinta had played a part in her abuse before.

That night as they sat in Jacinta's campervan, Jacinta sat searching through her wallet. She pulled two business cards from it and peered at them.

"Wa Kawai second-hand shop. Are they still there?"

'Yes," Frances said.

"What about Olden Times Antiques at Thames?" Jacinta continued.

"They are not at Thames. They are at Hamilton West."

"Oh, are they?"

At the end of the weekend, Frances told Jacinta that she wanted to leave early, to get a head start for the night before she found accommodation. "It would make driving easier for the next day," she told Jacinta.

"Why do you not stay with me another night?" Jacinta said.

In the end Jacinta won and Frances waited until Jacinta packed up, too. Frances followed Jacinta in her car to another camping ground further out from Wellington.

"I will show you some shops tomorrow. You would not know they are there," Jacinta told her.

The next morning Frances followed Jacinta in her car. Jacinta turned right into a small narrow street. She parked in an alley way and waited for Frances. They walked through the alleyway to an old, derelict building and into a shop.

"Salt and peppers," Jacinta yelled loudly to the owner as she entered the shop.

"Are you on the internet?" the man asked Jacinta.

"No," she said.

Strange conversation, Frances thought. Why mention salt and peppers?

After browsing the shop and making purchases, Frances left Jacinta and made her way home. She was exhausted when she arrived home and went to bed without unpacking.

The next morning the phone rang. "Shirley speaking," the woman's voice said. "I have an offer for you on your house."

"Oh, that's good," Frances replied.

"Can I come around now?"

"Yes, that's fine by me."

Ten minutes later, Shirley presented Frances with the contract.

"It is much better than the last offer," Shirley said.

Frances browsed the contract and put in a counter-offer. She felt sure it would be accepted, and she would certainly be pleased to leave this small, narrow-minded community.

Provocation. What did that really mean? Frances had been pushed beyond despair. She was desperate to eliminate the stalking and harassment from her. It was extremely distressing for her, and she pondered on how to eradicate this horrific abuse from her life.

Frances felt she would explode, although these people could not see that yet. She was calm outwardly, but underneath she smouldered with powerlessness and frustration. No one would help her, regardless of whom she tried to obtain help from. No one paid any attention to her pleas for help.

The contract for the sale of her house was finalized. She was pleased that at least now she could plan her getaway. She would make sure that no one would know where she moved.

She would go into hiding. It was the only way she could see. That way at least the stalking and horror of her life would cease.

Ten days later when the salt and peppers she had listed on eBay sold, she was still waiting for the bidder to contact her. She became suspicious when she remembered Jacinta and the salt and pepper episode in that shop near Wellington. These bids were a hoax, she was sure of that.

That night her powerlessness reached its peak. Frances rang Cindy for Harold's phone number. She wanted to ask him to stop these people. She felt she was going mad. Cindy refused to give her the phone number.

"What do you want me to do, go to Auckland and kill him?" Frances said in despair, then hung up and went to bed.

She took the phone with her. She lay helplessly on the bed, confused and desperate. She drifted in and out of sleep, and each time she woke, she hit the redial button on the phone and let it ring. Cindy answered every time, but Frances stayed silent. Let her see what it is like to be harassed, she thought as she drifted back to sleep.

Cindy pondered her predicament. Should she contact Mental Health? Mum had asked a question, talking about murdering her father. After a restless night, she decided to contact Mental Health, just to be on the safe side. She picked up the phone and dialled.

That morning Harold and his second wife Mary were watching TV when there was a loud knock on the door. Harold answered it. He was surprised to see a policeman there.

"I am Detective John Wilkins," he said. "Can I come inside to see Harold Jones?"

Harold let him in.

"I have come to warn you that your ex-wife has threatened to murder you," the cop said. "Do not open the doors to anyone until you have verified who they are. There is a warrant out to arrest Frances. She'll be committed to Mental Health."

"Oh," Harold said. "Sure thing, Detective. Thank you for coming to warn me."

When the detective was gone, Mary asked Harold what that was all about.

"It's worked," Harold said as he contemplated the news.

"What have you done?" Mary asked Harold. "No one threatens to murder someone unless they have done something to deserve it."

"I distributed a poster with Frances's photo and libellous remarks to coerce people to stalk and psychologically abuse her," Harold said with glee. "It is over five years since I did that, and it's still being distributed. I also rang all the companies to coerce them into stalking and abusing her. Money talks."

"What do you mean?" Mary asked him.

"Obviously these companies believe what I have said about Frances. Otherwise they wouldn't do it. I have a financier to help out when I need money."

"Who is the financier" Mary asked him.

"Don. He was a tenant of ours. I have his phone number and just need to ring him if I need more money. He has plenty of money. He made his fortune laundering money through the T.A.B. and the casino. He is a very bitter old man who likes to see women suffering because of what his wife did to him. As soon as they married, she left him and went to Australia to live. She left him supporting her child which was not his."

"I think what you have done is disgusting," Mary said. "How would you like it done to you?" Then she left the room to let Harold contemplate what he had done.

––––––––––

That same morning Frances was sitting on the couch in the lounge, gently hugging and patting Honey Boo, when she heard heavy footsteps on the deck. Many of them, and she wondered who they were.

There was a knock on the door and Frances opened the ranch slider and was amazed to find a burly policeman. He was swarthy, with dark grey hair and a white moustache. Beside him were Doctor Michaels and two women. She could not comprehend what they would want with her.

Who were these people who appeared to be swooping on her? Doctor Michaels stepped inside and said these two women wanted to take her to Mental Health for a talk. She was astounded. What had she done wrong?

"I will drive over in my car and meet you there," Frances told the women.

"You cannot do that. You must come with us," one of the women said. "You are being committed to the Henry Bennet mental clinic for assessment. The blond-haired woman said.

"But I am going away for the weekend. There is an auction I need to attend to pick up more stock," Frances replied.

"You must come with us," the woman insisted.

With foresight and foreboding, Frances grabbed her bag of evidence to take with her. There was no way she was leaving that behind. It had to stay with her.

After Frances locked the house, they departed down the driveway. Frances was stunned to see a police car and another car blocking the driveway. As they approached the cars, Doctor Michaels stuck his head out of the second car back seat and called out to the women.

"How do you get out of this car?" he asked them as he tried the handle which would not open.

"This car is a special car so people cannot escape," one of the women told him as she pressed a button to release the catch.

Frances's mind was in a turmoil. What did these people want of her? What had she done?

It was a long, slow drive over to Hamilton as Frances sat in the back seat with one of the women. She wearily eyed the two women, then she eyed the back-door handle. Why did they need that?

When they arrived at the Henry Bennet unit, one of the women used a swipe card as they walked through several doors. *This seems secure*, Frances thought as she noted there were no door handles at all. *What was going on here?*

This was in the city of Hamilton, it was a big building with very secure doors. The woman had to swipe each door as they walked through the unit.

They took Frances to a small room that had a desk and three chairs. A man and woman sat waiting for her.

"I am Doctor Wilkinson," one said, "and this is Doctor Erickson, a medical student."

Wilkinson had fine, dark hair and a short beard.

"What is going on here?" Frances cried out loudly in despair. "I have to go away to Thames for the weekend. I'm buying some stock at an auction there for my business."

"We want to examine you. It will not be possible for you to leave for Thames, not this weekend," Doctor Wilkinson told her.

"What is going on?" Frances yelled as her stress levels rose. "Why don't you lock me up!" she cried as she thrust both arms upwards and outwards towards the doctor.

Both doctors just sat and watched. Neither said a word.

"Do you want to ruin my small business?" she added.

"We want to help you, and you must stay here for the time being," Doctor Erickson told her.

After a short discussion that led nowhere, a woman entered the room and asked Frances to follow her. The woman introduced herself as Maryanne. "I am your key worker," she said. She was short with brown, curly hair.

They entered a small bedroom which was sparsely furnished with a cupboard and a very low bed. There was a light on the wall very low down just above the skirting board which was operated from outside the room which the staff used to check on the patients. The window was closed and Frances noted there was no way of opening the window at all. It was very secure. Frances dumped her bag on the shelving and sat on the bed.

"We will fill out this list I have," Maryanne told her, "Then I will take your belongings and put them in security for you."

"This," Frances told her, thrusting her evidence bag forward, "I will keep with me. this does not leave my person."

"It will be safe in the security area," Maryanne insisted.

"No, I will keep this with me even if I carry it everywhere."

After the form was filled in with Frances's belongings, Maryanne took her outside. There was an exercise yard where you could smoke or just chat with other people.

Frances stared around her as she was led outside. The walls around the yard were extremely tall, the boards at the top of them sloping upward and inward. There was no way anyone could escape from here. The scene reminded Frances of Mount Eden Prison. Even though she had never been inside, you could see the outline as you passed in the street.

There were several people milling around, some smoking. They looked like poor, wretched souls with nowhere to go. They stared into space, their eyes glazed and unfocused.

Her situation seemed futile. Why did they want her here?

What rights did they have to lock her up and throw away the key? Maryanne left Frances on her own, so she lit up and enjoyed her cigarette.

Later Maryanne approached her and asked her to go with her. She led Frances into the same small room. Doctor Wilkinson and Doctor Erickson were present, too.

"You have been committed under the Mental Health Act section sixteen, because you threatened to murder your former husband," Doctor Wilkinson told her.

"What?" she exclaimed. "Where did you get that information from?"

"Your daughter. She sectioned you after you repeatedly rang her last night," he said.

"I did that because I wanted her to know what it was like to be harassed," Frances told him. "I did not threaten to murder him. Here look at my report from last time." She grabbed her psychiatric report from her evidence bag.

"See here," she said, pointing to a portion of the report. 'Frances has been suffering paranoid delusional episodes for the last four years.'"

"How do you feel now?" Doctor Wilkinson asked her.

"I am fine and need to be released so I can travel to Thames for an auction to get items to sell for my business," she replied.

"I am sorry, but that is not possible. You need to go to court to see if you are fit to be released. You will go to court on Tuesday. Now you can go outside if you wish."

After a discussion, Frances was free within the unit to do what she wanted. She sat in the recreation room where the television was on and clutched her evidence closely to her chest.

There was a woman she noticed who kept walking around every fifteen minutes. She held a chart on a clipboard and stared intently at each client, then she wrote on the form.

Frances was intrigued. What was the woman doing? Spying on them and making notes.

Later Frances went to her room and just lay on the bed. Her mind wandered as she lay there, still and lifeless. What was going to happen to her? To Honey Boo? To her business?

She went to the office and demanded to use the internet.

"I need to keep in touch with my customers," she told the supervisor.

"You cannot use it," the woman told her sternly.

When Frances left the office, she noticed some pamphlets in a rack on the wall. "*Know your rights,*" glared back at her. She grabbed a copy and went to her room.

"You can apply to have an advocate speak for you," she read. There was a list of social workers who work for the government in the local area. Frances went to the phone and rang a woman, who said she would come out the next day.

The next morning at eleven o'clock Susan arrived. Susan was a pleasant woman, five foot three with straight, brown hair down to her shoulders. She was the advocate that Frances had rung.

"What is your problem?" Susan asked her.

"I need access to the internet," she replied, "and they will not give it to me. I need it for my business."

Susan took some details and then left. "I will contact you later," she said.

Later that day, Maryanne came and told Frances she could use the internet. So, Frances went and used the computer to check her business.

Back in her room, Frances searched her evidence bag for her psychiatric report. It wasn't there. She had relaxed her restriction on keeping the bag with her, and now the report was gone. "From now on I will keep this bag with me", she thought.

At four fifteen Frances was lying on her bed, when a woman came into the room.

"I am Lynette, your key worker for the night shift," she told Frances. "If there is anything you need, please see me."

Lynette was a kind, caring person, and Frances felt bonded to her. She cared about her clients, unlike Maryanne, who was obnoxious. She was five foot one, with lovely short, curly hair.

"You should not be in here," Lynette told her later that evening. "You will be going to court on Tuesday to apply to get out of here. Just go with the flow and they will have to let you out."

Later Lynette appeared beside her bed with her medication for the night.

"I need to wash some of my clothes," Frances told her. "They never told me to bring extra clothes. I did not know what was happening."

"I will show you the laundry and you can do it yourself," Lynette told her. "Just think of this episode of your life as time out. A cooling off period. You will be alright."

Lynette was so kind to Frances; she began to feel better. She no longer felt confused, although the horror she was facing caused her to feel chilly and she started shaking.

How am I going to manage in court? What do they do there?

CHAPTER
THIRTY-THREE

Frances passed the days by lying quietly on her bed pondering her situation, her mind in a whirl as to what was going to happen on Tuesday at the court hearing. Sometimes she went out into the garden enclosure for a cigarette. There was no one she could talk to. Most of her fellow patients were mentally unstable people. The wretched souls walked around the enclosure as though they were going somewhere. Their eyes were blank, staring at nothing in particular. They wore shabby clothes. One man kept looking up to where it looked like a basketball hoop used to be. Another who looked to be in his thirties held an ongoing conversation with himself. Still another had drawn a circle on the concrete pavement and walked around and around it.

Where did they think they were going? Some had visitors. Frances was not among those who did.

She refused to talk to her daughter after she tried to come and visit her. She wanted no part of her because of her betrayal. She blamed her for the loss of her business. She had been busy at home with her business, things were picking up, and she had been pleased with her efforts.

Cindy sent in some tobacco and tissues for Frances, but Frances refused them when Maryanne offered them to her.

"Where will you get more cigarettes when those have run out?" Maryanne asked her sternly.

One of the patients had run out of tobacco, so Frances got the tobacco from Maryanne and gave it to him. He was very grateful. Later she found out that the nurses could buy items that a patient required. Cigarettes and lighters were taken from the clients at eight p.m.; no lighters were allowed in the bedroom.

The light in each room, situated just above the skirting board, was operated from outside the room. When it was time for the night duty staff check each client through the small window in the door, the light in the room became brighter.

On Tuesday morning, as Frances lay on her bed waiting, Maryanne came in.

"Ms. Anderson, your appointed solicitor, will see you at nine a.m. before court," she said.

"Thank you," Frances replied.

"It is going to be a tough exercise for you," Maryanne said. "They may not let you out."

Frances lay still and cringed at the thought. *What say they never let me out? What say she was stuck in here with nothing to do?* She tried reading a book but could not concentrate. Her mind was now confused and fuzzy.

Frances met with Ms. Anderson, who had blonde hair and wore a light blue suit. They discussed the court procedure before the court hearing, and then it was just a matter of time until court began. Her face was pale. Her right leg was continually rocking, and she clenched and unclenched her hands.

"It's time to go to court," Maryanne told her as she popped her head in the door. "Come with me."

CHAPTER THIRTY-FOUR

Maryanne led Frances to the smokers' room which had been converted into a court room. It was a room set aside for people who wanted to have a cigarette inside. The tables had been rearranged. There was one table set against the wall of the sparse room. Three tables set opposite this table, with seating for seven people.

"Sit here," Maryanne told Frances as she seated her third from the end of the tables.

Ms. Anderson and the district inspector Mr. Watson came in. Watson had short brown hair and a moustache. He sat next to Frances. Maryanne seated herself on the other side of Frances. Nurses Sinclair and Paterson seated themselves next to Maryanne. Then Doctor Wilkinson head psychiatrist sat at the end.

Judge Macalister strode into the room and took her seat. She was a stern looking woman with grey hair, her lips pursed as though to speak her mind. She sat down and glared at the row of people seated in front of her.

"Let this session begin," she told them. "Frances, I understand that you were sectioned under the Mental Health

Act section sixteen for threating to murder your former husband."

"Yes, Your Honour."

"Did you threaten to murder him?"

"No, I did not," Frances replied emphatically. "I did not. I have been stalked and harassed for the last five years by my former husband, and I had reached the end of my tether."

"What did you say to your daughter?" the judge asked.

"I cannot remember, but it was not that."

"Why did you continually ring her during the night?"

"To let her see what harassment was like," Frances replied.

"I see," Judge Macalister said. "Doctor Wilkinson."

"Yes, Your Honour," he replied.

"What constitutes serious danger?" she asked him.

"When someone threatens or is a danger to either themselves or another person," he replied.

"How was Ms. Jones committed?"

"Her daughter sectioned her under the Mental Health Act section sixteen. The reason, as reported to me, was that Ms. Jones had threatened to murder her former husband."

"Do you believe that Ms. Jones is a serious danger?"

"I cannot state that. However, I do believe there is some danger."

The questioning went on and on. Frances was numb and shaking, devoid of emotion as she sat silently listening to the questioning.

"Nurse Maryanne, what have you to say?" the judge asked her.

"Frances claims she has laid a complaint with Human Rights. However, when I asked her to write down the list of people she had complained about to Human Rights, she refused. It is my opinion that she has lied about that."

Frances was astounded. She grabbed a pen and piece of paper from her solicitor and scribbled on it: *That is confidential information.*

"Frances also asked about some medication. She was unsure, she thought she had been given the wrong medication some months before," Maryann said. "I pointed out to her that this medication has two different names, Your Honour."

Finally, the summing up of the situation started. The judge sat up straight and flipped through some papers on her table.

"I have conducted an extensive examination of Ms. Jones. Her response throughout the course demonstrate to me unequivocally that she has a well-fixed delusional framework. As the examination progressed, Ms. Jones's comments consolidated the existences of that delusional framework. I think it is no exaggeration to say that the framework appears to be immovable."

Frances stared at the judge with disbelief. She tried not to show her distress. They did not believe her. They ignored her pleas for help to have Harold questioned. She was unable to focus on anything in the room.

"The requirement to find that a person has a mental health disorder," the judge said, "is one which involves two parts. First, there must be found an abnormal state of mind. Continuous or intermittent, characterised by delusions or certain other disorders. However, that abnormal state must be of such a degree that it poses a serious danger to the health and safety of that person or others. It must seriously diminish the capacity of that person to take care of himself, and it is what is usually described as the second limb of the definition that the difficulties arise in this particular review.

"The basis on which Ms. Jones was admitted was that she had made a number of harassing telephone calls to her daughter immediately before her admission and that in the course of one of those calls, she had threatened to murder her former husband.

"As I say, that was the basis upon which the application for assessment was made and upon which the admission was effected. Ms. Jones acknowledged perhaps an indication that there might have been such a threat. However, she certainly played it down.

"It was Doctor Wilkinson's evidence via the papers supporting the application for assessment and the report of the crisis team that there had been a threat to murder the former husband. In terms of danger—which is the word used in the Act—it is Doctor Wilkinson's view that there is danger to Ms. Jones's former husband. That danger arises because of a combination of delusional framework, a conception that no one is listening to her concerns, complete lack of insight, and a point apparently having been reached in her thinking that 'something must be done.' As I say, Doctor Wilkinson's assessment is a combination of all those factors and particularly given a clear and absolute focus on her former husband, given all those factors, there is a danger to the former husband.

"Doctor Wilkinson was clear, though, that he could not use the word *serious*. He made that comment in response to questions by Ms. Anderson, and I clarified with him afterwards whether the danger could be described as serious. Serious danger means an absolute certainty of danger, and he said that was a psychiatric definition, coming within the definition of mental disorder, because the act is quite clear. Any mental disorder in relation to any person must be of such a degree that it poses a serious danger to health and safety of others. And given the view expressed by Doctor Wilkinson, that cannot be said in this particular case. There is danger but there is not serious danger, and I am bound to follow the definition of the act in coming to any conclusion about finding a mental disorder. I find myself being reliant upon the expert opinion given by Doctor Wilkinson.

"It follows that I must find that Ms. Jones is fit to be released from compulsory status, because that means as far as the act is concerned that the person is no longer mentally disordered.

"That being my conclusion, Ms. Jones succeeds in her application for review, and she is to be discharged immediately."

The room was silent. Frances was ecstatic. The judge had let her out. She sat deep in thought. The tension was quickly swept away from her shoulders and her neck. Her pale face brightened. Her eyes rested nowhere in particular. She was released from this hideous nightmare. She could go home immediately.

All members of the court filed out of the room after the judge. Ms. Anderson and Mr. Watson took Frances into a small room and shut the door.

"Now remember the words of Judge Macalister," Ms. Anderson told her. "Make sure you keep yourself safe."

"You are free to go home anytime now. You will need to arrange your own transport," Mr. Watson told her as he opened the door to let Frances out.

Nurse Maryanne was waiting for her.

"I have found out that the bus to Wa Kawai leaves Hamilton at three 3 p.m. I will arrange for someone to take you to the bus stop," she told her.

Frances was unsure of herself. She disliked the tension in the atmosphere and the longer she stayed here, the worse the tension rose. She talked uneasily to Maryanne. She disliked her; she was the enemy here in a prison she had been taken to unwillingly.

"I tried to tell you what it would be like," Maryanne told her. "That it would be horrific."

Frances turned and went to her room. It was one p.m. She had an hour or more to pass before her release. She lay down on her bed and relived the most horrific time of her life.

At least she was free now.

Frances walked along those silent, still walls of the corridors and followed the case worker who was taking her to the bus stop. She could not wait to escape the terrible hospital where they locked you up with no thought or insight into why you were there. They judged you on what they were told. They did not want to know the truth. That was beyond their comprehension. They did not want to help you. They just patched you up until next time.

Frances sat in a seat on the dirty bus as it trundled towards Wa Kawai. She was deep in thought. She could not wait until she was back home with Honey Boo.

As she walked swiftly up the road to her home, Honey Boo came out to greet her. He sat by the gate waiting for her. Inside it became obvious that—despite the hospital authorities telling her that the local cop would feed him in her absence—Honey Boo was starving. He gobbled up the food she gave him and then looked for more. So much for help in the community, she thought

Frances sat on the couch, cuddling and stroking Honey Boo. He sat there lapping up the love she felt for him. He purred away like an engine softly idling.

The next day Frances eagerly ripped open the letter from

Human Rights. She was astounded. They stated there was insufficient information to proceed with the claim. "You do not have enough evidence for us to proceed with your claim," she read.

The sky was angry the following day. Dark grey clouds tinged with white edges covered the sky to the north. Frances was travelling to Whangarei to look at properties. Now that her house had sold, she had a month to find a new home.

A month to carefully plan her getaway from this horrendous environment that she now lived with.

No one, absolutely no one would know where she would escape to. Not even Cindy, because she had betrayed Frances by contacting Mental Health and had her committed. She would change her name and go on the run. She had sought to strive against all odds to prove herself innocent, yet the horror still simmered beneath the surface.

Frances had heard that houses were cheaper there, and god knew she had to buy a house with the little money she would get from the sale of her house. She was selling it well below what she had paid for it, including all the renovations that she had done. She was losing more than twenty-five thousand dollars.

When Frances arrived in Whangarei, she went around the land agents and picked up their booklets with properties for sale. That night she pondered them closely. One agent stood out from the others. There were properties listed that interested her immensely.

The next day she drove to the land agents' office and asked for Patricia, a woman who was amongst the agents listed. Patricia looked a kind person with a gentle look about her.

Patricia was very helpful and printed out information about a dozen properties. From there Patricia took Frances on a tour of these houses.

Early in the tour, one house stood out amongst the rest. It had a one-hundred-eighty-degree sea view. It needed some renovations, but it was isolated from the houses nearby, too. Just what Frances needed.

After touring all the houses, Frances decided on the house and the contract negotiations were implemented. The rest of the contract could be settled by fax or with her solicitor.

There was one other thing that Frances had to do for her escape from Wa Kawai. She approached the local post office and opened a post office box in an assumed name. She was pleased with her efforts and felt she had made good progress.

The next day she went to the Hamilton Post Office and made a redirect from Wa Kawai. She used the post office box number she had opened and left the street address blank as she did not want to be traced through carelessness.

All she had to do now was pack up her home and ready herself for the removal company on 27 July. She could not wait.

Two weeks later, as Frances cleared her letter box, the postie roared up to her on her scooter.

"I see your home is sold," the woman said.

"Yes, it is."

"Have you actioned a redirect?"

"Yes."

"Where?"

"At Hamilton," she replied and hastily walked away.

No one was going to find out where she was really moving to. This woman was too nosey by far. In addition, she had been involved in her abuse, too.

Was she spying for someone? Trying to pry the details from her so she would not escape the net they had placed around her.

The net of vile words and evil actions. A small, nasty community, hell bent on destroying her.

The day of her move finally arrived. A woman, Huia from the front house who had moved in after Anita moved out, came down and helped Frances pack the remaining items. Huia was a pleasant woman, and she cleaned out the kitchen for her. Her warmth and her friendliness took Frances in. She wistfully thought what a nice neighbour she would make. If only she did not have to move.

Frances managed to talk to the removal man before two neighbours came over to help with the big items.

"If anyone asks you, could you please tell them I am moving to Tauranga," Frances asked Tom.

"Yes, sure thing," he replied.

"I do not want my ex to know where I am going," she added.

That night after the removal van had left, Frances booked into the local hotel for the night. It was too late to start her journey into secretness. Too late to attend to Honey Boo. She left Honey Boo to stay around her home and she would pick him up the next morning before she dropped her keys off at the land agent's.

Early the next morning, Frances went to the local garage and filled up her tank with petrol. Lizzie served her. Lizzie, one of her harassers, had also been the person to buy her home. Forced out by the sheer horror of living in this mean-spirited community.

"I hear you are moving to Whangarei," Lizzie enquired with a sneer on her face. Frances cringed.

"No," she replied. "Who on earth told you that? I am moving to Tauranga," she added, pleased with herself. She had managed to act surprised.

It was obvious that Lizzie had got Whangarei from the local post mistress, as she had told no one where she was moving too.

Frances then drove to her old home and sedated Honey Boo for the long trip to Whangarei. She had to wait thirty minutes for the sedation to take effect. Then she took off, dropping the keys at the land agent before she left.

Thank goodness, she thought. I will never visit this place again. The tranquil scenery of the ocean and the trendy village hides the evil that lurks behind. People who should know better, who behaved in such a despicable manner.

I am so thankful I am able finally to be leaving this town.

THE END

EPILOGUE

On the 20th September 2022 Francis had three serious falls and ended up at the emergency department of the local hospital, Later that day she was clearing out old receipts and found a previous report from the hospital dated 2020 regarding a serious fall. When she received that report, she did not read it. When she read it there was a report from a hospital doctor who stated she thought that the medication Olanzapine could be the cause of the falls.

Francis then started to do research on the internet, and it says that if used long term the patient can be prone to falls, impaired thought processes, and Tardive Dyskinesia which is a form of brain damage. She had to go to a disability service to apply for discount taxi vouchers. The woman who attended to her said that she opened her mouth a lot and licked her lips a lot and advised her to see her doctor. These symptoms are for Tardive Dyskinesia. Francis then started thinking about what was happening to her. She wondered if her husband had contacted previous employers prior to 1997. She searched the internet for previous employers and managed to contact one of them from 1991. He emailed back and said that her husband used to ring him up and say not nice things about her, her husband had tense discussions with him. He wondered why this was happening because they shared a great interest rock 'n' roll. This employer did not abuse Francis...

She is still searching for previous employers and employees who she know will confirm the abuse that was inflicted on her by her early employers.

Francis decided to compile a file with all the applicable records including her mental health records and lodge complaints to the medical practitioners' service. She was misdiagnosed by the mental health units and is now lodging complaints for these doctors because of her long-term health problems. Francis has got an appointment with her lawyer for him to peruse her files to make sure they are OK to submit her complaints to the medical practitioners' service.

AFTERWORD

This book is written to expose the vindictive vendetta and serious crimes committed against me from 1998 until at least 2003 then continued until September 2022. And to expose the despicable people involved in my abuse. The only motivation they had was of a financial nature, greed.

I am not saying all people abused me but for those who did you Delighted in Playing Mind Games with me, a despicable trait to have and now the boot is on the other foot. LOL

You did not worry or care about how this abuse affected me nor the extra expenses this has cost me over the years and that these costs will continue for the rest of my life.

Nor did you care that I ended up under mental health all these years because of your despicable behavior and that the medication mental health prescribed turned me into a ZOMBIE for 20 years. I am now VERY ALERT and POWERFUL to finish my book which reveals your despicable attitude.

This is a SCATHING look at the dark side of society who treated me with contempt because of my vindictive narcissist ex-husband's attitude towards me.

These attitudes are absolutely appalling. Everything you did to me is documented in my book from the diary I kept over the years of stalking I suffered from, you will recognize yourselves when you read it.

You did not worry about how your attitude and behavior affected me, so now I won't worry about how you are affected by this disclosure about all the crimes you committed against me once this becomes public.

I have set out to expose the vindictive and despicable behavior of the following people in society. What my abusers never counted on was my obstinate tenacity to ensure they are exposed, and I fully intend to expose the many despicable crimes actioned against me over a long period of time.

I now have the POWER TO DO THIS.

First the corrupt cops from Henderson Police station Auckland in June 1998 who would not investigate my complaints of stalking and abuse. They fobbed me off with the lame excuse "they didn't have the funds to investigate" This is not so my husband and I JUST HAPPENED to know the two police workers involved and therefore would not investigate my serious complaints. I would not be at all surprised to know they accepted bribes for this because there was a financier involved in my abuse.

My husband had more than $800,000 to use in my abuse after the financier revealed himself and showed me his bank statement which had more than $800,000 in it.

I was informed by a psychiatrist on the phone that if the abuse was as bad as I told him there had to be a financier. That financier exposed himself 2 hours later and showed me his bank account. There was over $800,000 in it.

I know my phone was bugged because everything I did inside my home on the phone was used as abuse toward me. This was not the first time my phone had been bugged.

After our separation and divorce my vindictive narcissist ex-husband made it his business to make sure his vindictive vendettas continued for many years to come.

My ex-husband is a vindictive narcissist. When things don't go their way, they embark on a path of revenge to destroy your reputation, friends and family, your retirement fund, and your employment, all this happened to me.

After working hard for over 30 years I lost my well-earned retirement fund which is now valued at $1.7 million dollars. I lost everything including my home, I now live in a one-bedroom flat because of your despicable behavior.

HE contacted Catt West mental health Henderson Auckland in 1998 and gave them malicious and false information about me. They believed his lies and I was subjected to the most horrific treatment that anyone could endure from 1998 until 2022.

I was under Catt West Henderson Auckland, Henry Bennett Mental Health Hamilton, and Te Awhina Wanganui until I found out the reason why in September 2022.

Anything I told mental health they would not believe; they would not action my repeated requests for help which would have proven my claims to be correct.

From my experience Mental Health in NZ need a drastic shake up and so do the New Zealand Police, they do not honor the oath they swear on, they lack integrity and are not ethical. That is from my own personal experience of them from 1998 until 2023 as detailed in my story.

I suffered the following.

I am 77 years old.

No-one can give me back the 46 years of emotional & psychological abuse and coercive control which includes the despicable abuse by antique dealers from Wellington to Matakohe, Northland.

The time wasted in the care of mental health I endured at the hands of my vindictive narcissist husband.

That's over half my life.

For over 30 years I worked in very competitive employment and worked my way up the employment ladder to become a systems administrator for the last 10 years of my working life.

I was earning more than the average male in 1997, when my husband decided to contact them and gave them malicious information about me and coerced them into abusing me until I was forced to leave because of the stress.

He bragged about it when he told me what he had done.

This was a continual pattern after that, every job I had I was abused. I do not know what he was saying about me. Even the vindictive IRD data entry division in Hamilton got in on the act.

I have since found out that he was contacting companies I worked for since at least 1976 and probably longer than that. I have an email from a former employer in 2022 who told me when I worked for him in 1991 1992 my husband used to ring him and say not nice things about me, and he had very intense discussions with him about me. My employer did not know why this was happening.

I now know that this was happening since at least 1976 because of the way I was treated at work. I used to wonder how they knew so much about me even although I had never told them anything. It got so bad in the 1980's with a company I worked for, for over 8 years I hung notice on my wall ASSSUME NOTHING.

While I was earning good money, I managed to buy 2 rental units for our retirement fund. I also got a large redundancy payment from the Auckland Star when it finally ceased publishing. My husband obviously did not appreciate what I did for us and systematically destroyed everything I worked for. Those 2 units are now worth $1.7 million dollars in 2023, these units would have been mortgage free 2 years after I found out what he had been doing to me all these years.

So, in effect I worked hard for over 30 years only to be now living in a one-bedroom flat because I can no longer afford to buy my own house because of the abuse. Forced out of my homes because of the despicable attitude of New Zealanders.

I want appropriate compensation for the medical negligence and incompetent attitude of the mental health units associated with my care.

There was even a psychiatrist from Hamilton who admits in a letter that I found in my mental health files that he had never even consulted with me personally; he acted on the incompetent advice from a community nurse.

When I wrote to this psychiatrist many years ago, he did not action my complaints nor my request for his help or even reply to my letter. He wrote on the top right-hand side of the letter to his secretary," Please file – No Response" so that was his despicable attitude to his patients.

The medication Olanzapine should NEVER have been prescribed to me in June 2002 as outlined in my mental health records. I was on that medication until 2022 when I found out it was detrimental to my health. I now have serious ongoing health problems because of this GROSS MEDICAL ERROR. According to the research I did a patient should not be on this medication for longer than 5 years, I was on it for 20 years. So where does this leave me??

I discovered in 1997 that my husband had been controlling me since 1962 after reading the book Emotional Blackmail by Doctor Susan Forward.

I then took control of my life, and my husband could not

accept that so he left me because he could no longer control me.

He then began a vindictive and vicious campaign against me because he is a vindictive narcissist. He distributed a poster with my photo and libelous details on it to all place I was known to frequent especially antique fairs and shops, book shops and post offices etc. coercing people into emotionally and psychologically abusing me everywhere I went which you all did motivated by greed, the perpetrators of the many crimes committed against me over a long period of time. I was told about the poster by an antique dealer who unfortunately cannot confirm this because she is now deceased.

Especially antique fairs from Wellington to the Kauri Museum, Matakohe in Northland; psychological abuse and coercive control which include the despicable abuse by the antique dealers. These people engaged in the most horrific abuse anyone could encounter, all motivated by greed.

I am not motivated by greed for writing this book I want my story told so that everyone in New Zealand becomes aware of the extremely dark side of new Zealand's attitude and their desire for financial greed while they go about destroying a person because they are motivated by greed.

In 2001 I lodged the 2nd complaint regarding stalking with Kevin Holmes policeman in Raglan. Kevin refused to investigate with the LAME excuse "It was against my husband's right" so THEREFORE a VICTIM has no rights. Does he think anyone would believe that?

I was forced to sell my home in Raglan to escape the vicious atmosphere I was forced to live in for the sake of my mental health. I had to sell my home for a less than it was worth just to escape, the lady who brought my house was one of my stalkers and abusers' she got a lovey home which I had had redecorated fully except for the bathroom, including new floor coverings.

I moved to Wanganui, changed my name, went on the unpublished electoral roll, and have an unlisted phone number to ensure I could not be traced at all.

Before I moved the lady who brought my house made a point of telling me she knew where I was moving to, the only way she could have got that was from the NZ Post when I changed my postal details, she did this to alarm and frighten me.

I was stalked and abused in Wanganui for some time after I moved there but it finally died down.

I lived there peacefully or so I thought until September 2022 when I started having serious health problems. I found out that the reason was because of medication that Te Awhina Mental Health Wanganui prescribed me Olanzapine in 2002. This medication should not be taken long term, research on the internet shows that 5 years at most.

On the 18th December 2018 I phoned an antique dealer and asked her to confirm about the poster that was distributed about me. She denied this which was a lie because she was very good friends with the woman who told me about the poster. She told me to forget about the abuse and get on with my life. She did not have any right to say this to me after what I had suffered over all the years. She had no idea of the mental effects this had on me all these years.

Since I came off the medications that created me into a ZOMBIE, I am now very much alert and have been given the POWER to MAKE PUBLIC the abuse you all subjected me to.

For those from Hamilton who did not participate in my abuse, you are just as bad as the perpetrators of the crimes committed against me because when I wrote to you asking for you to substantiate my claims earlier this year 2023 you deliberately did not reply despite me sending you a Stamped addressed return envelope. You chose to remain on the side of my abusers.

The only antique dealer that I know of I cannot trace in Hamilton; I have lost his contact details and address. I think his name was John. I know he would vouch for me because we were great mates. I lived in Raglan at the time. I used to buy books from him at his home in Hamilton. He had a stall at the Hamilton Antique Market from around 2000 to 2003. His stall was in the middle of the hall, and I think the market was held in the church hall. Perhaps if you read this you are welcome to contact me.

So, this medication was causing my ill health. I immediately stopped taking the medication over a period of 3 months. I then became very alert and aware of what had happened to me. This was confirmed when I received my mental health files from the 3 mental health units, I had been under for such a long period of time. I was no longer the ZOMBIE that had been created by the medication.

I then lodged 5 Gross Medical Negligence complaints about 3 mental health units, 1 community health community nurse, and 1 psychiatrist. These complaints are still ongoing, it will be several months before I get the results.

I also lodged a historic complaint with the Wanganui Police regarding the stalking I suffered for 6 years. I can do this because I received a letter from the Solicitor General who advised me to lodge a complaint with the police. The police can get her consent to lodge these historic complaints.

The first time I lodge this complaint a police officer phoned me at 11.55 p.m. I was asleep and not alert when she rang. She had no right to ring me at that hour. She told me I could not do anything about it because it was over 5 years old. The next day I hand-delivered a letter to her with a copy of the solicitor general's letter. She did not do anything, so I lodged a complaint with IPCA, (Independent Police Conduct Authority).

In the end they advised Wanganui police to investigate.

A policeman then came to see me in 2023. It was very clear from the start that he did not want to investigate. He refused to take away my huge volume of evidence. I showed him a few documents then he said he would not investigate because there was no evidence. He had already seen my huge bag of evidence to show him so that was a complete lie. He lied because he could not be bothered to peruse my vast evidence.

I asked him to confirm in writing and gave him my email address.

He finally emailed me, and I asked him for the reason why he would not investigate. He said there was no evidence etc., I refer you to his email.

I now have the proof that he lied. He inferred that I was a silly old woman. He also said my health problems were a result of my age. This is not so and is reflected in my mental health files.

I have all the proof in these files but the police do not want to investigate my serious complaint.

He just did not want to know this.

I have legal documentation as well as my mental health records which are proof of what I went through and the story they tell.

I lodged another complaint with IPCA, and they advised me if they found further evidence, they would contact me. I never received a reply from them, so I emailed them on the 13th of April copy attached and asked them to advise me if the file is still open or have, they closed it. I have never received a reply.

I advised them if I did not hear anything from them, I would then plan my next strategy.

The following is the final email I sent them on the 13th April 2023

Urgent Reply Required - Attention Zac

Thu, Apr 13, 1:08 p.m.
to Independent

Hello Zac
I have not received a reply regarding the update of this complaint. I should have received a reply by now.

I received a reply on 13 February 2023 stating that if there was further evidence they would reply, you would only reply if it warranted it.

I don't think this is fair. I need to know if this complaint is still live, or you have closed the complaint.

I need to know this immediately so I can plan my next strategy.

I look forward to your reply.
Thank you!
Regards

To ALL the people I have approached for help over the years, and you refused to help me I hope you TOO can live with yourselves.

My next strategy is to get my story published worldwide.

First, I will get my first book published about the 6 years of stalking then I will sell the rights to print my story for the remaining 39 years of my domestic abuse.

My story is well documented through my mental health files and my writings; I also have an author in the UK who is interested in writing the next 39 years of my abuse once the book of stalking is published.

Two reviews of my book A Powerful Obsession.

"On reading A Powerful Obsession I concluded that this book would be a beneficial learning tool for its readers. The writer was very insightful to open a world of stalking and psychological abuse that one may not be aware of. This book was very hard to put down. Thank you, Mary, for the privilege of reading your book. Well done."
—Sheryl

Testimonial from Rob the solicitor who reviewed my manuscript A Powerful Obsession for libel.

"I found A Powerful Obsession a gripping and enlightening read. I believe the book is a great resource for any reader as it provides unique insight into a world that most people are not aware of and is deeply personal."

ACKNOWLEDGMENTS

I acknowledge Oprah Winfrey for her television program discussing the book *Emotional Blackmail*. Thank you, Oprah, for discussing this book on television. I acknowledge the work of Susan Forward with the book *Emotional Blackmail*. Without this book, I would never have known what was wrong with me. Thank you, Susan, for writing the book.

Christine Anne Borra from your books.co.nz for her input.

The following testimonials were processed after the third draft.

"On reading *A Powerful Obsession*, I came to the
conclusion that this book would be a beneficial
learning tool for its readers. The writer was very
insightful to open up a world of stalking and
psychological abuse that one may not be aware of. This
book was very hard to put down. Thank you, Mary, for
the privilege of reading your book. Well done."
—Sheryl

"I found *A Powerful Obsession* a gripping and
enlightening read. I believe the book is a great resource
for any reader as it provides insight into a world that
most people are not aware of."
—Rob

Thank you to three of the best editors from reedsy.com: Barry Hudock, for your exceptional editing and making my novel shine as promised, I hope I have done justice to Barry's suggestions. Alyssa Matesic, for your brilliant editing of the query letter, synopsis, and prologue. Well done. And Heather Rivera, another brilliant editor from Reedsy who took my book to completion and to publishing standard.

Barbara for her skilful proof reading and advice. She said the manuscript was riveting.

Arjan Van Woensel the BRILLIANT designer artist who interpreted my thoughts on how the cover should look and created my wonderful book cover and his great interior formatting so the book could have a pre publishing copy printed.